Leo Laporte's

2006 Gadget Guide

Leo Laporte with Michael Miller

800 East 96th Street
Indianapolis, Indiana 46240 USA

Leo Laporte's 2006 Gadget Guide

Copyright © 2006 by Que Publishing

All rights reserved. No part of this book shall be reproduced, stored in a retrieval system, or transmitted by any means, electronic, mechanical, photocopying, recording, or otherwise, without written permission from the publisher. No patent liability is assumed with respect to the use of the information contained herein. Although every precaution has been taken in the preparation of this book, the publisher and author assume no responsibility for errors or omissions. Nor is any liability assumed for damages resulting from the use of the information contained herein.

International Standard Book Number: 0-7897-3395-1

Library of Congress Catalog Card Number: 2005925001

Printed in the United States of America

First Printing: September 2005

08 07 06 05   4 3 2 1

Trademarks

All terms mentioned in this book that are known to be trademarks or service marks have been appropriately capitalized. Que Publishing cannot attest to the accuracy of this information. Use of a term in this book should not be regarded as affecting the validity of any trademark or service mark.

Warning and Disclaimer

Every effort has been made to make this book as complete and as accurate as possible, but no warranty or fitness is implied. The information provided is on an "as is" basis. The authors and the publisher shall have neither liability nor responsibility to any person or entity with respect to any loss or damages arising from the information contained in this book.

Bulk Sales

Que Publishing offers excellent discounts on this book when ordered in quantity for bulk purchases or special sales. For more information, please contact

U.S. Corporate and Government Sales
1-800-382-3419
corpsales@pearsontechgroup.com

For sales outside of the U.S., please contact

International Sales
international@pearsoned.com

Publisher
Paul Boger

Associate Publisher
Greg Wiegand

Executive Editor
Rick Kughen

Development Editor
Todd Brakke

Managing Editor
Charlotte Clapp

Project Editor
Tonya Simpson

Indexer
Aaron Black

Proofreader
Mindy Gutowski

Publishing Coordinator
Sharry Lee Gregory

Book Designer
Anne Jones

Page Layout
Kelly Maish

Graphics
Tammy Graham

Reviewer
Gareth Branwyn

Contents at a Glance

Table of Contents

About the Authors

Leo Laporte is an author, speaker, and broadcaster focusing on technology topics. The *San Jose Mercury News* called Leo the "best TV tech reporter in the nation." Leo currently hosts *The Tech Guy* technology talk show on Los Angeles radio station KFI AM 640 every Saturday and Sunday from noon to 3 p.m. He also appears regularly on many television and radio programs, including G4's *The Screen Savers*, ABC's *World News Now*, and *Live with Regis and Kelly*. Leo has also written three bestselling *Technology Almanacs*. More information can be found at his Leoville website, located at www.leoville.com.

Michael Miller has written more than 60 nonfiction books over the past 15 years. His books for Que include *Easy Computer Basics, Absolute Beginner's Guide to Computer Basics, Absolute Beginner's Guide to eBay,* and *Tricks of the eBay Masters*. He also co-wrote *Leo Laporte's 2005 Technology Almanac*.

Acknowledgments

Thanks to the usual suspects at Que, including but not limited to Greg Wiegand, Rick Kughen, Todd Brakke, and Tonya Simpson. Special thanks to Sharry Gregory, who wrangled all the pictures you see in these pages. And additional thanks to the companies who provided pictures, information, and—most important—the cool gadgets you're going to read about.

Photo Credits

All product photos used in this book are owned by the respective manufacturers, including, but not limited to ActionTec, AeroCool, AlienBees, Alienware, Alpine, Altec-Lansing, Apacer, APC, Apple, Archos, ARKON, Atari, ATN, Audio Technica, AudioTronic, AV123, Averatec, B&K, Belkin, Better Energy Systems, Blackberry, Bonica, Bose, Buffalo Technology, Burnham Brothers, Cambridge Soundworks, Camelbak, Canary Wireless, Canon, CH Products, Clarion, ClockBall, Couch Potato Tormentor, Creative, Dakota, D-Box, Definitive Technology, Dell, Delphi, Denon, Dension, Digital Dream, Digital Lifestyle Outfitters, Dive Alert, Dual, DVICO, Edirol, Epson, Escient, Etymotic, Eva Solo, Falcon Northwest, Fishpond, Flowlab, FreePlay, Furuno, Game Cabinets Inc., GameDeck, Garmin, Global Pet Finder, GloThong, GoDogGo, GPX, Gravis, Griffin Technology, Grundig, GSI, H20 Audio, Harman Kardon, Hasbro, HokeySpokes, Home Theater Master, Hoodman, HP, Humax, InFocus, i-O Display Systems, IOGEAR, iRiver, iRobot, Jabra, Jakks TV Games, Jawbone, JBL, JBL Enterprises, Jobo, Johnson & Johnson, JVC, Keynamics, Kingston, Klipsch, Konica Minolta, LaCie, Laserpod, Leupold, Lexar, LG, Linksys, LiteON, Logitech, Lotus Design, Lowrance, Macally, Magellan, MagPix, Marathon Computer, Mares, Maxtor, Maytag, Metz, Microsoft, Ministry of Sound, Mirage, Mobiblu, MOMO Design/Motorola, Monster, MonsterGecko, Motorola, MSI, Nature-Vision, Inc., Navman, Neoteric, Nextlink, Nielsen Kellerman, Nike, Nikon, Nintendo, Niveus Media, Nokia, Norazza, Oakley, Olympus, O'Neill, Onkyo, OpenX, Optronics, Oregon Scientific, Pacific Rim Technologies, PalmOne, Panasonic, Pentax, Philips, Photo3-D, Photoflex, Pinnacle Systems, Pioneer, Polar, Polk Audio, Precision Shots, Premiere, Princeton Tec, ProAim, Razer, RCA, REI, Rio, Road Safety, RoboDuk, Robosapien, Roku Labs, Saitek, Samsung, SanDisk, Sanyo, SavitMicro, ScanGauge, SCOTTeVEST, Sea Doo, Seagate, Sharp, Shure, Shuttle, Siemens, Silver Creek Industries, SIMA, SIRIUS, Sleeptracker, Slim Devices, SmartDisk, Smith Victor, Sonos, Sony, Sony Ericsson, Sound Kase, Spherex, SportVue, Stanton Magnetics, Sunbeam Technologies, Sunfire, Sunpak, SurfaceDive, Suunto, Targus, Taser International, TEN Technology, TG3 Electronics, ThrustMaster, Tiffen, Timex, TiVo, Tivoli, TomTom, Toshiba, TracVision, Trimble, Tube Surround, USBGeek, Vantec, VariZoom, Velocity Micro, Velox, Venexx, Veo, Verbatim, VidPro, VIOlight, VoiSec, Voodoo, Wacom, Wallflower Systems, Western Digital, Whistle Creek, X-Arcade, XM, XtremeMac, Yamaha, Zboard, ZIP-LINQ.

We Want to Hear from You!

As the reader of this book, *you* are our most important critic and commentator. We value your opinion and want to know what we're doing right, what we could do better, what areas you'd like to see us publish in, and any other words of wisdom you're willing to pass our way.

As an associate publisher for Que, I welcome your comments. You can email or write me directly to let me know what you did or didn't like about this book—as well as what we can do to make our books better.

Please note that I cannot help you with technical problems related to the topic of this book. We do have a User Services group, however, where I will forward specific technical questions related to the book.

When you write, please be sure to include this book's title and author as well as your name, email address, and phone number. I will carefully review your comments and share them with the author and editors who worked on the book.

Email: feedback@quepublishing.com

Mail: Greg Wiegand
           Associate Publisher
           Que Publishing
           800 East 96th Street
           Indianapolis, IN 46240 USA

For more information about this book or another Que title, visit our website at www.quepublishing.com. Type the ISBN (excluding hyphens) or the title of a book in the Search field to find the page you're looking for.

Introduction

Gadgets are fun.

It doesn't matter whether you're talking about one of those cheap little keychain memory gizmos or an expensive personal hovercraft, gadgets tickle my fancy. They don't even have to be practical—in fact, it's sometimes better if they're not. To capture my attention, a gadget only has to be interesting and innovative and imaginative—in a single word, *cool*.

So, this book is all about cool gadgets, of all shapes and sizes. Gadgets you attach to your computer. Gadgets you carry around on a belt clip. Gadgets that ride along with you in your car. Gadgets you talk into, or type on, or shoot pictures with. Gadgets that have absolutely no useful purpose at all, and gadgets that actually help you do something more efficiently.

In short, *Leo Laporte's 2006 Gadget Guide* is a "wish book" of more than 400 of my very favorite gadgets. I find all the gadgets here terribly interesting, and some of them either quite useful or hilariously funny—or both. (You can't beat the USB sushi drives for both novelty and practicality.) These are gizmos you can marvel at, laugh at, and drool over. With only a few exceptions, they're actual honest-to-goodness consumer products, which means you can purchase them for your own personal use. Or not.

How This Book Is Organized

This year's *Gadget Guide* is a little different from the one we did last year. This time around I approached the topic by examining what types of gadgets you'd want to become the "ultimate" enthusiast in a number of different categories. For example, if you want to become the ultimate home theater enthusiast, you need to assemble the coolest big-screen TVs, audio/video receivers, Media Center PCs, universal remote controls, and so on. Here are the categories I focused on:

- **Part 1, "The Ultimate Computer Geek"**—Includes computer displays, mice, keyboards, external hard disk drives, speaker systems, webcams and spycams, Internet phones, USB gizmos (always one of my favorite types of gadget), and other cool computer gadgets.

- **Part 2, "The Ultimate Gamer"**—Includes video game systems, PCs for gamers, game controllers, and other cool game gadgets.

- **Part 3, "The Ultimate Road Warrior"**—Includes notebook PCs, PDAs, PDA accessories, smartphones, cell phones, headsets, keychain storage devices, and other cool road warrior gadgets.

- **Part 4, "The Ultimate High-Tech Car Owner"**—Includes in-dash audio systems, satellite radio receivers, DVD entertainment systems, GPS navigation systems, and other cool car gadgets.

- **Part 5, "The Ultimate High-Tech Adventurer"**—Includes portable GPS devices, gadgets for runners, camping and hiking gadgets, gadgets for hunters, fishing-related gadgets, gadgets for boaters, scuba diving gadgets, and lot of other cool adventurer gadgets (including the aforementioned personal hovercraft).

- **Part 6, "The Ultimate Digital Photographer"**—Includes digital SLRs, prosumer digital cameras, specialty digital cameras, digital photo vaults, lighting and flash kits, and other cool digital photography gadgets.

- **Part 7, "The Ultimate Digital Movie Maker"**—Includes pro-level video cameras (including some new high-definition models), consumer-level video cameras, microphones, and other cool digital video gadgets.

- **Part 8, "The Ultimate Portable Music Fan"**—Includes hard-disk portable audio players, MicroDrive portable audio players, flash memory portable audio players, specialty portable audio players, portable video players, headphones and earbuds, iPod accessories (because the iPod is so popular!), and other cool portable audio gadgets.

- **Part 9, "The Ultimate Home Theater Enthusiast"**—Includes some really big and really expensive gadgets, such as big-screen televisions, audio/video receivers, speaker systems, DVD players and changers, digital video recorders, Media Center PCs, digital media servers, digital media hubs and extenders, universal remote controls, and other cool home theater gadgets.

- **Part 10, "The Ultimate Gadget Geek"**—Features gadgets that just didn't fit anyplace else, including wearable gadgets, desktop radios, gadgets for home and hearth, and lots and lots of other cool gadgets, from videophones to a *Star Trek*-like home communicator badge.

Within each category, I try to give you little bit of background info and lot of buying advice. Then I list my favorite gadgets within the category, organized by type of gadget. For each type of gadget, I've highlighted one "Leo's Pick;" this is, in my opinion, the absolute coolest gizmo of that type available today. (And, in case the Leo's Pick gadget isn't your cup of tea, I try to list another four or so similar gadgets that you should also consider.)

At the end of each individual gadget listing is a box with detailed information about that gadget, including the model number, manufacturer, website, price, and other important specifications. Given how things go, of course, all this information is subject to change. The price I list is generally the manufacturer's suggested retail price; if you shop around, you can probably find most of these gadgets for a bit less than that.

In case you're wondering, I've accepted no payment or consideration of any sort to list these particular gadgets in this book. The fact that I've included—or not included—a specific gadget reflects no objective review of the gadget's merit, only that it caught my fancy. In other words, these are my favorite gadgets at this point in time. That's all.

Where Does He Get Such Wonderful Toys?

If you see a gadget here that you think is particularly neat, you probably have one more question—where can I buy it? Well, many of these gadgets are available from major computer and consumer electronics retailers, such as Frye's Electronics (and their online counterpart at www.outpost.com), CompUSA, and Best Buy. Other gadgets—especially some of the more off-the-wall ones—can be purchased online at sites like Gadget Universe (www.gadgetuniverse.com) and ThinkGeek (www.thinkgeek.com). Finally, some gadgets can be purchased directly from the manufacturer; visit the company's website for more information.

And if you're a real gadget hound, take a gander at the Gizmodo (www.gizmodo.com) and GadgetMadess (www.gadgetmadness.com) blogs. These sites feature up-to-the-minute information about all sorts of new gadget releases, as well as links to the gadgets' manufacturers. They're the first places to read about the coolest new gadgets.

1

The Ultimate Computer Geek

HOW TO BECOME THE ULTIMATE COMPUTER GEEK

Everybody and his brother (and his brother's kids) have personal computers these days, so just owning a PC isn't a sign of tech geekdom—it's as normal as owning a toaster or a vacuum cleaner. But what distinguishes a gadget geek from a regular Joe is the *kind* of computer he has—how it performs, and how it's tricked out with various types of peripherals. The average Joe or Jane Consumer is happy with a $600 out-of-the-box PC they pick up at Best Buy; the ultimate computer geek spends two to three times as much on the basic unit, and then upgrades key components for better performance or more specialized needs. Since this book is all about being a high-tech major-domo, I'm going to ignore the boring mass market hardware and focus on the high-performance and specialty stuff instead. After all, that's the kind of stuff the ultimate computer geek is interested in.

Spec'ing the Perfect PC

We'll start by discussing what type of PC you might want to use as the core of your system. This implies, of course, that no out-of-the-box PC is going to do the entire job; you'll want to supplement this base unit with upgraded components and peripherals. But we'll start with the system unit itself, and go from there.

If I had my druthers, everybody and his brother (and his brother's kids) would all be using Apple computers. Not that I don't like Windows PCs; I don't dislike them, generally, it's just that I really don't like the Windows operating system. The Mac is my machine of choice, and what I recommend to anyone who'll listen.

So why am I pro-Apple and anti-Windows? It's a matter of security. The Windows operating system is notoriously exposed to all manner of viruses, spyware, hacks, and cracks. It's simply a holey operating system; if it didn't have so many holes, Microsoft wouldn't spend so much time issuing patches. I know this firsthand, because the most frequent calls to my radio show are about how to recover from spyware and virus infections on Windows machines. (I'm not exaggerating when I say that if we didn't weed out the calls out beforehand, I'd devote the entirety of every show to these same old Windows security problems.)

The Mac OS, on the other hand, is much more secure. It doesn't have near the number of holes and vulnerabilities that Windows has; you're much less likely to suffer from virus or spyware attacks if you're using a Mac. So if you want a safe computing experience, the simplest thing to do is to avoid Microsoft products. (And that includes the Internet Explorer browser, which is eminently exploitable.)

That said, I realize that 90% of you reading this book don't use a Mac, have never used a Mac, and don't intend to ever use a Mac. You work in a Windows office, share files with Windows friends, and correspond with Windows relatives; why in the world would you want to be a Mac maverick? I'm okay with that, really. Heck, I use a Windows computer, too—in addition to my main Apple computer, of course. I'm comfortable dealing with the Microsoft reality.

So, assuming that you don't want to switch to a powerful Power Mac G5 (perfect for video editing) or an affordable Mac Mini (ideal for browsing the Internet and managing digital audio files), let's focus our attention on building the ultimate Windows PC. When you're aiming to be the ultimate computer geek (Windows division), what kind of specs should you look for on a new PC?

I gotta tell you, asking how to spec a new PC is a loaded question. It all depends on how you intend to use it. Let me provide some examples:

- **Surfing and emailing**—The vast majority of people who have PCs in their homes use them primarily to connect to the Internet—that is, to surf the Web and send and receive email. These tasks really don't require a lot of power, which means you can typically get by with the lowest-priced PC you can find. Heck, even the lowest-priced PC today is overpowered for these applications. When you connect to the Internet what you really care about is connection speed, which your PC doesn't influence. You might be better off keeping an older PC and upgrading from a dial-up to a broadband connection.

- **Office applications**—In the pre-Internet days, most people used PCs for typical office applications—writing letters and memos with a word processor, crunching numbers in a spreadsheet, preparing presentations in

PowerPoint, and maybe managing your finances in Quicken or Microsoft Money. Well, sorry to tell you, but these applications don't require a lot of computing horsepower, either. Again, today's lowest-priced machines can run Word, Excel, and PowerPoint just as fast as a high-priced machine. If all you need to do is write, calculate, and present, you don't need to spring for a top-of-the-line model. A low-priced box with a decent keyboard and monitor is all you need.

- **Digital music management**—So if the most common computing tasks don't require a lot of computing power (in today's terms, anyway), who's buying all those $1,500 machines—and why? Well, outside of simple surfing and word processing, everything else you want to do with your PC *does* require a little extra horsepower, in one form or another. Case in point: digital music management. Now, you don't need a super-fast microprocessor to download MP3 files from Napster, but you do need a large hard disk to store all those files. (I recommend going with at least a 100GB drive, which can hold over 3,000 hours of MP3 files—much more than most folks have in their entire CD collections.) You'll also need a decent speaker system; a good 2.1-channel system (left and right speakers and a separate sub-woofer) will do the trick. Since most $600 PCs don't have that much hard disk storage or a decent speaker system (if they come with speakers at all), this means buying a better system or going with a cheap system and then upgrading the hard drive and speakers.

- **Digital photo editing**—Digital photo editing is lot like digital music management, in that you need a big hard drive to hold all your digital picture files. In fact, if you like to take and store your photos in high-resolution format, you'll need an even bigger hard drive—think 200GB, or maybe an external hard drive dedicated to photo storage. A little extra horsepower in the CPU department and a little extra memory wouldn't hurt, either, especially if you're editing large files in Photoshop. And, since the picture's the thing, investing in a larger monitor is a necessity. (A 19" LCD is nice for photo editing.) Again, you won't find all this on a $600 PC; you'll probably spend between $1,200 and $1,500 to get all the features you need.

- **Digital movie editing**—Even more demanding than digital photo editing is the task of digital movie editing. You'll want to connect your Digital Video (DV) camcorder directly to your PC, which means your PC has to have a FireWire port. You'll also need a big (200GB or more), dedicated hard drive just for your digital movie files, and a big widescreen LCD monitor for viewing. You'll also want to upgrade to the fastest CPU you can afford, with at least 2GB of memory. In other words, you need the fastest, most powerful, highest-capacity PC you can afford if you want the movie editing process to be anything less than painful.

- **Playing games**—If there's any task more demanding than video editing, it's game playing. That's right, playing games takes more processing power than editing photos or movies. That's because today's state-of-the-art PC games require state-of-the-art processing to display their state-of-the-art graphics and game play. I'll go into more detail about gaming PCs in Part 2, "The Ultimate Gamer;" suffice to say, if you're a serious gamer, you want to buy the most powerful PC that your budget can afford.

- **Home theater use**—There's one final PC use that warrants mention here, and that's using your PC in your home theater system. As you'll learn in Part 9, "The Ultimate Home Theater Enthusiast," a home theater or Media Center PC can function as a CD player, DVD player, hard disk video recorder, and digital music server, all in one box. Naturally, you need a PC spec'd for all these purposes—a huge hard drive, TV tuner card, and the like. You'll also want a PC that's relatively quiet, since you don't want the normally loud PC fans disturbing your TV viewing; this means investing in some sort of quiet PC design, using water cooling or some similar technology. And you'll want this PC to come with Windows XP Media Center Edition pre-installed, since it's Media Center (and its accompanying remote control unit) that you'll use to control everything from the comfort of your living room couch.

So you see why answering the "what kind of PC should I buy?" question is so tricky. Depending on what you want to do with it, you might want anything from a $600 plain-Jane machine to a $2,500 custom job. Just make sure you think through how you'll be using it before you buy, and then shop for a machine that fits your specific needs.

Of course, the PC you get out of the box isn't necessarily the PC that you'll be using. There are lots of ways to customize even a stock PC, which means upgrading peripherals and adding new components, as necessary.

Picking the Right Monitor

One of the things that helps a manufacturer get PC prices down to the $600 range is that they don't always give you a full system. In fact, most $600 PCs don't come with monitors. Which means that one of the first peripherals you'll be adding to your system is a new video display.

When it comes to computer monitors, you have two basic choices. You can go with a CRT-based unit or with an LCD display. CRT displays are big and bulky and are becoming less popular with each passing day. They're also less expensive than LCD displays, so they're still an option if you're building a budget system. For most users, however, an LCD monitor is a better choice.

LCD displays are flat-screen displays, which means you get more free desk space than with a CRT model. Early LCD displays weren't quite as accurate, color-wise, as their CRT cousins, which made them less-than-ideal for sensitive photo editing work. They were also a little slow and prone to streaking with fast-moving images, which didn't endear them to serious game players. Both of these issues have been pretty much resolved in the latest models, so it's not that hard to find accurate and fast LCD displays. Make sure you try before you buy, however, especially if you do a lot of pro-level photo editing or are a heavy gamer.

(That said, some digital photo pros and gaming geeks still swear by high-end CRT monitors, although these expensive beasts are getting harder and harder to find.)

When you're shopping for a monitor, you should look at the unit's contrast ratio, response time (for gaming), and color accuracy (for graphics editing). I prefer to actually examine the LCD I'm going to buy in person, just in case there are any dead pixels. I also recommend putting up some black text on a white screen to see how crisp the text looks; this is especially important if you do a lot of word processing or number crunching, where you're looking at small text and numbers all day.

And remember that a video display is one instance where size matters. Doing a lot of photo editing or Excel number crunching on a 14" display is tantamount to cruel and unusual punishment; spending a few more bucks to upgrade to a 17" or 19" LCD is often money well-spent. (And if you're doing fancy movie editing, consider a really big widescreen model, to better reproduce the picture that others will be viewing.)

Replacing the Mouse and Keyboard

If you're still using the standard-issue mouse and keyboard that came with your PC, you're missing out on some really cool input devices. Despite what you might think, not all mice and keyboards are alike; some perform bet-
ter than others, some offer unique features, and some are hip and trendy looking. You just have to know what's available and what you really want and need.

In fact, the very first change I make when I get a new PC is to replace the standard mouse and keyboard (which typically pretty much suck—PC manufacturers don't spend a lot on their input devices) with something a bit better. I look for a keyboard with a nice firm feel and a good "click;" I want my mouse to feel solid, have decent accuracy, and offer a lot of one-hand control options.

And, for what it's worth, I really like cordless models. If you like to lean back and put your feet up while computing, you know how constricting it is to be tethered to your computer by the standard too-short connecting cable. When you go cordless, you can put your keyboard on your lap and your mouse on a coffee table, if that's what you want. Cordless equals more flexibility.

Cordless mice and keyboards can use either traditional RF or the newer Bluetooth technology. Bluetooth tends to cost a bit more, but I've found that it doesn't always work as well; for some reason, it's been a less-reliable technology for me. For this reason, I warn against buying Bluetooth mice and keyboards, and recommend going with standard RF models.

Beyond cordless connectivity, look for mice and keyboards with enhanced ergonomics, as well as those cool-looking (if not always useful) lights and colors. And don't limit yourself to mice and keyboards; some of the neatest input devices break the paradigm completely, letting you communicate with your computer via trackball or pen.

By the way, not that I'm on the payroll or anything, but some of the most innovative input devices come from a single company—Logitech. I don't want to sound like a shill for the company, but it's hard not to be impressed by Logitech's offerings. Even the company's run-of-the-mill mice and keyboards have a better feel than most competing products, and their cutting-edge models show you what all the other manufacturers will be producing next year.

Sound Matters

Back when I was a youngster, our PCs had just one small, tinny-sounding speaker—and we were glad to have it! (I also walked five miles to school every day, uphill, in the snow.) Of course, all the speaker did was bleep and bloop a little, so the fact that it sucked wasn't that big a deal.

Today, however, we expect our PC speakers to do a lot more than bleep and bloop. We use our PCs to listen to CDs and the digital music we download; we use our PCs to watch surround sound movies on DVD; and we use our PCs to play ultra-realistic games with heart-pounding sounds. And you can't do any of that—or at least, not well—with a tinny-sounding built-in speaker.

For that reason, multiple-speaker systems are some of the most popular add-ons for personal computers today. Ideally, you want a speaker system that sounds good when you're playing music, when you're watching movies, and when you're playing games.

Music reproduction is probably the simplest task for a speaker system. You need two speakers, right and left, and maybe a third speaker—called a subwoofer—for the low bass. This type of system is called a 2.1 system; the right and left speakers are the 2, the subwoofer is the 1, and the dot is a separator.

When you start talking about movies and games, you get into surround sound, which requires two or more speakers to be placed behind you. A 4.1 system has right and left front speakers, right and left rear speakers, and a subwoofer; this used to be the type of system used by high-end PC games. A 5.1 system adds a fifth speaker center front; this is the most common system for movie watching, and nowadays for cutting-edge PC games. A 6.1 system adds a center rear speaker to the mix, and a 7.1 system has the three front speakers plus two surrounds on the left and right sides and two in the rear. (Just wait; in a few years we'll be talking about 9.1 systems with two more speakers even further back in the room!)

All PC speaker systems are built around powered speakers. Unlike home audio systems that use a power amplifier (sometimes built in to a multifunction receiver) to power the speakers, your PC doesn't have a power amplifier built in. Instead, the amps are in the speakers themselves or, in some cases, in a control unit to which the speakers are connected. It's not always a truism, but in most cases more power means better sound.

If you decide on a surround sound system, make sure you have the wherewithal to run the proper cables from the front to the rear. Also make sure your PC's sound card supports multichannel sound; you'll need a card with digital outputs to feed most high-end surround sound speaker systems. Otherwise, if all you care about is music listening, a 2.1 system (with standard mini-plug analog output) should do the trick.

Essential Accessories

Beyond monitor, mouse, keyboard, and speakers, there are lots of other accessories you can add to your computer system, depending on what types of tasks you'll be performing. Computer peripherals are fun gadgets to buy, so make sure you have lots of extra room on your desktop—as well as an appropriate number of open USB ports on your system unit. (That's because most external peripherals today—in the Windows world, at least—connect via USB.)

One of the most necessary peripherals is an external hard disk, which you can use to back up all the important programs and files on your PC's main drive. Back in the caveman days of personal computing, you could back up all your important files on a single floppy disk. But in today's world of 200+GB internal drives, you'd need literally thousands of floppies to do a full backup—and that's simply not practical. Fortunately, hard drive prices have dropped to such a degree that external hard drives can be had for well under $200, and that's money very well spent. These drives connect to your PC via either USB 2.0 or FireWire (the latter being the better connection method for large data transfers), and totally automate the backup process via included backup software. Get a big enough external drive (200GB or larger) and you can copy all the files from your main drive, turning the backup drive into a mirror of your main drive. What could be easier than that?

Beyond the external hard drive, what other peripherals might you be interested in? There are lots, from webcams to drawing tablets to AM/FM radio receivers. The thing that most of these gadgets have in common is that they connect to your PC via USB. USB is a unique type of connector in that it not only transfers computer signals and data, but also passes through a small amount of electricity. That electricity is used to provide power to the USB devices you connect to your computer. So, if you connect a webcam via USB, for example, you don't have to plug the webcam in to a power outlet; the USB connection provides all the operating power it needs.

That simple fact has inspired designers the world over—but particularly in Japan, for some reason—to come up with all manner of devices that can feed off the USB power source. The devices don't have to be particularly useful; the only common denominator is that they don't have separate power connections, just a simple USB connector. As you'll see, manufacturers use USB power to feed everything from USB beverage warmers to USB aquariums. Most of these gizmos are fairly useless, but some actually perform a useful function—and they're all pretty fun!

COMPUTER DISPLAYS

Apple 30" HD Cinema Display

Leo's Pick

Now this is one mongo-sized computer display. Apple's 30" Cinema Display is a widescreen (16:10 aspect ratio) LCD display, perfect for playing or editing movies. It's a high-resolution display, with more than four million pixels in a 2560 × 1600 pixel configuration. Do the math and you see that this display offers better-than-HDTV specs, which is saying something.

While the display is great for editing widescreen movies, it's also extremely useful for regular computing. It's big enough that you can fit two full-page documents on the screen, side by side—or work on a photo full-size in Photoshop, with room for all the various palettes docked around the sides. What other display can you say that about?

The display has a big screen, but it won't take up that much space on your desktop—depth-wise, that is. The display fits on a hinged connector, so it's easy to swivel it up or down for the best viewing angle. (You can also take it off the stand and mount it on your wall, if you like.)

Even though it comes from Apple, you can use the Cinema Display with just about any Windows PC. (Or with any Mac, of course.) All your PC needs is a DVI connection, and you're ready to go.

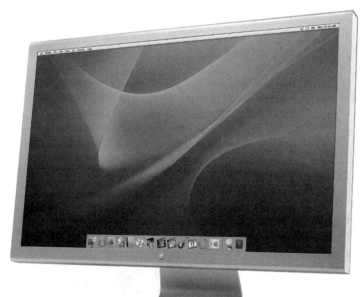

To make the Cinema Display even more usable, Apple was thoughtful enough to include 2 USB and 2 FireWire ports, so your display can act as a hub for other peripherals. It's a convenient way to connect all your desktop peripherals without running additional cables to your PC.

Oh, and if a 30" display is just too much for your desktop, check out Apple's smaller Cinema Displays, in 20" and 23" versions. The picture quality will be just as good, just on a smaller scale—and at a lower price ($799 and $1,499, respectively).

Model: M-9179LL/A **Manufacturer:** Apple (www.apple.com) **Screen size:** 30" diagonal **Aspect ratio:** 16:10 **Resolutions:** 2560 × 1600, 2048 × 1280, 1920 × 1200, 1280 × 800, 1024 × 640 **Display colors:** 16.7 million **Viewing angle:** 170° **Contrast ratio:** 400:1 **Pixel pitch:** 0.250 mm **Cable:** DVI **Dimensions** 21.3" (h) × 27.2" (w) × 8.46" (d) **Weight:** 27.5 lbs. **Price:** $2,999

Dell UltraSharp 24" LCD Display

Here's a slightly smaller and considerably more affordable alternative to the 30" Apple Cinema Display. This Dell UltraSharp LCD display is a 24" widescreen model that also functions as a remote hub with 4 USB ports and a 9-in-1 flash card reader. Maximum resolution is 1920 × 1200 (HDTV quality), and the picture is first-rate, with a 1000:1 contrast ratio. It's a good choice for movie editing tasks.

Model: 2405FPW Manufacturer: Dell (www.dell.com) Screen size: 24" diagonal Aspect ratio: 16.10 Dimensions: 22" (h) × 22" (w) × 9" (d) Price: $1,199

HP 23" LCD Display

Another way to go is with HP's 23" widescreen LCD display. Native resolution is 1920 × 1200, and it offers both analog and digital (DVI) connections. What I particularly like about this unit is the ultra-thin bezel, which lets you tile two or more monitors together for an almost-seamless effect. It's also highly adjustable; the neck telescopes 3 1/2", the panel swivels 35° right or left, and the whole shebang tilts 5° forward and 25° back. This is one flexible display!

Model: L2335 Manufacturer: HP (www.hp.com) Screen size: 23" diagonal Aspect ratio: 16:10 Dimensions: 20.9" (h) × 21.46" (w) × 8.27" (d) Pixel pitch: 0.258 mm Price: $1,399

LG Flatron 19" LCD Display

If you don't have the space (or the budget) for an uber-large display, check out LG's 19" Flatron. This is a standard 4:3 aspect ratio display, but with an exceptionally sharp and vivid picture. Native resolution is 1280 × 1024, with a 160° viewing angle and 500:1 contrast ratio. You get both analog and digital (DVI) connections, and it comes on a very attractive swivel base. It's the best standard display out there today, in terms of both price and performance.

Model: L1980Q Manufacturer: LG (us.lge.com) Screen size: 19" diagonal Aspect ratio: 4:3 Dimensions: 16.1" (h) × 16.6" (w) × 10.3" (d) Pixel pitch: 0.292 mm Price: $599.99

Wacom Cintiq 21" Touchscreen Display

Wacom's Cintiq 21UX combines a standard 21" LCD display with a pen tablet—which means you can "draw" directly onscreen with a pressure-sensitive pen. This is ideal for graphics artists, who can use the display as a drawing tablet for illustrations, CAD blueprints, and the like. Screen resolution is a tasty 1600 × 1200, in a standard 4:3 aspect ratio; connection is either analog or digital (DVI).

Model: Cintiq 21UX Manufacturer: Wacom (www.wacom.com) Screen size: 21.3" diagonal Aspect ratio: 4:3 Dimensions: 16.5" (h) × 21.1" (w) × 5.2" (d) Pixel pitch: 0.27 mm Price: $2,999

MICE

Logitech MX1000 Laser Cordless Mouse

Leo's Pick

First there was the one-button mouse. Then there was the two-button mouse. Then the two-button mouse with scroll wheel. Then the wireless two-button mouse with scroll wheel. Then the optical wireless two-button mouse with scroll wheel—no moving parts and no wires.

Now Logitech goes one better and moves beyond traditional optical technology with a laser-operated mouse. That's right, the MX1000 uses a tiny laser beam to "read" the desktop below, providing 20 times the tracking resolution of a typical optical mouse. That's damned precise, great for either traditional application mousing or high-performance gaming. And the laser technology lets you roll the mouse over any surface with equal precision (really!), no mouse pad required.

The cordless part of the MX1000 uses RF technology, which is pretty well perfected by now. The mouse is recharged in a separate desktop charger/receiver stand; there's a four-level LED battery indicator on the mouse itself which lets you know when it's time to recharge.

Of course, no state-of-the-art mouse would be state-of-the-art without more than the standard left and right buttons. In the case of the MX1000, you get a tilt-wheel for side-to-side scrolling, Cruise Clocker buttons for rapid up-and-down scrolling, thumb-button back and forward buttons, and an extra application switcher button that's surprisingly useful. Even better, all these buttons don't make the mouse feel crowded; everything is just where you expect it to be.

Best of all, this is a very solid-feeling mouse. It feels good in your hand, with a nice heft and a comforting solidity. All the wheels and buttons work in an exceedingly crisp manner, and don't feel mushy (like most Microsoft mice do). Logitech has pulled out all the stops with this one—great performance, solid feel, you name it. It's not cheap, but you get what you pay for. It's head and shoulders above the type of mouse that comes standard with the typical desktop PC.

Model: MX1000 **Manufacturer:** Logitech (www.logitech.com) **Connections (base station):** USB or PS/2 mouse port **Accessories:** Base station/recharger, USB-to-PS/2 adapter, AC power adapter **Price:** $79.95

Logitech MediaPlay Cordless Mouse

Logitech's MediaPlay is more than just a mouse; in addition to scrolling around your desktop, you can pick it up and use it like a television remote control. You get all the standard (and not-so-standard) mouse buttons, including tilt-wheel and page navigation buttons, along with special buttons to control your Windows Media Center PC. Naturally, it's cordless; the wireless receiver connects to your PC via USB.

Model: MediaPlay Cordless Manufacturer: Logitech (www.logitech.com) Price: $49.95

Razer Diamondback Mouse

Razer's Diamondback is the ultimate gaming mouse. It's a wired mouse with the ultra-precision necessary for playing today's PC games, provided by a high-quality infrared optical sensor. It features 7 programmable buttons optimized for gaming response, and connects to your PC via USB. The Diamondback is also way-cool looking, available in translucent Chameleon Green and Salamander Red.

Model: Diamondback Manufacturer: Razer (www.razerzone.com) Price: $59.99

Microsoft Optical Mouse by S+ARCK

Microsoft is known more for functionality than for style, but this mouse is an exception. The Microsofties partnered with European designer Philippe Starck to create this cool-looking rodent. It's a symmetrical design, inspired by the two hemispheres of the human brain—if the human brain had a glowing blue or orange strip down the middle. Feature-wise, this is a standard two-button corded optical mouse with scroll wheel, so it'll do everything you need it to do—and look cool doing it.

Model: Optical Mouse by S+ARCK Manufacturer: Microsoft (www.microsoft.com) Price: $16.99

Logitech Football Mouse for Kids

Okay, it's cool enough that this is a mouse that looks like a football. But the really neat thing is that this is a mouse designed for little kids—it's just 2/3 the size of a standard mouse, perfect for small hands. And even though it's small, it works just like its big brothers, with corded optical technology. The football thing is just a bonus!

Model: Football Mouse Manufacturer: Logitech (www.logitech.com) Price: $14.95

KEYBOARDS

Logitech MX3100 Cordless Desktop

Leo's Pick

Now this is one state-of-the-art keyboard.

First of all, it's not just a keyboard, but a keyboard/mouse combo. And it's wireless, using RF technology. (The wireless receiver doubles as the mouse recharger.) Set up is as easy as plugging the recharger into your PC's mouse and keyboard ports (via PS/2 connectors) or into a single USB port. Click the Connect buttons on the recharger, keyboard, and mouse, and you're ready to go.

Once you're up and running, there's a lot of running you can do. They keyboard itself has a nice feel, and an attractive dark blue-on-black color scheme. It also has a ton of extra buttons, in addition to the standard typewriter and numeric keys. I'm fairly certain it was Logitech's intent to let you control all your web browsing and music listening from the keyboard, no mouse required.

What kinds of extra keys and buttons are we talking about? Well, there are keys to launch and control your instant messaging program; to open your email, word processing, and spreadsheet programs; to play, pause, fast forward, and rewind through your digital music; to rip and burn CDs; to tune directly to your favorite Internet radio stations; to increase or decrease your speakers' volume level; and to scroll through (and back and forward through) web pages.

In fact, I think the MX3100 has more special keys than it has regular keys. That's okay; I find most (but not all) of these keys at least sporadically useful. What matters more to me, however, is the feel of the keyboard, and here is where the MX3100 shines. It's firm without being clickity, with none of the mushiness you get with some competing keyboards. (Are you listening, Microsoft?) Bottom line, the keys feel good under your fingertips, and all the special stuff doesn't get in the way of normal typing. (In fact, all of the extra traditional keys—Delete, Insert, and so on—are extremely well-organized.)

The fact that you also get Logitech's MX1000 laser mouse is just icing on the cake. I talked about this puppy a couple pages back; suffice to say, the MX1000 is the most accurate mouse on the market today, with a terrific in-hand feel. The combination of keyboard and mouse gives you a state-of-the-art PC control center that you can use to do just about everything—with no cords to get in the way.

Model: MX3100 **Manufacturer:** Logitech (www.logitech.com) **Connections (base station):** USB or PS/2 mouse/keyboard ports **Accessories:** Base station/recharger, USB-to-PS/2 adapter, AC power adapter **Price:** $149.95

Logitech diNovo Cordless Desktop

When every mouse and keyboard starts to resemble every other mouse and keyboard, Logitech's diNovo Cordless Desktop stands out from the crowd; this mouse and keyboard combo features hip styling and the latest cordless technology. The unique part of the diNovo is a separate piece that docks to the keyboard, called the MediaPad. It's more than just a numeric keypad, although it's that, too; you can use the MediaPad to control all your digital media—to play music files, display digital photos, and so on. It also displays email and instant message notifications and includes a time and date display.

Model: diNovo Cordless Desktop **Manufacturer:** Logitech (www.logitech.com) **Price:** $149.95

Microsoft Wireless Optical Desktop Comfort Edition

Too much typing can result in severe wrist disorders, such as carpel tunnel syndrome. You can alleviate this problem by using an ergonomic keyboard, such as the one in Microsoft's Wireless Optical Desktop Comfort Edition. In addition to the comfortable split keyboard, you get a variety of media control buttons, cordless RF technology, an optical tilt-wheel mouse, and lots more. This is probably the most comfortable keyboard on the market today.

Model: Wireless Optical Desktop Comfort Edition **Manufacturer:** Microsoft (www.microsoft.com) **Price:** $84.95

Deck Keyboard

This is one cool-looking keyboard. There's nothing fancy about the key layout or connections (it's a standard USB wired model), but what counts is how it looks. The entire Deck keyboard—including the individual keys—is backlit in either Gold, Fire (red), or Ice (blue). You can see this one from across the room, and use it to work in total darkness. (Well, you'd still need to have the display on, but you know what I mean.) The lighting is via LEDs under a tough polycarbonate housing, great for heavy-handed typists.

Model: Deck Keyboard **Manufacturer:** TG3 Electronics (www.deckkeyboards.com) **Price:** $99

Eclipse Keyboard

This is another lighted keyboard, designed specifically for PC gamers. The Eclipse features blue LED illumination, with two levels of lighting (they say three, counting off as a lighting level). It's a perfectly flat keyboard with an adjustable wrist rest, and it's all very heavy-duty for hard-core gaming.

Model: Eclipse **Manufacturer:** Saitek (www.saitekusa.com) **Price:** $59.95

EXTERNAL HARD DISK DRIVES

Seagate External Hard Drives

Leo's Pick

With hard disk prices continuing to drop, there's no excuse for not having a back up hard drive for all your valuable data. And the bigger your PC's built-in hard drive, the bigger your backup drive needs to be.

My favorite external hard drives are those from Seagate. What I like most about Seagate's drives is their form factor. These 3.5" drives are compact and lightweight; you can position them vertically or lay them horizontally. And if you go the horizontal route, they're stackable!

Backing up your hard drive is literally a pushbutton operation. You can initiate a backup by pressing the big button on the front of the unit, or by using the included BounceBack Express software. The software also lets you schedule automatic backups on any schedule you devise.

Performance-wise, we're talking 7200 rpm with an 8MB cache, and they connect via either USB 2.0 or FireWire. Seagate is even nice enough to include both USB and FireWire cables in the box—a nice touch you won't find from all manufacturers. Even better, Seagate offers capacities up to 400GB—one of the largest external drives on the market today. All the drives are hot-swappable, of course.

Seagate's hard drives are also very quiet, which makes them good choices as backup for a Media Center PC. The 400GB model can hold more than 100,000 JPG photos, 6,500 hours of digital music, or 400 hours of digital video—more than enough for most needs. I have one in my home theater system, tucked quietly out of the way, making nightly backups of all my digital music. It does its job so well, I don't even know it's there.

Manufacturer: Seagate (www.seagate.com) **Capacity:** 200GB, 300GB, 400GB **Speed:** 7200 rpm **Cache buffer:** 8MB **Dimensions:** 7.125" × 6.5" × 2.25" **Price:** $249.99 (200GB USB/FireWire), $264.99 (300GB USB/FireWire), $349.99 (400GB USB/FireWire)

Maxtor OneTouch II

Another good one-button backup drive is Maxtor's OneTouch II. In addition to pushbutton backups, automatic backups can be scheduled via the included Dantz Retrospect Express software. Performance-wise, the OneTouch II is extremely fast; it functions at 7200 rpm (with a 16MB cache), for an average seek time of less than 9 ms. Maxtor offers four different OneTouch II models, with either USB or USB/FireWire connectivity, in capacities from 100GB to 300GB.

Model: OneTouch II **Manufacturer:** Maxtor (www.maxtor.com) **Capacity:** 100GB, 200GB, 250GB, 300GB **Price:** $159.95 (100GB USB), $229.95 (200GB USB), $279.95 (250GB USB/FireWire), $299.95 (300GB USB/FireWire)

Western Digital Dual-Option Media Center

What makes Western Digital's Media Center unique is that it's more than just a backup device; it also functions as an 8-in-1 digital media reader, two-port USB hub, and two-port FireWire hub. Use it to download your latest digital photos via memory card or to connect other USB peripherals. It connects to your PC via either USB 2.0 or FireWire and offers 250GB of capacity. The drive itself has a rotational speed of 7200 rpm, with an 8MB cache, and can be positioned either vertically or horizontally.

Model: WDFX2500JB **Manufacturer:** Western Digital (www.wdc.com) **Capacity:** 250GB **Price:** $259.95

LaCie 2 Terrabyte Bigger Disk Extreme

If you're storing lots of digital movies or thousands of CDs (in lossless format), you need more capacity than a typical external hard disk can provide. For you storage hounds, LaCie offers the Bigger Disk Extreme, a one-box solution containing multiple hard disks in a RAID array. Capacity is truly humongous; the Big Disk Extreme comes in 1 terrabyte, 1.6 terrabyte, and 2 terrabyte versions, all with high-speed FireWire 400 and 800 connections. Yowsers, these are big disks!

Model: Bigger Disk Extreme **Manufacturer:** LaCie (www.lacie.com) **Capacity:** 1.0TB, 1.6TB, 2.0TB **Price:** $979.00 (1.0TB), $1,699.00 (1.6TB), $2,299.00 (2.0TB)

Buffalo TeraStation Network Attached Storage Drive

You don't have to connect your external storage to a single computer; if you have a whole-house network, you can use a single network-attached storage drive to back up all the PCs on your network. Buffalo's TeraStation NAS is easy to set up and practically invisible when in use, and it comes in three extra-large capacities, with either 0.6 terrabytes (600MB), 1.0 terrabytes (1,000MB), or 1.6 terrabytes (1,600MB) of storage.

Manufacturer: Buffalo Technologies (www.buffalotech.com) **Capacity:** 0.6TB, 1.0TB, 1.6TB **Price:** $799.99 (0.6TB), $999.99 (1.0TB), $1,999.99 (1.6TB)

SPEAKER SYSTEMS

Logitech Z-5500 5.1 Speaker System

Leo's Pick

Now here's one fine-sounding speaker system, perfect for both music and games. The Z-5500 is the updated version of my last year's Leo's Pick in this category, the memorable Z-680 system, updated to sound even better than ever.

What you get here is a THX-certified 5.1 system with fairly powerful amplification—505 watts in total. The center speaker checks in at 69 watts, the four satellites are 62 watts/channel, and the subwoofer delivers a floor-shaking 188 watts. The system includes both Dolby Digital and DTS surround sound decoding, as well as Dolby Pro Logic II technology to simulate surround sound from a stereo input. (You can also listen in pure stereo, of course, just in case you're finicky about such things.)

The Z-5500 lets you connect up to four audio sources simultaneously; the unit includes digital optical, digital coaxial, six-channel direct, and stereo-mini connectors. That means you can use it not only with your PC, but also with any video game system, DVD player, CD player, and satellite receiver. And the speakers won't look out of place in your living room; leave the cloth grills on for a pro-audio look, or take them off to show off the aluminum speaker drivers.

All that said, the absolutely coolest thing about the Z-5500 system is the Digital SurroundTouch Control Center, an outboard controller with its own LCD display. You can use the controller to select which input to listen to, the desired digital surround sound effect, volume level, and other settings (surround delay, center channel width,

and so on). It also features an auxiliary jack you can use to connect a portable music player. And in case that's too overwhelming, you get a simplified wireless remote control, too—great for operating the system in a home theater environment.

Great sound, great connections, great control—any wonder why this is my new Leo's Pick system?

Model: Z5500 **Manufacturer:** Logitech (www.logitech.com) **System:** 5.1 **Drivers:** 3" polished aluminum (satellites), 10" ported bass reflex (subwoofer) **Total RMS power:** 505 watts **Signal to noise ratio:** >93.5dB **Surround sound formats/effects:** Dolby Digital, DTS, DTS 96/24, Dolby Pro Logic II (Movie and Music modes), 6-channel direct, stereo x2, stereo, PCM (44.1kHz through 96kHz) **Inputs:** Digital optical, digital coaxial, 6-channel direct (3 stereo mini-connectors), analog stereo-mini **Price:** $399.95

Creative GigaWorks 7.1 Speaker System

If five speakers (plus a sub) aren't enough, go whole hog with the THX-certified GigaWorks 7.1 system from Creative. You get six two-way satellite speakers (front, surround, and rear lefts and rights), a center channel speaker, and a powerful subwoofer that combine to create a truly enveloping sound field. Naturally, the Inspire system features a full complement of digital and analog inputs, and handles all the popular 7.1-channel surround-sound formats.

Model: S750 **Manufacturer:** Creative (www.creative. com) **System:** 7.1 **Total RMS power:** 700 watts **Price:** $499.99

Creative I-Trigue 2.1 Speaker System

If you don't use your PC to listen to movies or play surround sound games, you don't need all those speakers; instead, you want a quality 2.1 system optimized for music listening. The best music-oriented system, IMHO, is Creative's I-Trigue L3500. The left and right speakers each feature two Titanium drivers and a lateral firing transducer, and they sound extremely neutral and open. The deep bass is provided by the separate subwoofer, and the result is a full-range system ideal for listening to your favorite digital music files.

Model: L3500 **Manufacturer:** Creative (www.creative. com) **System:** 2.1 **Total RMS power:** 350 watts **Price:** $99.99

Klipsch ProMedia Ultra 5.1 Speaker System

This system demonstrates just what a traditional audio manufacturer can do in the PC speaker arena. Klipsch is well-known for its high-end home speakers, and the ProMedia Ultra 5.1 system delivers that same award-winning sound to any PC-based sound source. The center and satellite speakers feature a horn tweeter and a 3" midrange; the subwoofer has dual 8" side-firing drivers. All this is driven by a 500-watt BASH amplifier, making this one of the most powerful speaker systems available today.

Model: Ultra 5.1 **Manufacturer:** Klipsch (www.klipsch. com) **System:** 5.1 **Total RMS power:** 470 watts **Price:** $399.99

Harman Kardon Soundsticks II

They may not offer audiophile-quality sound, but Harman Kardon's Soundsticks II might be the coolest-looking PC speakers made today. Look closely at that picture; that's right, these are *transparent* speakers—and they sound as good as they look. The left and right speakers each feature four 1" drivers and the bass is delivered by the separate 6" subwoofer, although you probably want to rethink the typical under-the-desk placement. The darned thing is too cool-looking to hide away in a corner!

Model: Soundsticks II **Manufacturer:** Harman Kardon (www.harmankardon.com) **Speakers:** 2.1 **Total RMS power:** 40 watts **Price:** $169.95

WEBCAMS AND SPYCAMS

Logitech QuickCam Orbit

Leo's Pick

Let's face it; most PC-mounted webcams are pretty much the same. The little eye fastens on top of your monitor or on your desktop, and it sits there and stares at you as you sit there and stare back. Yeah, some are wired and some are wireless, but come on—where's the cool factor?

Well, here's the cool factor. Logitech's QuickCam Orbit is a webcam that doesn't just sit there and stare, it actually rotates and zooms and follows you as you move around the room. That's right, this camera features automatic face tracking software and a mechanical pan-and-tilt mechanism with digital zoom to keep the camera focused on your face, no matter where your face might be.

You know, it's almost creepy how this webcam twists and turns to follow your every movement. It can automatically turn 128° side-to-side and 54° up and down, which provides a fairly wide stage. Feel like dancing while you're online? No problem with this puppy.

Performance-wise, the QuickCam Pro delivers 640 × 480 video resolution (at 30 frames per second) and 1.3 megapixel photo resolution. It includes a built-in microphone, so others can both see and hear you online. The connection to your PC is via USB.

Software-wise, Logitech provides programs that let you add live video to MSN Messenger and Yahoo! Messenger, send live video to mobile phones, send video email, edit movies and photos, and make live video calls. You can even add video to your eBay auctions and conduct online videoconferences, if you so desire.

But let's not gloss over the real reason to get this Webcam—it's way cool! The QuickCam Orbit is very futuristic-looking, like a sleek, black robot arm with a mechanical eye on the end. And the way the arm whirs and rotates as it follows you around...it's like you're being watched by the HAL 9000 computer from *2001: A Space Odyssey*. You'll want to dance around the room just to see it work!

Model: QuickCam Orbit **Manufacturer:** Logitech (www.logitech.com) **Resolution:** 1.3 megapixels (photo), 640 × 480 pixels (video) **Connection:** USB **Features:** Built-in microphone, digital zoom, mechanical pan and tilt **Price:** $129.99

Logitech QuickCam Pro 4000

It's not as gee-whiz as the QuickCam Orbit, but if you don't mind positioning your webcam manually, Logitech's QuickCam Pro will get the job done. It's the best-selling Webcam today, and for good reason—the QuickCam Pro is a solid performer in a compact package that's easy to use, is easy to connect, and delivers a host of useful features. It also includes a built-in digital zoom, as well as mechanical (not automatic) panning and tilting, all controlled from your PC via the included software. The PC connection is via USB.

Model: QuickCam Pro 4000 **Manufacturer:** Logitech (www.logitech.com) **Resolution:** 1.3 megapixels (photo), 640 × 480 pixels (video) **Price:** $99.95

ActionTec Wireless Network Camera

Webcams aren't just for instant messaging; you can also use them for monitoring and surveillance. Case in point is ActionTec's Wireless Network Camera, which you can mount anywhere inside or outside your house and connect to your home WiFi network. This puppy even offers a combination of live video streaming and multiple recording and alert options (including motion detection), so you can watch things now or later—or over the Internet. And, best of all, it's wireless, so there are no messy cables to run, wherever you put the thing.

Model: Wireless Network Camera **Manufacturer:** ActionTec (www.actiontec.com) **Resolution:** 640 × 480 (video) **Networking:** 10/100BaseT Ethernet, 802.11g WiFi **Price:** $199.99

Creative WebCam Live Ultra

In the world of webcams, Creative's WebCam Live Ultra is a dependable performer with some useful and unusual features. Performance-wise, you get 1.3 megapixel resolution (for 640 × 480 full-motion video), a 76° wide-angle view, and 4X digital zoom. Feature-wise, check out the smart face tracking, to keep you centered in the picture. And, as an extra bonus, you get a microphone headset, for clearer sound than with most built-in microphones. What's not to like?

Model: WebCam Live Ultra **Manufacturer:** Creative (www.creative.com) **Resolution:** 1.3 megapixels (photo), 640 × 480 pixels (video) **Price:** $99.99

Panasonic BL-C30A Network Camera

The neat thing about this Panasonic network camera is that you can control it when you're away from home, via a simple Internet connection. It operates over an 802.11b or g WiFi connection, so you can place it anywhere within range of your wireless network. Then use your web browser, cell phone, or PDA to control panning (up to 120°) and tilting (up to 90°), or go directly to one of eight preset shooting positions. This makes this camera the ideal remote webcam—either indoors or outdoors.

Model: BL-C30A **Manufacturer:** Panasonic (www.panasonic.com) **Resolution:** 640 × 480 (video) **Networking:** 10/100BaseT Ethernet, 802.11b/g WiFi **Price:** $299.95

USB GIZMOS

AeroCool AeroBase UFO Gaming Pad

How to describe this gadget? It's a mouse pad that looks like a flying saucer, it connects to your PC via USB, and it has 11 blue LEDs around its perimeter that flash in fifteen different sequences. Why, I'm not exactly sure. But I do know that the lights can sense your cell phone, and flash faster when you have an incoming call. Again, I'm not sure why, but that's not the point of these USB gizmos. All I know is that it looks really cool!

Model: AeroBase UFO **Manufacturer:** AeroCool (www.aerocool.us) **Price:** $18

USB Café Pad

The USB Cafe[as] Pad isn't a mouse pad—it's a drink warmer. Just plug it into your PC's USB port, sit your coffee mug on top, flip the switch, and your hot beverage will stay relatively hot. Oh, I suppose you *could* use it as a mouse pad—but things would heat up pretty quickly!

Model: Café Pad **Distributor:** USB Geek.com (www.usbgeek.com) **Price:** $15

USB Alarm Clock

Finally, a somewhat practical USB gadget. The USB Alarm Clock is a small analog clock that you can set as a desktop alarm. The neat part is that the alarm can be programmed from any sound file stored on your PC's hard disk—including MP3 and WMA music files!

Model: USB Alarm Clock **Manufacturer:** Elecom **Distributor:** JBOX (www.jbox.com) **Price:** $48

USB Massage Ball

This gizmo is the cure for all those tiring late-night sessions in front of the PC. When your muscles get tired, massage them with this USB-powered massage ball. One touch of the one-off button and you're holding a vibrating rubber ball in your hand, which you can use to massage any body part you so desire. For what it's worth, you can also order this gadget with a USB-to-car adapter, so you can make your massages mobile.

Model: USB Massage Ball **Distributors:** Everything USB (www.everythingusb.com) and USB Geek.com (www.usbgeek.com) **Price:** $14

USB Mini-Aquarium

What you have here is a miniature fake aquarium, complete with fake fish, powered from your computer's USB port. The USB powers the aquarium's high-intensity blue LED light, as well as the small motor used to generate the small water current. The aquarium comes with the plexiglass tank, two "fish," and a USB cable. Just add water to the tank, attach it to your computer via USB, and watch the fake fish swim around. It's just kitschy enough to be cool.

Model: USB Mini-Aquarium **Distributor:** USB Geek.com (www.usbgeek.com) **Price:** $19

USB Mini Vacuum

The USB Mini Vacuum is a small handheld vac sized just right for cleaning your computer keyboard and the front of your system unit. It comes with a fairly long coiled cord, so you have a little bit of flexibility. The USB connection provides adequate power for sucking dust off the keys. Don't laugh at this one—just take a look at your keyboard and see how much dust you have building up at the corners. Why not use USB power to clean things up a bit?

Model: USB Vacuum Cleaner **Distributor:** Everything USB (www.everythingusb.com) and USB Geek.com (www.usbgeek.com) **Price:** $12

USB Christmas Tree

The perfect gadget for the holidays, this festive little gizmo is just what it says—a USB-powered Christmas tree. It stands a little over 5" tall, is lit by a series of miniature LEDs, and cycles through six different colors. Ho ho ho!

Model: USB Christmas Tree **Distributors:** Everything USB (www.everythingusb.com) and USB Geek.com (www.usbgeek.com) **Price:** $17

Griffin PowerMate USB Controller

Griffin's PowerMate is easy to describe—it's a big knob for your PC. So why do you need a big knob? (No snickers, please.) Well, you can program the PowerMate to control just about anything you want on you computer—volume, window scrolling, video editing functions, and so on. It looks cool, it feels cool, and it actually does something useful—which is more than you can say for most USB gadgets.

Model: PowerMate **Manufacturer:** Griffin Technology (www.griffintechnology.com) **Price:** $45

MORE COOL COMPUTER GADGETS

Sunbeam 20-in-1 Superior Panel

Whether you're building a new PC from scratch or upgrading an older system, it's nice to add some extra connections to the front panel. That's where Sunbeam's 20-in-1 Superior Panel comes in. It takes up a normal 5.25" drive bay and offers a combination of card readers (all popular formats), FireWire, USB (2), SATA 2, RCA audio, and headphone connections, along with a fan controller and cool blue LCD display. It comes in either black or silver fronts, whichever works best with your machine.

Model: 20-in-1 Superior Panel **Manufacturer:** Sunbeam Company (www.sunbeamtech.com) **Price:** $34.99

IOGEAR MiniView Micro USB PLUS KVM Switch

When you need to share USB devices between two PCs, you need a KVM switch. (KVM stands for "keyboard, video, and mouse.") It's a great way to control two PCs from the same keyboard or mouse or use two PCs with the same monitor. IOGEAR's MiniView Micro offers connections for audio, USB keyboard and mouse, and video monitor; just flip a switch to make all these peripherals work on one or another PC.

Model: MiniView Micro USB PLUS **Manufacturer:** IOGEAR (www.iogear.com) **Connectors:** Audio speaker (2), USB (2), monitor (2) **Price:** $69.95

Marathon Computer RePorter

Tired of pulling your PC out to access those back-panel connections? Then use Marathon Computer's RePorter to move those connections in plain sight on top of your desk. The RePorter is essentially a big ol' extension cable that plugs into the rear of your computer and replicates those ports on the opposite end. You get two USB ports, FireWire 400 and 800 ports, and audio in and out connections—all on a five-foot cable. No more aching backs!

Model: RePorter **Manufacturer:** Marathon Computer (www.marathoncomputer.com) **Ports:** USB (2), FireWire (2), audio in/out **Price:** $59

MSI Bluetooth Star USB Hub

Here's a USB hub that's more than a USB hub. Yes, the Bluetooth Star hub provides three extra USB connections, but it also is a Bluetooth receiver that supports up to seven separate Bluetooth wireless devices. A very nice idea for integrating a variety of peripherals in one device.

Model: MSI **Manufacturer:** MSI (www.msicomputer.com) **Connections:** USB (3), Bluetooth **Price:** $50

Wacom Graphire Bluetooth Tablet

If you're a graphic artist, you'll like this one. The Graphire Bluetooth is a drawing tablet without the wires—it operates via Bluetooth technology. It's nice to sit on your couch with the tablet in your lap while you draw and paint and whatever at your convenience. It's a quality product, as you'd expect from Wacom, and the Bluetooth connection lets you get up to 30 feet away from your PC. Nice!

Model: Graphire Bluetooth **Manufacturer:** Wacom (www.wacom.com) **Connection:** Bluetooth wireless **Drawing area:** 6" × 8" **Price:** $249.95

APC Back-UPS Uninterruptible Power Source

A simple power strip or surge protector just won't cut it these days. Provide full backup power to your PC with APC's Back-UPS battery-powered power source. The ES 725 Broadband is a 450 watt unit that offers a typical backup time of 4.3 minutes (14.0 minutes at half-load), long enough to get your system shut down properly during a power outage—or last you through a short brownout. It also functions as a power cleaner and surge protector, with four power outlets for your key devices.

Model: Back-UPS ES 725 Broadband **Manufacturer:** APC (www.apc.com) **Output power:** 450 watts **Backup time:** 4.3 minutes **Outlets:** 4 **Price:** $99.99

Griffin AirClick USB Remote Control

Want to operate your PC's media functions (audio playback, etc.) via remote control? Then check out Griffin's AirClick USB. The receiver connects to your PC or Mac via USB; the hand unit has five buttons for play/pause, next track, previous track, volume up, and volume down—everything you need for music playback. It works via RF signals, so line-of-sight isn't necessary.

Model: AirClick USB **Manufacturer:** Griffin Technology (www.griffintechnology.com) **Wireless:** RF **PC Connection:** USB **Price:** $39.99

Griffin radio SHARK AM/FM Radio/Recorder

Even with all that music on the Internet, sometimes you still want to listen to traditional AM or FM radio. Now you can add radio reception to your PC or Mac, thanks to Griffin's radio SHARK. It's an add-on radio antenna and receiver that connects to your computer via USB, and also functions as a radio recorder (so you can time-shift your favorite radio programming). It's easy to use and, with it's Jaws-fin design, even easier on the eyes. Check it out!

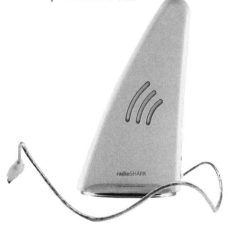

Model: radio SHARK **Manufacturer:** Griffin Technology (www.griffintechnology.com) **PC connection:** USB **Price:** $69.99

2

The Ultimate Gamer

HOW TO BECOME THE ULTIMATE GAMER

Playing games is serious business, and to be the ultimate gamer you're going to need some serious equipment. Today's top gamers have a ton of hardware at their disposal, including multiple video game consoles, a couple of handheld systems, and a powerful gaming PC—as well as all the necessary peripherals, game controllers, and gadgets. You'll spend a lot of cash on hardware alone before you start busting your budget with the games themselves, so you might think about getting a paper route or something to bolster your on-hand cash.

Choosing the Best Video Game System(s)

Serious gamers don't limit themselves to a single gaming system. Great games are available for all the major video game systems, and since it's the games that drive things, you need to be prepared to play any new game that comes along. This means investing in all the current game consoles—Sony's market-leading PlayStation 2, Microsoft's Xbox, and Nintendo's GameCube. Yeah, it's a pain to have all of these systems hooked up to your TV, but that's the price you pay.

You don't want to limit your game playing to your living room, which means you'll also need to invest in a couple of portable game systems—specifically, Sony's PSP and Nintendo's DS. The nice thing about one of these gadgets—well, about the PSP, anyway—is that you can use it for more than just playing games. The PSP is an eminently hackable little gizmo, capable of being used as a portable music player, video player, and who knows what all else.

All that said, we're on the cusp of a new generation of video gaming. These things go in cycles, starting with the original PONG game through the Atari 2600 and the first Nintendo Entertainment System, on through today's three major video game systems. Well, the big three game systems are about ready to be upgraded, which means that if you're a serious gamer, you should start saving your money now for the next-generation video game systems—Microsoft's Xbox 360, Sony's PlayStation 3, and Nintendo's Revolution.

These next-generation systems will be much more powerful than the current-generation systems (and also more powerful than your average desktop PC, believe it or not), and offer a lot more features, especially in the digital entertainment realm. All will be able to play music CDs and DVD movies, and to connect to your home network (wirelessly) and the Internet. Sit one of these puppies next to your living room TV and you have a full-fledged digital entertainment hub. (In fact, Microsoft's Xbox 360 functions as a Windows XP Media Center Extender, right out of the box.) In other words, you'll be able to use your video game system to replace your VCR, CD player, and DVD player—and to play games, as well.

Building the Perfect Gaming PC

The serious gamer plays more than just video games, of course; he also plays a lot of PC-based games. And the thing with the latest PC games is that they require a lot of computing horsepower, in terms of both basic processing and graphics display. In fact, playing games is probably the most demanding thing you can do with your PC, more demanding even than editing digital movies and photographs.

So the ultimate gamer has to have the ultimate gaming PC—a computing powerhouse with an ultra-fast processor, tons of memory and hard disk storage, state-of-the art graphics card, and digital surround-sound processing (along with five or more satellite speakers and a subwoofer, of course). This isn't your typical $600 chain-store machine; most serious gamers buy their PCs from boutique manufacturers, or just hunker down and build their own from the finest parts available.

I won't get into build-it-yourself PCs here, other than to mention the growing trend of PC "modding." This involves taking either a from-scratch or out-of-the-box PC and modifying its case in much the way that a serious hot-rodder will customize his ride. I'm talking about custom paint jobs, see-through side panels, lots of fancy lights, colored water cooling, and the like. PC mods are very cool, and you learn more about them on my friend Yoshi DeHerrera's Mod Times website (www.yoshi.us).

I mention modding because many gamer PC manufacturers do a bit of case modding on the pre-manufactured units they sell. The ultimate gaming PC, whether you build it yourself or buy it, comes with something a bit more interesting than the standard beige or black case. I particularly like the alien-looking cases from Alienware, as well as the cool custom paint jobs available from Falcon Northwest. If you can't do it yourself, at least start with something cool out of the box!

Now, as to spec'ing that perfect game PC. You can go as wild as your imagination (and your pocketbook) permits, but here's a good place to start:

- First and most important, you need a fairly powerful processor to handle today's complex game play. Think Pentium 4 or AMD Athlon64, running at 3GHz or more. Consider upgrading to an extreme edition chip with hyper-threading technology, so that multiple pipes can run simultaneously.

- You'll need at least 1GB of memory, with 2GB or more being ideal.

- You'll also need a lot of hard disk storage. Go for at least a 200GB hard disk, and consider the two-disk option—one hard drive for your operating system and basic programs, with a second hard drive dedicated to games.

- The capability to handle rapidly moving graphics is essential. Today's hottest games require a 256MB video card with 3D graphics accelerator and DirectX 9 compatibility, but that's just the minimum. The best gaming PCs feature 512MB NVIDIA or ATI graphics cards.

- All this computing power generates a lot of heat, so make sure your PC has a fairly large power supply and an adequate number of cooling fans.

- For the ultimate gaming experience, go with a high-quality 3D sound card with built-in surround sound, and be sure you have a quality speaker system, complete with subwoofer.

- Big games look better on a big screen, so think about a 21" CRT or 19" LCD monitor.

Finally, you need something other than your mouse to control your games. You'll want to invest in a good-quality joystick or similar game controller.

Selecting the Ideal Game Controller

Back when I was your age (I know, I was never your age), back when the Atari 2600 was all the rage and *so* much better than plain old PONG, there were only two types of game controllers—joysticks and paddles. Nothing fancy, just a joystick or rotating knob with a single fire button somewhere on the thing. None of this "press button A while holding down button B and firing button C" nonsense; life was a lot simpler back then.

But I'm just showing my age. Today, not only are game controllers a lot more sophisticated (re: complex), but there are also many different types of game controllers, each designed for specific types of games. Gamers are used to disconnecting one controller and connecting another when they switch from first person shooters to flight games to racing games; each type of game demands its own type of controller.

When you're shopping for a controller, here are the major styles to choose from:

- **Gamepad**—The default controller for most videogame consoles, complete with a variety of buttons and the directional D-pad. It's versatile enough for just about any type of game.

- **Flight/combat stick**—A type of joystick with 360° movement and firing buttons; it's ideal for flight games.

- **Racing wheel**—Combines a full-function steering wheel, gear shift, and gas and brake pedals for playing racing games. (Some wheels implement the gas and brake functions as buttons on the wheel.)

And, of course, some games actually use the computer keyboard and mouse as input devices, so you have that to take into consideration, as well.

Most important, make sure you like how the controller feels and how it plays. Make sure it's sturdy enough to hold up through intense game play, comfortable enough for long gaming sessions, and has a quality feel. Then plug it in, settle back, and start playing!

VIDEO GAME SYSTEMS

Sony PSP

Leo's Pick

The hottest game system this year isn't a traditional console game, it's a hand-held unit—Sony's first. The PSP is essentially the portable version of the popular Sony PlayStation 2; in fact, the name "PSP" stands for "PlayStation Portable."

Size-wise, the PSP is everything you want it to be. It's slim enough (less than an inch deep) to fit into a shirt pocket, and light enough (a little over a half pound) not to make your pocket sag. Most of the front of the unit is taken up by the big 4.3" diagonal 16:9 ratio screen, with four-button thumb controllers on either side for game play. Additional memory can be had by using Sony's Memory Stick Duo-format flash drives. There's also a WiFi connection, for multi-player gaming.

Games are available on miniature DVD-like disks that Sony calls Universal Media Disks (UMDs). This is a 2.4" disk that can hold up to 1.8GB of data—almost three times the capacity of a larger CD-ROM disk. It's impressive technology, even if it's more proprietary than universal.

As for game play, prepare to be wowed. The PSP is every bit as powerful as its older PS2 sibling, and the graphics are amazing for a unit this size. Game play itself is fluid, and the thumb controllers are surprisingly ergonomic. Bottom line, the PSP is a great little game-playing device.

But the PSP is more than just a game system. You can also use your PSP to play MPEG-4 videos, which you can find at PSP Connect (psp.connect.com) and other sites. Sony even offers Image Converter software to convert videos stored on your PC to a PSP-compatible format. And, of course, there are plenty of prerecorded movies for the PSP, on Sony's UMD-format disks. It's actually a nice little movie player, all things considered.

While the PSP won't replace your PS2 console, it will let you achieve the same level of game play when you're out of the living room. And the added features—especially the video playback and ability to store and display digital photos—make the PSP a good choice for an all-around media player. It definitely puts the more limited Nintendo DS to shame!

Model: PSP **Manufacturer:** Sony (www.us.playstation.com) **Memory:** 32MB **CPU:** MIPS R4000 32-bit **Screen:** 4.3 diagonal 16:9 ratio color TFT LCD **Resolution:** 480 × 272 pixels **Connections:** 802.11b WiFi, USB, Memory Stick Duo, infrared **Dimensions:** 6.7" (w) × 2.9" (h) × 0.9" (d) **Weight:** 0.62 lbs. **Price:** $249.95

Sony PlayStation 2

The PS2 is the premiere home video game system today, leaving both Microsoft and Nintendo in the dust. Is it because the PS2 is such a high-performance system, or because there are so many great PS2 games available? That's a chicken-and-egg question, and who really cares—in the case of the PS2, you gotta like both the chicken and the eggs! BTW, the latest version of the PS2 is exceedingly sleek; it's 75% smaller than the original console, only about an inch thick.

Model: PlayStation 2 Manufacturer: Sony (www.us.playstation.com) Dimensions: 9" (w) × 6" (d) × 1.1" (h) Weight: 2 lbs. Price: $149.99

Microsoft Xbox 360

Despite achieving the number two spot in U.S. console sales, Microsoft's Xbox video game system never quite took off the way some folks expected. Microsoft hopes that all will change with the launch of the second-generation Xbox 360 in November 2005. Features include a detachable 20GB hard drive, three 3.2GHz processors, 512MB RAM, a custom ATI graphics processor with 10MB embedded DRAM, wireless controllers, and surround sound; games display in full 720p/1080i 16:9 ratio high definition.

Model: Xbox 360 Manufacturer: Microsoft (www.xbox.com) Price: $299

Nintendo GameCube

Nintendo's GameCube might be starting to look and feel a little long in the tooth, but it's still a formidable video game system—not least because of the wide variety of quality games available. It's actually a snazzy little system, small and compact, and you can't beat the game play. It may not be as graphically advanced as Microsoft's Xbox or upcoming Xbox 360, but who cares when the games are this good? (Also, you can't beat the hundred-dollar price!)

Model: GameCube Manufacturer: Nintendo (www.nintendo.com) Dimensions: 4.3" (h) × 5.9" (w) × 6.3" (d) Price: $99.99

Atari Flashback Classic Game Console

Now we're talkin' retro-cool. The Atari Flashback is a new millennium version of the classic 1980s Atari 7800 game console, complete with 20 classic games built-in. The console looks and feels like a genuine Atari 7800 (the successor to the popular 2600), and features two classic 7800-style controllers. The built-in games include Atari 2600 classics like Adventure and Yars' Revenge, as well as 7800 hits like Asteroids and Centipede. And you get it all for a twenty-dollar bill—sweet!

Model: Flashback Manufacturer: Atari (www.atari.com) Players: 1 or 2 Price: $19.95

GAMING PCs

Alienware Area 51 ALX

Leo's Pick

PCs for gamers are all about the power—and all about the cool factor, both of which the Alienware Area 51 ALX has in spades.

Performance first. You can get an Area 51 ALX in any one of a number of powerful configurations, but I'll outline a typical one here. My dream system is built around an Intel Pentium 4 840 Extreme Edition CPU, which is a dual-core processor on a single chip. Performance is enhanced ever further with Intel's Hyper-Threading technology, which supports up to four threads simultaneously.

That super-fast CPU is accompanied by up to 2GB of high-speed DDR2 memory and up to 1TB of hard disk space. (That's right—a *terabyte* of storage.) Graphics performance is similarly state-of-the-art, thanks to the NVIDIA GeForce 6800 Ultra 512MB graphics card. You'll also get two DVD/CD drives standard, along with a 550-watt power supply.

All this power is accomplished in relative quiet, the result of Alienware's silent liquid cooling technology. Excess heat is absorbed by the internal coolant, which is moved through the chassis via two pumps and cooled by a high-performance heat exchanger. In addition, a proprietary power control board constantly monitors the unit's internal temperature and dynamically reports system temperatures and operational status. If temperatures heat up to uncomfortable levels, an alarm sounds and the system will automatically shut down.

The result of all this power is a PC that can play virtually any PC game ever made, at blazing-fast speeds. No graphics freezes, no game play slowdowns, no choppy control. This PC can handle everything you throw at it—including other high-demand tasks, such as video editing.

As to the cool factor, this is another area where Alienware shines. The Alienware case looks… well, a little alien-like. The stylish cabinet combines subtle contours with dramatic highlights for a look

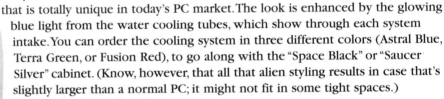

that is totally unique in today's PC market. The look is enhanced by the glowing blue light from the water cooling tubes, which show through each system intake. You can order the cooling system in three different colors (Astral Blue, Terra Green, or Fusion Red), to go along with the "Space Black" or "Saucer Silver" cabinet. (Know, however, that all that alien styling results in case that's slightly larger than a normal PC; it might not fit in some tight spaces.)

However you configure it, this is a true state-of-the-art PC, for game use or otherwise. It's also just a tad more expensive than your typical PC; it costs a little more to get such a forward-thinking piece of equipment.

Model: Area 51 ALX **Manufacturer:** Alienware (www.alienware.com) **Processor:** 3.2GHz Intel Pentium 4 Extreme Edition 840 **Memory:** 1GB–2GB **Hard disk:** 74GB–1,050GB **Graphics:** NVIDIA GeForce 6800 Ultra 512MB **Dimensions:** 22.3" (h) × 9.5" (w) × 22.5" (d) **Price:** $4,681–$6,000

Falcon Northwest Mach V

Like Alienware, Falcon Northwest is a popular high-end computer manufacturer, especially among gamers. The Mach V is Falcon's top-of-the-line model, running an AMD Athlon64 FX-55 64-bit processor. You also get 2GB memory, two NVIDIA GeForce 6800 Ultra 512MB graphics cards, and up to 1.6TB of storage across four hard disk drives. What makes Falcon's PC especially cool is that you can order a custom paint job or opt for laser cutting and lighting for the case. The Mach V is a truly custom PC—and Falcon is highly regarded in terms of the documentation and support they provide.

Model: Mach V **Manufacturer:** Falcon Northwest (www.falcon-nw.com) **Processor:** AMD Athlon64 FX-55 **Memory:** 1GB-2GB **Hard disk:** 74GB-1,600GB **Graphics:** NVIDIA GeForce 6800 Ultra 512MB (2) **Price:** $6,800-$9,300

Velocity Micro Raptor 64 Dual X

Velocity Micro is another high-end niche PC manufacturer, and the Raptor 64 Dual X is their state-of-the-art gaming machine. It's powered by an AMD Athlon64 FX-55 processor, up to 2GB of memory, up to 1.2TB of storage across three hard drives, and two NVIDIA GeForce 6800 Ultra 256MB graphics cards. Pricing is a little more affordable than with Alienware or Falcon Northwest, but still not cheap.

Model: Raptor 64 Dual X **Manufacturer:** Velocity Micro (www.velocitymicro.com) **Processor:** AMD Athlon64 FX-55 **Memory:** 1GB-2GB **Hard disk:** 74GB-1,200GB **Graphics:** NVIDIA GeForce 6800 Ultra 256MB (2) **Price:** $3,795-$5,900

Shuttle Gaming XPC

Some gamers prefer a small form factor PC, which is portable enough to take to LAN and gaming parties. Shuttle is the premiere manufacturer of these smaller PCs, and their Gaming XPC offers big-box performance in a relatively small package. The top-of-the-line P9500g Gaming XPC runs a 3.4GHz Pentium 4 550 processor with 1GB memory and a 200GB hard drive; the graphics card is an NVIDIA GeForce 6800 GT 256MB. You can customize the system with more memory and storage space, and it's still an affordable—and portable—alternative to the big boys.

Model: Gaming XPC P9500g **Manufacturer:** Shuttle (www.shuttle.com) **Processor:** 3.4GHz Pentium 4 550 **Memory:** 1GB-2GB **Hard disk:** 74GB-960GB **Graphics:** NVIDIA GeForce 6800 GT 256MB **Price:** $1,999-$3,700

Voodoo Envy u:703

Here's another alternative for gaming on the go—a laptop PC souped up for high-performance gaming. Voodoo's Envy u:703 is a lot more powerful than the typical business laptop, and also runs a lot hotter (and eats through batteries like their potato chips). It features a huge 17" 1900 × 1200 display, 3.6GHz Intel Pentium 4 560 processor, up to 2GB of memory, and up to 200GB of hard disk storage—all in a hefty 13-pound package. Still, it's smaller and lighter than lugging around a desktop model, and it performs just about as well.

Model: Envy m:870 **Manufacturer:** Voodoo Computers (www.voodoopc.com) **Processor:** 3.6GHZ Intel Pentium 4 560 **Memory:** 512MB-2GB **Hard disk:** 60GB-200GB **Graphics:** NVIDIA GeForce 6800 Go 256MB **Price:** $3,895-$4,600

PC GAME CONTROLLERS

Logitech Cordless Rumblepad 2

This award-winning game controller is one of the best general gamepads on the market—and it's wireless, to boot! The Cordless Rumblepad 2 connects to your PC via 2.4GHz RF signals and has a 30-foot range (50% longer than the previous version), so you can put some space between you and the screen. And the wireless operation gives you the freedom to twist, turn, and move around without tangling or unplugging any cables.

As to the gamepad itself, the Rumblepad 2 incorporates realistic vibration feedback effects that let you feel every explosion as you play. Two independent vibration feedback motors provide maximum tactile feedback, and you can customize the amount of feedback generated.

The gamepad features dual analog mini-sticks, an eight-way D-pad, 11 programmable buttons, and a slide throttle. The mini-sticks are particularly responsive, with precise 360° movement. Even better, you can customize all the buttons and double the number of buttons by using the shift button.

Logitech's software lets you quickly switch between different controller configurations for different games. The Rumblepad 2 includes profiles for hundreds of popular games, and you can easily download new game profiles from the Internet.

All in all, a great force feedback game controller—with the added bonus of wireless operation.

Model: Cordless Rumblepad 2 **Manufacturer:** Logitech (www.logitech.com) **Price:** $39.99

Gravis Xterminator Force Feedback Gamepad

If you want a no-compromise high-quality game controller, check out the Gravis Xterminator Force, one of the most popular controllers among hardcore gamers. The Xterminator Force offers one of the best force feedback systems today, with proportional-control D-pad and flippers. Just push the D-pad—and it pushes back! This rugged gamepad also offers six programmable buttons, a Precision button for hyper-accurate play, and an ultra-comfortable design. It connects to your PC via USB.

Model: Xterminator Force **Manufacturer:** Gravis (www.gravis.com) **Price:** $69.99

Saitek X52 Flight Control System

Saitek's X52 is a two-piece control system for flying games, like Microsoft Flight Simulator. Piece one is a precision joystick with two-stage trigger, 4 fire buttons, and 3D rudder twist. Piece two is a progressive throttle with tension adjustment, 2 fire buttons, scroll wheel, and a clutch button. Put them together and it's just like flying a real airplane—on your own PC, of course.

Model: X52 **Manufacturer:** Saitek (www.saitekusa.com) **Price:** $129.95

CH FighterStick USB

The FighterStick USB is simply the best joystick/flightstick controller available today. It's modeled after the Air Force's F-16 control column, and features 3-axis control, a side slide throttle wheel, 24 buttons, and three separate programming modes. You even get dual rotary trim controls for precision adjustment of ailerons and elevators. But the best thing about this flight stick is its sturdy base and solid feel; this is one controller that just feels right.

Model: FighterStick USB **Manufacturer:** CH Products (www.chproducts.com) **Price:** $149.95

X-Arcade Solo

When you're playing old school, you want a controller that feels like those classic arcade games of the past—which is what the X-Arcade Solo delivers. The X-Arcade Solo is an accurate reproduction of a classic arcade controller, complete with joystick and 9 operation buttons. It's an industrial-grade controller, coming in at a hefty 12 pounds—it'll take all the punishment you can give it. And you can purchase adapters to use with any current game system, as well as your PC.

Model: X-Arcade Solo **Manufacturer:** X-Arcade (www.x-arcade.com) **Price:** $99.95

PC GAME CONTROLLERS

Saitek Cyborg evo Wireless

Here's a cool joystick controller, fully customizable and wireless, as well.

Saitek's Cyborg evo Wireless claims to be the world's only fully adjustable wireless stick, and that claim may be justified. For starters, you can customize both the head and the stick for either left- or right-hand play; there's also a three-way handle adjustment to make the controller fit all hand sizes. In addition, Saitek's software offers more advanced programmability of all the joystick's functions. I don't know of any other game controller that offers this type of physical and virtual customization.

As to the controller itself, it's wireless, of course, which means you can sit up to 30 feet away from your PC. The wireless receiver is actually a small dongle (about the size of a USB flash drive) that attaches to a USB port on your PC. When you move from one PC to another, the dongle slides into a slot on bottom of the controller, so it won't be easily lost.

Operationally, the controller features a rapid-fire trigger, 5 fire buttons, 2 shift buttons, 4 base buttons, an 8-way point-of-view hat switch, a lever throttle, and 3D twist for rudder control. This makes the control great for both action and flight games.

Feel-wise, there's a lot to like here. The Cyborg evo is a very sturdy stick, it doesn't feel cheap or plasticky, as some competitors do. Even the physical adjustments are heavy duty, such as the knobs (attached to worm gears) that tilt the stick left-to-right and front-to-rear. Comfort is achieved by an adjustable hand rest that flares out from the bottom of the stick.

Solid feel, extreme customability, and wireless operation. That's why the Cyborg evo Wireless is a Leo's Pick controller!

Model: Cyborg evo Wireless **Manufacturer:** Saitek (www.saitekusa.com) **Price:** $59.99

MonsterGecko PistolMouse FPS

My preferred controller for shooting games is MonsterGecko's PistolMouse. It's a stylish pistol controller with an 800 dpi high-resolution optical sensor built into the base, for high-precision performance. The trigger is heavy-duty aluminum, there's an oversized scroll wheel on the side, and—best of all—it looks and feels like a real handgun. When you want to excel at first person shooter games, this is the gun to get.

Model: PistolMouse FPS **Manufacturer:** MonsterGecko (www.monstergecko.com) **Price:** $39.95

Zboard Modular Keyset

The problem with playing games on your PC is that the control keys are typically spread all across the keyboard. Wouldn't it be nice to design a keyboard with the appropriate keys for a given game all in one place? Well, that's what the Zboard Modular Keyset does; it turns your keyboard into a kind of high-tech Lego game, where you can design your own key layouts for different PC games. Just move this module here and that one there, and you have a whole new keyboard to play with; special predesigned keysets are available for the most popular games.

Model: Zboard **Manufacturer:** Zboard (www.zboard.com) **Price:** $49.99

Logitech MOMO Racing Wheel

From Logitech comes a force-feedback racing wheel designed by the racing professionals at MOMO—one of the world's leading designers of automotive accessories. The steering wheel includes two paddle shifters, just like the F1 drivers use, so you can shift without taking your hands off the wheel—or you can use the manual shifter for precise sequential shifting. The advanced force feedback lets you feel every turn, slide, and bump, and the comfortable grip offers precise steering; the foot pedals are mounted on a large stable base with a unique carpet grip system.

Model: MOMO Racing **Manufacturer:** Logitech (www.logitech.com) **Price:** $99.95

ThrustMaster Enzo Ferrari Force Feedback Wheel

Ever want to trade in your Ford Escort for a Ferrari racer? Here's the next best thing, an exact replica of the steering wheel on the latest Enzo Ferrari. You get powerful force feedback effects, an 8-way D-pad, 9 action buttons, and progressive gas and brake control. The gearshift levers are mounted on the wheel itself, just like in the real car. It's a classy, cool, and high-performance racing wheel—just like the big boys use.

Model: Enzo Ferrari Force Feedback Wheel **Manufacturer:** ThrustMaster (www.thrustmaster.com) **Price:** $79.99

MORE COOL GAME GADGETS

GameDeck NAVIS

Leo's Pick

If you're really serious about PC gaming, you need a dedicated game desk/cockpit, such as the GameDeck NAVIS. It starts out as kind of a high-tech PC workstation, but then morphs, Transformer-like, into the ultimate arcade pod. In its workstation mode, it's highly ergonomic; swing the game controllers into place, and it's a tailor-fitted gaming environment.

Slide down into the NAVIS' attached seat and you're ready to play. Your PC mounts below your seat, the LCD monitor mounts right in front of you, surround sound speakers are positioned fore and aft, control pedals are directly under your feet, and built-in wiring hides unsightly cables. The seat features a pneumatic lift for over 4" in height adjustment, as well as a synchronized tilt feature that slides the seat forward when you lean back (or back when you lean forward).

When you want to switch from work to play modes, just slide the keyboard drawer in and pull down one of the two pivoting game controller arms. One arm holds a steering wheel controller; the other arm slides down on either side of the main section to hold joysticks, rudders, and other hand controllers. The pivoting arms contain gas springs to dampen their swing.

The base frame is constructed from aluminum, and comes in three different color combinations—red/gray/black, yellow/gray/black, and charcoal/gray/black. Various accessory kits are available, including a Driving Sim Kit and Flying Sim Kit. You can also purchase an optional adjustable footrest, leather upholstery, and other upgrades.

This is a serious workstation/cockpit, and costs serious money—the base price is $4,395, but it's easy to trick it up closer to five grand. Once you sit down in a NAVIS, however, you'll never want to get up!

Model: NAVIS **Manufacturer:** GameDeck (www.thegamedeck.com) **Dimensions:** 48" (d) × 37" (w) × 54" (h)
Price: $4,395

Spherex RX2 Surround Sound Game Chair

Gaming becomes an immersive experience with this unique surround-sound game chair. The RX features its own 5.1 speaker system and 300 watt power amplifier installed into the frame of the chair. It's surprisingly effective, thanks to the built-in Dolby Digital and DTS surround sound processors and ButtKicker tactile transducer (that lets you feel, as well as hear, the low bass frequencies). Just plug the RX2 into the audio out jacks of your PC or game consoler, then settle back for some long and intense gaming sessions.

Model: RX2 **Manufacturer:** Spherex (www.spherexinc.com) **Price:** $1,599.99

Spherex Xbox 5.1 Surround Sound System

Add surround sound to your Xbox games with Spherex's Xbox 5.1 Surround Sound System. (It will also work with PC games, DVD players, and other digital media devices.) You get five satellite speakers and a big subwoofer, all powered by a 300 watt amplifier and controlled via infrared remote. The sound is surprisingly good; you'd be surprised how much more intense your games are with surround sound enabled.

Model: Xbox 5.1 **Manufacturer:** Spherex (www.spherexinc.com) **System:** 5.1
Total RMS power: 300 watts **Price:** $429.95

Classicade Upright Game System

The Classicade Upright is an honest-to-goodness replica of a classic arcade game, complete with wooden cabinet, 21" television display, and multi-function controllers. Each unit is a two-player machine and comes with 21 games pre-installed, including Asteroids, Centipede, Lunar Lander, Missile Command, Super Breakout, Tempest, Dragon's Lair, and Space Ace. (The games are loaded onto a PC located inside the cabinet; it's easy to add more games, as you like.) It's just like having a gaming arcade in your living room!

Model: Classicade Upright **Manufacturer:** Game Cabinets Inc. (www.gamecabinetsinc.com)
Dimensions: 64" (h) × 28" (w) × 37" (d)
Price: $4,095

Jakks Classic Arcade Games

TV Games let you experience old-school gaming on any TV—no PC or game console required. These are portable, self-contained game systems; everything is contained in the joystick controller device. Just connect the joystick to your TV and start playing; each joystick device contains six or so popular games. Different models include Activision, Atari, Atari Paddle, Classic Arcade Pinball, Ms. Pac-Man, and NAMCO collections.

Manufacturer: Jakks TV Games (www.jakkstvgames.com) **Price:** $20

3

The Ultimate Road Warrior

HOW TO BECOME THE
ULTIMATE ROAD WARRIOR

The good thing about portable technology is that we're no longer chained to our desks. The bad thing about portable technology is that we're no longer chained to our desks. Go figure.

In days of yore (yore being a dozen or so years ago) you did your work at your desk, and when you were away from your desk, you were away from your work. Not so today, and you can thank all the major technology companies for this dubious advancement. Used to be that if you were driving, or out for a walk, or shopping for groceries, you were out of touch, communications-wise. Today, however, thanks to cell phones and wireless PDAs and other such gizmos, you're never out of touch. You can conduct sensitive business negotiations (or be badgered by your spouse) while shopping for liverwurst or sipping on a latte, much to the annoyance of everyone around you. For better or for worse, you just can't get away from it all anymore; no matter where you are, you're still connected, probably wirelessly.

So if the ubiquitous connection is now the rule rather than the exception, you might as well go with the flow—and have a little fun with it. After all, this influx of portable technology is a great excuse to buy all sorts of portable gadgets. And gadgets are definitely fun!

Choosing the Right Gadgets to Fit Your Road Warrior Lifestyle

The big question is, exactly which portable gadgets you need? If you bought one of everything, you'd need Batman's utility belt to carry them all around—which sort of negates the concept of portability. No, the savvy road warrior picks and chooses his gadgets, to maximize his portable computing and communicating efficiency. It's possible, after all, to have a single gadget perform multiple functions.

So, which portable gadgets do you need? It all depends on your individual road warrior lifestyle. Here are some hints:

- **If you breathe oxygen, you need a cell phone**—That's another way of saying that everybody has one, whether they want it or not. A basic cell phone (or *mobile*, with the accent on the second syllable, as they say across the pond) is the minimum high-tech gadget for just about anyone today.

- **If you're sixteen years old, you need a cell phone with text messaging service**—Kids like text messaging. Adults not so much, possibly because our thumbs are bigger and less flexible. In any case, txt msg r kwl—unless you can't decipher message-speak, that is.

- **If you have a blog, you need a camera phone**—Mobile blogs (moblogs, for short) are the latest rage, where you use your mobile phone to take pictures of wherever you're at, and then post them online for all to see. (You can see my personal moblog at www.leoville.com/blog/; just click the Pictures link at the top of the page.) Camera phones are also great for savvy businesspeople; imagine going to a trade show or a client's presentation and camera-phoning product shots back to the office. And it goes without saying that if you have kids, you have to have a camera phone; kids do the cutest things, and you absolutely *must* capture every thing they do for posterity, even if you don't have your big digital camera handy.

- **If you have to juggle a ton of contacts and appointments, you need a PDA... or maybe a smartphone**—A personal digital assistant (PDA) is a handheld gizmo with the brains of a computer, minus the keyboard. (They use touch-screen input, instead.) PDAs are great for storing contacts and schedules, and for playing solitaire during boring meetings. Every self-respecting road warrior has one, unless you decide to go with a smartphone instead. A smartphone is a cell phone with PDA functions, or sometimes it's a PDA that makes phone calls. In any case, one smartphone can take the place of a separate cell phone and PDA, even though it's enough larger than a cell phone to be somewhat inconvenient for calling, and enough smaller than a PDA to be somewhat unusable for data entry, which makes it pretty much the worst of both worlds, or the best, depending.

- **If you make a lot of notes to yourself, you need a PDA**—Ah, another good use for a PDA, to jot down notes during meetings and such. You could just use a yellow legal pad, of course, but then you wouldn't have to deal with finicky handwriting recognition systems and storage capacity limits, and what's the fun in that?

- **If you travel a lot, you need a laptop PC… or maybe a PDA… or perhaps a smart-phone**—When you're away from the office, you not only need to get a little work done, you also have to check your emails—otherwise, the spam quickly builds up to insurmountable levels. So you need to carry something along with you that you can hook up to a phone line (or, ideally, to a wireless hotspot) and check your inbox. The notebook PC is a good workhouse for this task, as you can also use it to write memos and crunch numbers. If you don't need to write memos and crunch numbers, however, you could always use a PDA (with built-in WiFi) to do the email thing. For that matter, a smartphone can also connect to a WiFi hotspot and send and receive email, if you don't mind typing on those little Chiclet keys. It's up to you how big a device you want to carry around, and whether or not you need to do industrial-strength computing while you're on the road. Or you could be a real geek and carry both a laptop PC and PDA, although that's kind of a belt-and-suspenders approach to road warrioring, IMHO.

- **If you take work home from the office, you need a USB memory device**—Now here's a gadget I really like—and one that actually works as promised. In the old days, you transferred data from one location to another via floppy disk, which held a whopping 1.44MB of data. Today, some email messages are larger than this, so you need a portable storage device with more capacity, which is what you get with a USB memory device (sometimes called flash storage, or keychain storage, or a USB drive, or "that little plug-in thingie"). With storage capacities up to 2GB, these little gizmos plug into any PC's USB port and are instantly recognized as an extra storage drive. Best of all, it's simple technology that almost always works. Hard to beat, especially when you need to take files back and forth from one location to another.

You get the idea. There's lots of gadgets you *can* carry, although you don't *have* to carry each and every one. Since many portable gadgets due double and triple duty, it's a matter of determining what types of tasks you'll need to do, and picking the right devices for those specific tasks. Do your planning, and you could end up with a single device in your briefcase. Don't, and you'll need an assistant to juggle all the different gadgets you carry along!

Shopping for a Laptop PC

For most businesspeople, a laptop PC is an essential portable gadget. With the right laptop, you can do practically any work you would normally do in your office from just about anywhere on the road.

Buying a laptop PC isn't all that simple, however, because there are so many different types on the market today. At the very least, you'll have to choose from these types of models:

- **Ultracompact**—If you primarily use your notebook for email and running the occasional PowerPoint presentation (using an external projector), and not for heavy-duty typing or number-crunching, this might be the type of machine for you. An ultracompact has a smaller screen (10"–12") and cozier keyboard than larger laptops, and consequently is smaller and weighs less—and also uses less power, which results in longer battery life. These puppies are easier to slide into a briefcase than larger models.

- **Business laptop**—For most non-executive road warriors, you actually need to do some real work when you travel—which means that a bigger screen and full-size keyboard are important. What we're talking about here is the traditional business laptop, with a 14"–15" screen, full-sized keyboard, combo CD/DVD drive, and enough computing horsepower for typical Word and Excel use. Do your homework and you can find a model that's relatively thin and not too heavy; you should also look for a unit that offers decent (3+ hours) battery life.

- **Desktop replacement**—If power matters more to you than portability, you want a laptop that can function as a full-featured desktop PC. These so-called desktop replacement models use standard Pentium 4 processors (instead of the portable-oriented Pentium M) and provide extra-large 15.4" or larger screens (typically widescreen) and CD/DVD burning capabilities. You also get more memory, bigger hard drives, and just about everything else you'd expect in a larger PC. The tradeoff comes in terms of size (bigger), weight (heavier), and battery life (none to speak of). A desktop replacement really isn't an option for a true road warrior, unless you're always in reach of a power outlet. (BTW, if you're looking for a laptop for game playing, as discussed in the previous chapter, this is the type of laptop you're looking for.)

- **Tablet PC**—This is a subspecies of the notebook PC, with a touch screen you can write on—with a stylus, that is, not a real pen. Tablets are great for specific tasks, such as meter reading or checking inventory in a warehouse. For most of us, they're totally unnecessary for standard computing tasks.

Whichever type of laptop you decide on, you'll want to make sure it meets some minimal performance specs. Assuming you don't go the Apple route (which I prefer, but you probably don't), you should look for a laptop that uses a Pentium M processor (runs cooler and uses less power than standard desktop Pentium 4 processors), has at least 512MB memory, offers built-in 802.11b/g WiFi wireless connectivity, and has a combo CD burner/DVD player drive.

By the way, machines billed as using Intel Centrino technology use Intel's Pentium M/WiFi chips, which is a sure-fire way to go—but not the only way. Some manufacturers use non-Intel WiFi chips, and even though they use the Pentium M processor, can't use the official Centrino logo. No big deal, as long as you get some sort of Pentium M/WiFi combination.

Looking forward, we're just about due for notebooks that use Intel's next-generation Centrino technology, dubbed Sonoma. These notebooks will have improved performance thanks to a 533Mhz bus, DDR2 RAM, PCI Express, and improved audio and video. Sonoma will also support something called stack execution disabling, which will improve security on next-generation notebooks. Look for it.

Choosing the Right PDA

Even though some experts say the traditional PDA is on the way out (to be replaced by smartphones and semi-smart cell phones), there's still a market for these little gizmos. No self-respectable gadget geek is without a clunky PDA clipped to his belt, after all.

Now, you wouldn't expect the PDA market to be any less confusing than other high-tech markets, which is why you have your choice of units that use the Palm operating system (Palm OS) or Microsoft's Pocket PC operating system. Palm OS devices tend to be a little lower-priced than Pocket PCs, although some of the high-end Palm models are every bit as expensive. Features tend to be comparable between the two types of devices, although you should go the Pocket PC route if you need to work with Word or Excel files; Pocket PCs incorporate "pocket" versions of both programs.

The big player in the Palm OS market is palmOne, as the old Palm company now calls itself. (Well, actually, they're going to go back to calling themselves just Palm again, but we'll stick with the PalmOne name just to be stubborn.) PalmOne manufactures two different lines of devices (three, if you count the Treo smartphones), the Tungsten line for business users and the Zire line for general consumer use.

The Pocket PC is Microsoft's answer to the Palm PDA. Pocket PCs tend to be a little more business-oriented and a little more powerful than Palm PDAs—and little more expensive, as well. The major Pocket PC manufacturers are HP and Dell.

Most users use their PDAs pretty much for managing contacts, scheduling appointments, and making to-do lists. (Oh, and playing games—never forget the games!) Palm OS PDAs synch with the Palm Desktop software for all these functions; Pocket PCs synch your Pocket PC contact and appointment lists with Microsoft Outlook. (Most Palm PDAs also come with utility programs that let you synch with Microsoft Outlook, if that's your preference.) In addition, Pocket PCs are a little more oriented towards traditional office tasks; they come with Pocket Word, Pocket Excel, and Pocket Money, so you can use your Pocket PC to edit the same files you use on your desktop PC.

Which type of PDA should you buy—Palm OS or Pocket PC? My general advice is that if all you need is basic calendar and address book functions, go with the lower-priced Palm OS. If you need to integrate with various Windows applications—Outlook, especially—then spring for a Pocket PC.

Whichever type of PDA you choose, here are some of the things to look for when shopping:

- **Size and weight**—You'll actually pay more for less—that is, the smaller units come at a premium. That said, some of the most expensive units are the largest, as they incorporate mini-keyboards and built-in cameras, which add to a unit's heft.

- **Speed and storage**—Even the least expensive PDA is fast enough and has enough built-in storage for all your contacts and scheduling information. If you want to play games, however, you'll want to consider a unit with a faster processor.

- **Screen**—Color is more expensive than monochrome, of course—but a lot easier on the eye. Some models have a slightly larger display, which is always nice.

- **Keyboard**—Most units feature stylus-based entry. If you prefer to type, consider a unit that features a mini-QWERTY keyboard.

- **Wireless connectivity**—If you're into connecting on the go, look for either Bluetooth or WiFi wireless connectivity.

- **Digital music players**—Many PDAs also function as digital music players, with built-in media player software. Because the built-in speaker typically leaves a lot to be desired, you'll probably want to do your listening via headphones.

- **Digital cameras**—For the ultimate in coolness, check out the models with built-in digital cameras. Just make sure you have plenty of storage capacity for all the photos you take!

Of Cell Phones and Smart Phones

Choosing a cell phone is a major lifestyle decision. Do you prefer a flip phone or a candy bar phone? Do you use it strictly for conversations, or do you do text messaging? Do you want to play games on your phone, or watch videos? How about taking pictures? And do you prefer a silver case or a blue one?

More important—well, equally important—is the cell phone provider, and the network technology used. As you've no doubt discovered, phones that work with one provider don't work with another provider. That's because different providers use different cell phone technologies. In the pre-digital days, analog cell phones used a technology called FDMA (frequency division multiple access). Today's digital networks (in the U.S., anyway) use different technologies. Sprint and Verizon use 800MHz or 1900MHz CDMA (code division multiple access) technology; Cingular and T-Mobile use 1900MHz GSM (global system for mobile communications) technology. Naturally, they're all incompatible with each other.

And that's just within the United States. Overseas (over any sea, actually), GSM technology is standard. However, since European and Asian providers use the 900MHz and 1800MHz bands, these systems are incompatible with the U.S. providers' 1900MHz GSM systems.

Confused yet?

It gets better, especially when you discover that different cell phone manufacturers produce different models for different systems. You might see a particular cell phone you like, but then find out it isn't available for your particular service provider. So you have to pick a model that works with your particular provider, and vice versa.

Then we have the topic of smartphones. A smartphone is a combination PDA and cell phone; that is, it's device that makes cellular calls and stores contact and scheduling information. Most smartphones offer a larger display than a normal cell phone (more like a PDA display), as well as a mini-QWERTY keyboard (for data entry).

Why would you want a smartphone? Well, if you carry both a PDA and a mobile phone, a smartphone lets you cut your number of portable gadgets by half—that's if you don't mind the compromises inherent in such a combo device, of course. You see, the typical smartphone is somewhat larger than a typical cell phone, shaped and sized more like a PDA. This makes for a somewhat awkward phone, but if you think of it as a PDA plus, then you're okay.

In any case, before you purchase any smartphone, you should give it a full try-out. Make sure it does everything you need it to do, in a way that's intuitive and comfortable to you. And definitely be sure you like the size and heft; whichever model you choose, you'll be using it a lot!

And, no matter which type of phone (smart or otherwise) you choose, check out all the various accessories available—especially headsets. If you use your cell phone for extended periods at a time, you know how uncomfortable it can get. That's why many people use some sort of headset, so they don't have to hold the handset to the side of their heads all the time.

All cell phone headsets include an earphone for listening and a microphone for talking. They're very popular among people who work all day on the phone, such as call center professionals. They're also great for using a cell phone in the car, which you really shouldn't be doing anyway, although I know you do.

Until recently, all headsets attached to the phone via a long cord—easy to connect, if somewhat inconvenient. Today, many new headsets attach cordlessly, thanks to Bluetooth wireless technology. If your phone is already Bluetooth-enabled (and more and more are), just synch a Bluetooth headset with your phone and you're ready to go. If you don't have a Bluetooth phone, you'll have to attach a Bluetooth adapter to it to use a wireless headset.

When you're shopping for a headset, whether wired or wireless, the main thing to look for is comfort. Do you like the way it hangs on your ear? You should also check the performance; those mini-mics don't always work that well, especially if you're a quiet speaker. You might have to evaluate several models to find one you really like. And then there's the style issue; some of these puppies are ultra-stylish, others look like giant plastic bugs growing out of your ear canal. Style is in the eye of the beholder (and the ear of the beholden), so choose accordingly.

Portable Storage for the Portable Lifestyle

Then there's the gadget for every road warrior—and even for those warriors who don't hit the road all that much. I'm talking about so-called USB memory devices, which are terrific gizmos for transferring data from one PC to another. These gadgets contain various amounts of flash memory and connect to any computer via a free USB port. When connected, your computer views the device just like another disk drive. You can then transfer files from your computer to the flash memory and back again.

What's especially cool about these USB memory devices is that they pack so much storage into such a small form factor. Most of these gizmos are truly keychain-sized; you can slip them in your pocket and easily carry them from PC to PC, which makes for truly portable mass storage. And, because they're pretty much plug-and-play, transferring your files from one computer to another is easy, which is great if you use multiple PCs or travel to various locations.

Some of the early USB memory devices didn't have much memory onboard—8MB and 16MB devices were common back then. But as the price of flash memory has come down, manufacturers have packed more and more memory into these little doodads. Some models today have 2GB or more capacity, which is big enough to store all but the biggest files. (Heck, that's big enough to hold a couple of CDs worth of music—uncompressed!)

Of course, the more storage offered, the higher the price. Today's lowest-priced USB memory devices give you 256MB of storage for $50 or less. Double that price and you'll get into the 1GB range; 2GB devices typically run over two bills. Choose the right size for your needs, as well as a form factor that you like, and you'll be a happy warrior.

NOTEBOOK PCS

Apple PowerBook G4

Leo's Pick

If you've ever heard me on the radio or on TV, you know that I'm an Apple fan. So it's no surprise that my favorite laptop is an Apple, in particular the PowerBook G4. I gotta tell ya, Apple knows how to do laptops right.

Let's start with the form factor, which is Apple's real forte. The PowerBook is sleek and slim, and looks as good with the case closed as it does in operation. The keyboard has a nice solid feel, and the screen (no matter which size you go with) is bright with a wide viewing angle. It's just a nice-looking machine, no matter how you look at it.

Apple offers three sizes of PowerBooks, for different on-the-go needs. The 12" model packs a lot of power into a case that's just 10.9" × 8.6" when closed; at just 4.6 pounds, it's ideal for users who like to travel light. The 15" model is more of a full-featured business machine, but still thin and relatively light (5.6 pounds). The big 17" model is a multimedia powerhouse, ideal for watching and editing video movies; it's not as portable as the others, but it's a true desktop replacement machine.

All three of the PowerBooks are super-thin, only 1.18" from top to bottom with the case closed. They all come with 512MB memory and Apple's DVD/CD SuperDrive; depending on the model, you get either a 1.5GHz or 1.67GHz PowerPC G4 processor. Hard disk capacities range from 60GB in the 12" model to 100GB in the 17" machine. (And here's something super-neat; the 15" and 17" models come with full-size illuminated keyboards!)

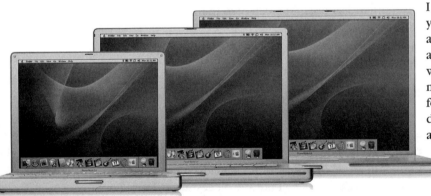

I could go on and on, but you get the picture. Apples are notoriously easy to use, and not as incompatible with Windows PCs as you might think. I know lots of folks who use a Windows desktop PC in the office and an Apple PowerBook on the road; it's a workable—and stylish—combination.

Model: PowerBook G4 **Manufacturer:** Apple (www.apple.com) **Models:** 12-inch Combo Drive (12.1" screen, 1024 × 768 resolution, 1.5GHz PowerPC G4 processor, 512MB memory, 60GB hard drive, 10.9" × 8.6" × 1.18"), 15-inch SuperDrive (15.2" screen, 1280 × 854 resolution, 1.67GHz PowerPC G4 processor, 512 memory, 80GB hard drive, 13.7" × 9.5" × 1.1"), 17-inch SuperDrive (17" screen, 1440 × 990 resolution, 1.67GHz PowerPC G4 processor, 512MB memory, 100GB hard drive, 15.4" × 10.2" × 1.0") **Price:** $1,499 (12-inch Combo Drive), $2,299 (15-inch SuperDrive), $2,699 (17-inch SuperDrive)

HP Compaq nc8230

Okay, so most of you prefer a Windows machine to an Apple, and that's okay. When you want a business-oriented Windows laptop, you can't do much better than HP's Compaq nc8230 series. You get a nice big 15.4" screen, 1.86GHz Intel Pentium M 750 processor, 1GB memory, 60GB hard drive, DVD/CD-R drive, and built-in 802.11g WiFi—all for less than two grand. The whole thing weighs just 5.8 pounds, and it's only 1.1" deep—a decent compromise between size/weight and performance.

Model: Compaq nc8230 **Manufacturer:** HP (www.hp.com) **Screen:** 15.4" **Processor:** 1.86GHz Intel Pentium M 750 **Memory:** 1GB **Hard drive:** 60GB **Weight:** 5.8 lbs. **Price:** $1,849

Sony VAIO T250

Many road warriors prefer an ultracompact laptop, like the Sony VAIO T250. This puppy measures just 10.7" (w) × 8.1" (d) × 1" (h) with the case closed, and weighs in at a paltry 3 pounds—just the right size and weight to carry in your briefcase. It features a 10.6" screen and Intel Centrino technology, so you get extremely long battery life—even with the DVD/CD burner. The only drawback is that the T250 is a tad pricy, but you gotta pay extra to make something this good this small.

Model: VAIO T250 **Manufacturer:** Sony (www.sonystyle.com) **Screen:** 10.6" **Processor:** 1.2GHz Intel Pentium M 753 **Memory:** 512MB **Hard drive:** 60GB **Weight:** 3 lbs. **Price:** $2,299

Averatec 6240

You might not have heard of Averatec, but I have, and I really like their products. What you get with the 6240 is a lot of performance in a decent-sized package (1.18" thick)—and an extremely affordable price. Even better, Averatec's PCs don't use a lot of power, so you get lots of battery time—more than 7 hours, if you're listening to audio CDs. Spec-wise, you get a 15.4" screen, 512MB RAM, 80GB hard drive, dual DVD burner, and built-in 802.11g WiFi. It might not be a name brand, but you get a lot for your money!

Model: 6240 **Manufacturer:** Averatec (www.averatec.com) **Screen:** 15.4" **Processor:** Mobile AMD Athlon64 3000+ **Memory:** 512MB **Hard drive:** 80GB **Weight:** 6 lbs. **Price:** $1,199

Toshiba Portege M200

And now for something completely different. Toshiba's Portege M200 is a combination tablet/notebook PC; just swivel the 12" screen around to write on it with a stylus, or leave it in place for regular typing. For tablet use, the screen rotates into either portrait or landscape orientation. Feature-wise, you get Centrino technology with built-in 802.11g WiFi and a 60GB hard drive; one drawback is that the base machine doesn't come with an optical drive (Toshiba offers an external USB DVD/CD drive, if you like).

Model: Portege M200 **Manufacturer:** Toshiba (www.toshiba.com) **Screen:** 12" **Processor:** 1.7GHz Intel Pentium M 735 **Memory:** 512MB **Hard drive:** 60GB **Weight:** 4.5 lbs. **Price:** $1,899

PDAS

palmOne LifeDrive

Leo's Pick

This new Palm OS gizmo is more than a simple PDA. The LifeDrive contains a 4GB hard drive that lets it store and transport PC files, as well as play digital audio and video files. To that end, palmOne doesn't call the LifeDrive a PDA, instead opting for the "Mobile Manager" moniker. Whatever you call it, it's a pretty impressive device.

Let's dispense with all the specs first. You get a 4G MicroDrive for storage, a big 320 × 480 pixel color display, built-in 802.11b WiFi and Bluetooth wireless, an SD/MMC expansion slot, and built-in voice recorder with microphone. It runs the Palm OS 5.4 ("Garnet") operating system, has 64MB RAM, and is powered by a 416MHz Intel XScale processor, which makes it every bit as powerful as competing Pocket PCs.

What makes the LifeDrive stand out from the average PDA is it's hard disk. The LifeDrive's 4GB drive is big enough to hold thousands of Word documents, 1,200 PowerPoint presentations, 1,000 digital photos, 2 1/2 hours of digital video, and such. File management is a drag and drop affair, with selected files easily synced to your PC. The LifeDrive has built-in support for Word, Excel, PowerPoint, and Adobe Acrobat files; it also syncs with Microsoft Outlook.

Another unique feature is the LifeDrive's capability as a digital media player. The LifeDrive's hard drive is the same size as the one in an iPod Mini, so there's plenty of storage for MP3 and WMA files—as well as an audio out jack to connect your earphones. The big color screen makes the LifeDrive a decent portable video player, as well, so you're all set for both music and movie playback.

So if you want one unit that can function as a PDA, portable audio player, portable video player, and wireless Internet access device, the LifeDrive does the job—it does all the jobs, actually. The only thing it doesn't do is function as a cell phone, but hey, you can't have everything!

Model: LifeDrive **Manufacturer:** palmOne (www.palmone.com) **Operating system:** Palm OS 5.4 **Display:** 320 × 480 **Dimensions:** 4.76" (h) × 2.87" (w) × 0.74" (d) **Weight:** 6.8 oz. **Price:** $499

palmOne Tungsten T5

If you don't want to splurge for the hard drive-enabled LifeDrive, the Tungsten T5 is an equally full-featured Palm OS PDA. It uses the same extra-large 320 × 480 display as the LifeDrive, which you can view in either portrait or landscape mode—just turn the T5 on its side, and the screen rotates into landscape mode. You also get built-in Bluetooth capability and an astounding 256MB memory—a lot of PDA for your money.

Model: Tungsten T5 **Manufacturer:** palmOne (www.palmone.com) **Operating system:** Palm OS 5.4 **Display:** 320 × 480 **Dimensions:** 4.76" (h) × 3.08" (w) × 0.61" (d) **Weight:** 5.1 oz. **Price:** $399

palmOne Zire 72

Tungsten is palmOne's business line; Zire models are aimed at the general consumer market, which means they're a little hipper and more stylish. Case in point: the Zire 72, a feature-packed PDA in a cool blue, rubberized case. The Zire 72's entertainment focus is evident from the built-in 1.2-megapixel digital camera that lets you shoot photos and video clips. You can also record voice memos and play digital audio files; Bluetooth wireless connectivity is built-in.

Model: Zire 72 **Manufacturer:** palmOne (www.palmone.com) **Operating system:** Palm OS 5.2.8 **Display:** 320 × 320 **Dimensions:** 4.6" (h) × 2.95" (w) × 0.67" (d) **Weight:** 4.8 oz. **Price:** $299

Dell Axim X50v

If a Pocket PC is what you want, Dell's Axim X50v is one fine PDA. First off, you get a beautiful 3.7" color screen, really big and sharp with 640 × 480 resolution—twice that of most handhelds. Second, you get both WiFi and Bluetooth wireless built-in, so you can connect to WiFi hotspots and sync up with Bluetooth accessories. Third, it just looks cool; this is one of the most stylish PDAs on the market today.

Model: Axim X50v **Manufacturer:** Dell (www.dell.com) **Operating system:** Windows Mobile 2003 Second Edition **Display:** 640 × 480 **Dimensions:** 4.7" (h) × 2.9" (w) × 0.7" (d) **Weight:** 6.2 oz. **Price:** $424

HP iPaq h4350

The iPaq h4350 is a full-featured model with a miniature QWERTY keyboard at the bottom of the unit, which makes entering data a snap. (Even cooler, the keys have blue backlighting for typing in the dark!) You also get dual WiFi and Bluetooth wireless, 64MB memory, and a nice 3.5" color display. Naturally, it runs all the standard Pocket PC applications, and lets you stay in touch at any public WiFi hotspot.

Model: iPaq h4350 **Manufacturer:** HP (www.hp.com) **Operating system:** Windows Mobile 2003 Premium Edition **Display:** 240 × 320 **Dimensions:** 5.4" (h) × 2.9" (w) × 0.6" (d) **Weight:** 5.8 oz. **Price:** $449

PDA ACCESSORIES

TomTom Navigator 2004

Leo's Pick

For the second year running, my Leo's Pick PDA accessory is the TomTom Navigator. This is a cool little gizmo that turns your PDA into a full-fledged GPS navigation system. It offers all the features you'd find in a handheld GPS device, but routes all the information and maps through your PDA.

The Navigator connects to your PDA via Bluetooth wireless technology; you can carry the remote GPS unit in your hand or mount it on your dashboard and then read the results on your PDA's screen. This means that you can use the Navigator as either a handheld or automotive GPS device. TomTom offers models for both Palm and Pocket PC units, as well as lower-priced wired models that forego the wireless Bluetooth connection.

TomTom's navigation software includes tons of U.S. maps, liberally sprinkled with gas stations, restaurants, and other points of interest. The TomTom Navigator not only shows you where you are, but also offers door-to-door 2D or 3D navigation and voice-guided turn-by-turn instructions.

Obviously, you want to plan your route before you start driving, and you can do so by selecting your start and destination from the currently displayed map, entering the start and end addresses manually, or simply tapping the name of the person you want to visit in your PDA's address book. It's really that easy.

I particularly like the "avoid roadblock" feature that provides instant rerouting around major construction and traffic congestion. The Navigator even displays the total distance for your trip and your estimated time of arrival. And if you take a wrong turn, it takes that into account and recalculates your route automatically.

Model: TomTom Navigator 2004 **Manufacturer:** TomTom (www.tomtom.com) **Price:** $299

HP Bluetooth iPaq Headphones

If you're an HP iPaq user, here's a neat little accessory. These headphones let you use your iPaq as a portable music player, while you listen in private—without any cord between your headphones and your PDA. Connection is via Bluetooth wireless technology, and the headphone itself is a comfortable behind-the-head design.

Model: Bluetooth iPaq Headphones **Manufacturer:** HP (www.hp.com) **Price:** $99.99

palmOne Universal Wireless Keyboard

Inputting data via stylus is a pain; it's much easier to type in large amounts of data, which is where palmOne's Universal Wireless Keyboard comes in. As the name implies, it's a full-size keyboard that connects to your PDA via Bluetooth wireless connection. And, even though this accessory comes from palmOne, it works with any type of PDA—even Pocket PC models.

Model: Universal Wireless Keyboard **Manufacturer:** palmOne (www.palmone.com) **Price:** $69.99

Veo Photo Traveler Camera

Add a digital camera to your PDA with Veo's Photo Traveler. The Photo Traveler is a 1.3-megapixel camera with 4X digital zoom; it can also be used to shoot moving videos. You can fine-tune your image with the unit's focus dial. The Photo Traveler connects to the expansion slot on the top of your PDA. Versions are available for most major Palm and Pocket PC models.

Model: Photo Traveler **Manufacturer:** Veo Products (www.veo.com) **Price:** $99.99

ZIP-LINQ Sync-n-Charge Cables

Here's a neat idea: Recharge your PDA from your laptop PC, so you don't have to carry that bulky PDA recharger with you when you travel. Instead, use ZIP-LINQ's Sync-N-Charge cable to connect your PDA to your PC, via USB. Once connected, the cable automatically syncs your data and recharges your PDA. The cable itself includes a retractable doohickey, so when you're not using it it's nice and compact. Sync-N-Charge cables are available for most major Palm and Pocket PC models, as well as selected smart phones.

Model: Sync-n-Charge **Manufacturer:** ZIP-LINQ (www.ziplinq.com) **Price:** $9.99

SMARTPHONES

palmOne Treo 650

Leo's Pick

A smartphone is a mobile phone that adds PDA functionality. That is, it's a cell phone you can use like a PDA—or a PDA you can use like a phone.

My favorite smartphone is the Treo 650, the latest update of my last year's Leo's Pick, the venerable Treo 600. The nice thing about the Treo 650, like its predecessor, is that it does both things well—it's a good phone *and* a good Palm OS PDA, no compromises on either side.

Design-wise, the Treo 650 looks like a PDA with a miniature QWERTY keyboard at the bottom. While it's a little bigger than a standard cell phone, it's still small enough to fit nicely in your hand—and, when you're talking, against your ear.

As you might expect, the Treo 650 functions both as a cell phone and as a Palm OS PDA. That means you can use it to manage all your appointments and contacts—and dial directly from your Palm address book.

But, as the carnival barker used to say, that's not all, folks. The Treo 650 also has a built-in camera, complete with picture caller ID on the big touch-screen display. You can also use the touch-screen to display an onscreen dial pad for push-button dialing.

And there's more. The Treo 650 has an integrated speaker phone, a built-in MP3 player, an SD/MMC expansion slot, and Bluetooth wireless connectivity. You also get all the applications that come with the Palm OS operating system, as well as Internet email, SMS text messaging, and MMS multimedia messaging. It's Internet-enabled with a color Web browser. Lots of features in a handy all-in-one device; pretty smart, eh?

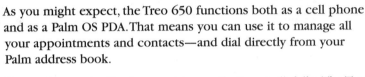

Model: Treo 650 **Manufacturer:** palmOne (www.palmone.com) **Operating system:** Palm OS 5.4 **Display:** 320 × 320 touchscreen **Cellular operation:** 850/900/1800/1900MHz (GSM/GPRS model), 800/1900MHz (CDMA model) **Dimensions:** 4.4" (h) × 2.3" (w) × 0.9" (d) **Weight:** 6.3 oz. **Price:** $449

Blackberry 7100T

Here's another PDA/smartphone from the folks who make those cool little BlackBerry email/pager devices. This gadget comes with a high-resolution 65,000-color touchscreen display, as well as a mini-QWERTY keyboard, in a non-flip form factor. And it's a little smaller and a lot lighter than the competing Treo, so it feels a little more like a standard cell phone in your hand.

Model: 7100T **Manufacturer:** Blackberry (www.blackberry.com) **Cellular operation:** 850/900/1800/1900MHz GSM/GPRS **Dimensions:** 4.7" (h) × 2.3" (w) × 0.8" (d) **Weight:** 4.2 oz. **Price:** $249.95

Sony Ericsson P910a

The Sony Ericsson P910a is a cell phone that's also a PDA that's also a digital camera that's also a game playing machine, all in a flip-phone form factor. When closed, the flip portion contains the dialing keypad. Flip it open to get access to the full 65,000-color touchscreen display and QWERTY keyboard. Turn the unit sideways to play games, including the preinstalled V-Rally racing game. You also get a digital still/video camera and the ability to save photos and video clips to Memory Stick media.

Model: P910a **Manufacturer:** Sony Ericsson (www.sonyericsson.com) **Display:** 208 × 320 touchscreen **Cellular operation:** 850/1800/1900MHz GSM/GPRS **Dimensions:** 4.5" (h) × 2.3" (w) × 1" (d) **Weight:** 5.5 oz. **Price:** $649

Siemens SX66

What I like about the Siemens SX66 smartphone is the slide-out QWERTY keyboard. Push the keyboard in, and you have a fairly compact candy bar design—with a big 3.5" color screen, of course. Pull it out, and you can enter text and other data. Feature-wise, check out the dual WiFi/Bluetooth wireless, as well as USB connectivity. The SX66 also has a built-in speakerphone, and the ability to play MP3, WMA, and WAV audio files.

Model: SX66 **Manufacturer:** Siemens (www. siemens-mobile.com) **Display:** 240 × 320 **Operating system:** Windows Mobile 2003 Second Edition **Cellular service:** 850/1800/1900MHz GSM/GPRS **Dimensions:** 4.92" (h) × 2.82" (w) × 0.74" (d) **Weight:** 7.4 oz. **Price:** $549.99

Motorola A630

This is a different-looking smartphone, kind of like a little candy bar that flips open horizontally to reveal a bigger-than-normal QWERTY keyboard and decent-sized color display. Keep it closed to use it like a normal (and normal-sized) cell phone. It's heavily feature-laden, as you might expect, including a built-in speaker phone. Stylish, practical, and well-designed—it's worth a look-see.

Model: A630 **Manufacturer:** Motorola (www. motorola.com) **Display:** 176 × 200 **Cellular service:** 850/1800/1900 or 900/1800/1900 GSM/GPRS **Dimensions:** 3.74" (h) × 1.91" (w) × 0.93" (d) **Weight:** 3.95 oz. **Price:** $299.99

CELL PHONES

Motorola Razr V3

Leo's Pick

With the current trend in cell phones being bigger and bulkier with more and more useless features, it's nice to find a stylish phone in an ultra-small form factor—which precisely describes this season's hottest model, Motorola's Razr V3.

First off, there's no denying the visual appeal of this slick little phone—it's small and thin and light and very sexy. At just a half-inch thick, it's small enough to fit in any pocket, including one in a tight pair of jeans. And the anodized aluminum case and cool-blue touch keypad are the height of 21st-century high-tech.

What's really amazing is how much technology Motorola crammed into this little gizmo. You get Bluetooth wireless connectivity, MPEG4 video playback, a VGA-quality digital camera, and a built-in speakerphone. The color display is an ample 2.2" diagonal, big enough for watching those videos or playing downloaded games. (Did I mention you can download and play 3D Java games? The Razr has 5MB of memory you can fill up with useless stuff like this.)

Of course, the Razr has all the expected cell phone functions, including MP3 ringtones, 1,000-entry phone book, VibraCall alert, and MMS/SMS messaging. It also has basic PIM functionality, along with a calendar and alarm clock. And, surprisingly, battery life isn't bad, with up to 430 minutes of talk time.

You don't buy a phone like this for its features, however—no matter how useful those features might be. You buy it because it looks cool, and when it comes to cell-phone cool, there's nothing out there that beats the Razr V3. All the trendsetters have one!

Model: Razr V3 **Manufacturer:** Motorola (www.motorola.com) **Display:** 176 × 200 (internal), 96 × 80 (external) **Cellular service:** 850/900/1800/1900 GSM/GPRS **Dimensions:** 3.86" (h) × 2.08" (w) × 0.54" (d) **Specs:** 3.35 oz. **Price:** $599.99

Sony Ericsson S710a

Not all phones have to flip open; some swivel. My favorite swivel phone is the Sony Ericsson S710z, which hides its keypad until you swivel it open. The display (visible all the time) is an oversized 2.3" diagonal with 240×320 resolution. You also get a built-in digital camera, unique five-way directional button to control the phone's operations, slot for Memory Stick DUO flash memory, and Bluetooth wireless connectivity. Lots of features, unique design—definitely high on the gadget cool factor.

Model: S710a **Manufacturer:** Sony Ericsson (www.sonyericsson.com) **Display:** 240×320 **Cellular service:** 850/1800/1900Mhz GSM/GPRS/EDGE **Dimensions:** 4.23" (h) × 1.93" (w) × 0.96" (d) **Weight:** 4.83 oz. **Price:** $499.99

Nokia N90

Nokia's N90 is another swivel phone, but this one swivels in a much different fashion. The top portion of the clamshell twists and turns to turn the phone into a digital camera or camcorder-like device. (It also has an extra-sharp 352×416 color display.) The N90 features a 2 megapixel digital camera with Carl Zeiss lens and integrated flash, 352×288 pixel video camera, Bluetooth wireless, and (surprise!) a USB connection. It's a little bigger than the average phone, but look at everything it packs in!

Model: N90 **Manufacturer:** Nokia (www.nokia.com) **Display:** 352×416 **Cellular service:** 900/1800/1900 GSM/GPRS/EDGE **Dimensions:** 4.4" (h) × 2.0" (w) × 0.9" (d) **Weight:** 6.1 oz. **Price:** $249.95

Sanyo MM-5600

Sanyo's MM-5600 is a good choice for a compact camera phone. It features a 1.3 megapixel digital camera, built-in speakerphone, and 2.1" color display, and supports Sprint's Ready Link walkie-talkie service. You even get an internal voice recorder with 60 minutes of record time—great for recording important conversations and interviews.

Model: MM-5600 **Manufacturer:** Sanyo (www.sanyo.com) **Display:** 240×320 (internal), 72×96 (external) **Cellular service:** 800/1900MHz GSM **Dimensions:** 3.66" (h) × 1.91" (w) × 1.04" (d) **Weight:** 4.52 oz. **Price:** $429.99

Siemens S66

The Siemens S66 (not to be confused with the SX66 smartphone) is a good-looking candy bar phone with strong multimedia features. You get a 1.3 megapixel digital camera, integrated video recorder, video player, and digital music player—all in a compact package. Phone-wise, there's Bluetooth wireless connectivity, MMS and text messaging, and—believe it or not—a built-in calculator and currency converter (!). Quite a performer—and quite stylish, as well.

Model: S66 **Manufacturer:** Siemens (www.siemens-mobile.com) **Cellular service:** 850/1800/1900MHz GSM **Dimensions:** 4.3" (h) × 1.9" (w) × 0.7" (d) **Weight:** 3.45 oz. **Price:** $299.99

HEADSETS

Nextlink Bluespoon Digital

Leo's Pick

Nextlink claims that its Bluespoon headsets are the smallest and lightest in the world, and that's not an idle claim. Using technology that Nextlink perfected for the military, the Bluespoon Digital weighs just 10 grams, and fits on the inside the curve of your ear. It's really that small!

Nextlink's military technology also enables superior performance for the Bluespoon Digital. What you get is adaptive digital noise cancellation that filters out unwanted background noise, for an extra-quiet listening experience. It's the quietest phone headset I've ever used.

What's really neat about the Bluespoon is that it uses a spring to place the headset in your ear, for perfect placement. It's safe, it's secure, and it won't pop out if you wear it while running, dancing, or jumping around like a madman. As the company says, this makes the headset the "natural choice for active people with the need for quality communication while on the move." Yeah, man.

Naturally, the Bluespoon Digital uses Bluetooth technology for a hands-free wireless connection to your Bluetooth-compatible phone. For added convenience, the headset features voice dialing—no need to touch your phone at all.

The headset comes with four different recharging cables, including a USB cable that lets you recharged from your notebook PC. Fully charged, the Bluespoon Digital should provide up to six hours of talk time, or 200 hours on standby.

Small, light, and quiet. It's everything you want in a wireless phone headset—even if it does look like you have a big ladybug in your ear.

Model: Bluespoon Digital **Manufacturer:** Nextlink (www.nextlink.to/) **Connection:** Bluetooth
Dimensions: 1.85" × 0.98" × 9.98" **Weight:** 0.35 oz. (10 grams) **Price:** $350

Jabra BT800

Here's a stylish and functional little wireless headset. The Jabra BT800 puts all of your phone's important controls on the headset itself—mute button, jog wheel, and answer and end buttons. You even get a blue backlit LCD screen that displays incoming caller ID—although how you're supposed to read the display when it's in your ear escapes me. Still, it's a nice design (aside from the LCD) for a good-performing Bluetooth headset.

Model: BT800 **Manufacturer:** Jabra (www.jabra.com) **Connection:** Bluetooth **Dimensions:** 2.7" × 1.3" × 1" **Weight:** 0.8 oz. **Price:** $149.99

Logitech Mobile Pro

Logitech put one of the first cordless headsets on the market, and company is still a market leader. The Mobile Pro is an affordable headset that connects cordlessly to any Bluetooth-enabled cell phone and has a long 7-hour talk time. This unit has a flexible, soft-touch headset for comfortable fit on either ear, and the microphone is of the noise-canceling type.

Model: Mobile Pro **Manufacturer:** Logitech (www.logitech.com) **Connection:** Bluetooth **Specs:** 1 oz. **Price:** $99.99

Jawbone Adaptive Headset

The Jawbone is a corded headset with adaptive noise reduction technology. It constantly adapts the incoming audio to the room's background noise, raising the sound level when necessary and lowering it when not. The adaptive technology even works with the microphone, to filter out background noise from your voice. The result is crystal-clear sound quality that makes you sound better to your callers—and hear better, too.

Model: Jawbone **Manufacturer:** Jawbone (www.jawbone.com) **Connection:** Corded **Weight:** 0.5 oz. **Price:** $149.95

Shure QuietSpot Boom

If you want a more affordable noise-blocking headset, go with Shure's QuietSpot Boom. The NoiseBlocker earphone reduces outside noise by 80%, while the noise-canceling boom microphone (with foam windscreen) blocks 70% of extraneous noise. The result is remarkably quiet sound at a decent price—if you don't mind going the corded route.

Model: QSHB3 **Manufacturer:** Shure (www.shure.com) **Connection:** Corded **Weight:** 0.8 oz. **Price:** $39.99

KEYCHAIN STORAGE DEVICES

Verbatim Store 'n' Go Pro

Leo's Pick

Most USB storage devices look alike, but that doesn't mean they all perform alike. Verbatim's Store 'n' Go Pro drives are just a little faster than the average drive, which makes transferring large amounts of data a little less of a chore. Read speeds approach 23MB/second, with write speeds in the 14MB/second neighborhood (on a USB 2.0 connection), which makes the Store 'n' Go Pro one of the fastest USB drives out there. And, as you know, a second or two here and a second or two there add up over time.

Physically, the Store 'n' Go Pro occupies an attractive transparent colored plastic case, complete with a dual-color LED that flashes while data is being transferred. The device itself is ultra slim, especially when compared to similar keychain devices, which makes it easier to plug into stacked USB ports on your PC.

Each drive comes with V-Safe security software and V-Key file software, on an accompanying mini-CD. Install the software on each PC on which you use the Store 'n' Go drive, and you can format your USB drive with a password-protection section for added security.

The Store 'n' Go Pro is available in 256MB, 512MB, 1GB, and 2GB sizes. For the price you also get a lanyard to carry the device around your neck, as well as a set of personal identification labels.

Model: Store 'n' Go Pro **Manufacturer:** Verbatim (www.verbatim.com) **Capacity/price:** 256MB ($50), 512MB ($70), 1GB ($135), 2GB ($170)

Kingston DataTraveler Elite

Kingston's DataTraveler Elite is another good high-speed USB memory device. Read speed is 24MB/second; write speed is 14MB/second. TravelerSafe+ software lets you set password access control; My Traveler software helps you organize the drive's contents.

Model: DataTraveler Elite **Manufacturer:** Kingston (www.kingston.com) **Capacity/price:** 256MB ($50), 512MB ($65), 1GB ($130), 2GB ($230)

Lexar JumpDrive Lightning

Lexar's JumpDrive Lightning comes in a stylish stainless steel case, with file synchronization and security software pre-loaded. The 2GB version offers 24MB/second read and 18MB/second write speed; the 1GB version is almost as fast.

Model: JumpDrive Lightning **Manufacturer:** Lexar (www.lexar.com) **Capacity/price:** 1GB ($139.99), 2GB ($270)

Apacer Handy Steno

Apacer offers the highest-capacity USB drives around, topping out at 4GB of storage. Read speed is 20MB/second; write speed is 14MB/second.

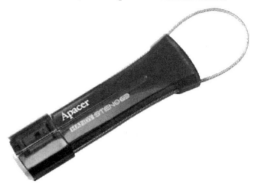

Model: HT203 **Manufacturer:** Apacer (www.apacer.com) **Capacity/price:** 256MB ($40), 512MB ($60), 1GB ($100), 2GB ($200), 4GB ($380)

USB Sushi Drives

USB drives don't have to be practical—they can also be fun! And what's more fun than a USB storage device in the shape of a piece of sushi? These "sushi disks" are available in various shapes—shuumai, ebi, salmon, futomaki, cucumber maki, and so on. And, unusual as they look, they really work.

Distributor: Dynamism (www.dynamism.com/sushidisk/) **Capacity/price:** 32MB ($59), 128MB ($99)

MORE COOL ROAD WARRIOR GADGETS

Canary Wireless Digital Hotspotter

The Digital Hotspotter is a second-generation device that not only senses WiFi hotspots, but also tells you (via its LCD display) the name (SSID) of the available network, signal strength, and encryption status. It's a great little gadget to carry when you're traveling, and need wireless Internet access.

Model: HS10 **Manufacturer:** Canary Wireless (www.canarywireless.com) **Price:** $59.95

Targus DEFCON MDP Motion Sensor

The DEFCON MDP is a PC card you insert into your notebook computer to deter theft. The card contains a tiny tilt motion sensor which senses when a thief is making off with your PC; it then sounds a 110dB alarm and prohibits unapproved access. It includes its own rechargeable battery, so your PC is protected even if it's turned off.

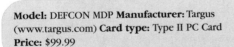

Model: DEFCON MDP **Manufacturer:** Targus (www.targus.com) **Card type:** Type II PC Card **Price:** $99.99

Keynamics Reclinable Laptop Stand

Most notebook PCs are something less than ergonomic. To provide a more comfortable typing position, check out the Keynamics Reclinable Laptop Stand. This stand puts your PC at a comfortable angle, and even provides better access to the back-of-unit ports. Even better, the stand itself is on rollers, so it's easy to move in and out of position on your desktop.

Model: Reclinable Laptop Stand **Manufacturer:** Keynamics (www.keynamics.com) **Price:** $79.99

Vantec LapCool 2 Notebook Cooler

Here's a really cool notebook PC gadget—obvious pun intended. The LapCool 2 notebook cooler helps cool down hot-running notebooks, thanks to two ultra-quiet fans in the base. The LapCool has a flat 11.8" × 10.3" surface, so just about any notebook fits on top and stays cool while doing so. Added bonus— the LapCool 2 also functions as a four-port USB 2.0 hub, so you can get double duty from the desktop footprint.

Model: LPC-305 **Manufacturer:** Vantec (www. vantecusa.com) **Dimensions:** 11.8" × 10.3" × 0.8" **Price:** $39.99

FreePlay FreeCharge

When your cell phone battery runs out, what do you do? Well, with the FreePlay FreeCharge, you crank it up—that is, you turn the crank to recharge the battery. The FreeCharge provides emergency power to your phone; you get 2–3 minutes of talk time per 45-second crank. It's better than not having any power at all!

Model: FreeCharge **Manufacturer:** FreePlay (www.freeplayenergy.com) **Price:** $65

Western Digital WD Passport Pocket Hard Drive

USB flash drives are nice, but sometimes you just need more storage than you get with those little gizmos. The answer is to carry around a portable hard drive, like the WD Passport. This is an 80GB hard drive that's small enough to fit in your pocket; it connects to any PC via USB, which makes it ideal for transferring data from PC to PC.

Model: WDXML800UETN **Manufacturer:** Western Digital (www.wdc.com) **Capacity:** 80GB **Dimensions:** 5.68" × 3.51" × 0.83" **Price:** $199.99

Creative WebCam Notebook

I covered desktop webcams back in the computer gadgets section, but let's take a quick look at a webcam specifically designed for notebook PCs. I'm talking about Creative's WebCam Notebook, which is a super-small penlight-style camera that clips to the top of your notebook screen and connects to any open USB port. It shoots a 640 × 480 resolution picture, and tilts vertically a total of 270°.

Model: WebCam Notebook **Manufacturer:** Creative (www.creative.com) **Resolution:** 640 × 480 **Dimensions:** 2.3" × 1" × 1.6" **Price:** $49.99

Bose QuietComfort 2 Noise Canceling Headphones

The Bose QuietComfort 2 is, without a doubt, the quietest headphone on the market today—which is why you see so many of them in use on long business flights. Bose's Acoustic Noise Canceling technology electronically identifies and then reduces unwanted noise. You don't even have to listen to music to use these phones; just put them on, turn them on, and hear virtually all background noise disappear. Connectors include a standard mini-plug for use with portable devices, a 1/4" adapter for home audio equipment, and a dual plug adapter to use when flying.

Model: QuietComfort 2 **Manufacturer:** Bose (www.bose.com) **Weight:** 6.9 oz. **Price:** $299

The Ultimate High-Tech Car Owner

HOW TO BECOME THE ULTIMATE HIGH-TECH CAR OWNER

Cars are becoming more and more computerized. If you don't believe me, take a new mid-priced car to an older independent mechanic; unless you need your oil changed or your brakes relined, the poor guy will quickly be over his head. Take the same car to the repair shop at your local car dealer, and you'll find all sorts of high-tech gizmos sitting around, just waiting to be plugged into the waiting vehicle. A surprising number of vehicular functions are controlled by microchips and electronic circuits; problems are diagnosed by computer, and sometimes fixed by reprogramming or replacing the chips. It's all very gee-whiz 21st-century stuff, light-years away from banging on the cylinder block with a monkey wrench.

High-performance car owners know that their vehicles can be tuned by reconfiguring various electronics, or by replacing stock chips with high-performance versions. It kind of amazes me that you can get a few extra horsepower out of the same engine just by changing control chips, but that's the way things are today. Whether you know it or not, you *are* a high-tech car owner.

The electronics under the hood aren't the only high-tech gadgets inside your car, however. There are plenty more gizmos in your dash, controlling your car's display, heating/cooling system, and audio system. In fact, the audio system in your car is every bit as high-tech as the audio system in your home, if not more so. After all, if you're like me you spend a lot more time listening to music in your car than you do in your home; it makes sense to have the best audio system possible in your traveling listening pod!

Choosing the Right In-Dash Audio System

As good as some factory audio systems are, the ultimate high-tech car owner doesn't settle for what Ford or Chevrolet or even BMW supplies. Much better sound can come by putting your own audio components in the dash—and your own speakers in the doors. In addition, when you go the custom route you can choose which functions you want; you're not limited to simple AM/FM/CD sources.

One such function is satellite radio. As I'll discuss in a minute, satellite radio offers more programming choices and higher quality sound than you get from standard AM/FM radio. Many in-dash systems today come with either SIRIUS or XM radio built-in; other systems are XM or SIRIUS compatible, meaning that they have a plug in for an optional satellite receiver. Even if you choose not to add satellite radio at the moment, it's good to have a system that can be upgraded in the future, if you choose.

Another popular feature is iPod compatibility. These systems have an input jack for an Apple iPod or other portable music player, so that you can listen to your iPod through your car's audio system. This is a much better option than beaming your iPod via an FM transmitter, which sometimes works and sometimes doesn't, depending on adjacent FM stations in the area. If you're an iPod junky, this sort of adaptability is crucial.

You should also make the upfront choice of whether you want an audio-only system or whether you want a system that can also play DVD movies. A DVD entertainment system has a big dash-mounted color LCD display, which also doubles as a control panel for the regular audio functions. DVD playback capability is not something you can easily add to an existing system; you'll need to choose this option upfront.

A final option to consider is HD radio. This high-definition format is actually digital radio—traditional terrestrial AM and FM radio broadcast in digital (rather than traditional analog) format. HD radio dramatically increases the quality of the broadcast signal, making AM sound like traditional FM, and giving FM CD-quality sound. Unfortunately, there aren't a whole lot of radio stations broadcasting in the HD format, so check to see what's available in your area before you invest in this technology.

As to choosing one in-dash audio system over another, the three things to consider are sound quality, features, and usability. Sound quality is typically reflected in the unit's power rating; the more power, the better the sound. (Although, to be honest, most high-end systems promise a similar 50 watts per channel peak power, so where's the difference in that?) Features we just discussed, and usability is something you have to determine for yourself. Remember, you'll typi-

cally be changing channels while driving, so make sure the unit can be easily operated by touch. You don't want to have to take your eyes off the road just to scan to the next station!

Adding Satellite Radio

If you're on the road a lot, you know how frustrating it is to have radio stations fade in and out as you drive through (and out of) their broadcast areas. Satellite radio offers the much better alternative of fade-free nationwide coverage—you're never out of range. Plus, you get over a hundred channels of entertainment, with a good mix of music and talk, all with high-quality digital sound.

In the United States, there are two similar but competing satellite radio services: SIRIUS Satellite Radio and XM Radio. Both offer satellite radio receivers for in-home and in-car listening, both offer similar programming packages, and both charge a similar monthly subscription fee.

Both XM and SIRIUS work in a similar, deceptively simple, manner. In essence, they bounce digital signals off orbiting satellites; the signals are then received and decoded by compatible satellite receivers back on Earth. XM uses two Boeing HS 702 satellites (dubbed "Rock" and "Roll") in geostationary orbit approximately 22,000 miles above the Earth. Instead of geosynchronous satellites, SIRIUS uses three Space Systems/Loral satellites in an inclined elliptical constellation; this configuration puts at least one satellite over the U.S. at all times.

One of the things I really like about both the XM and Sirius systems is that the digital stream transmits more than music; there's room for the service to transmit data about the music that's playing, including artist and song information. Most satellite radio receivers have big multiline LCD displays for just this purpose.

To listen to either XM or Sirius in your car, you need to invest in a satellite radio receiver. You can choose to replace your old car radio with an XM- or Sirius-capable model, add a separate XM or Sirius tuner to your existing in-dash receiver, or use a portable radio "shuttle" unit that sends the satellite radio signals through your car's FM radio or cassette deck. The advantage of a portable unit is that you can move it between your car and home, with an optional home adapter. Of course, you'll also need to install a satellite antenna, which is one more thing to hang on the outside of your car.

The big question, however, is which satellite system you should go with—XM or Sirius. In some ways, you can't go wrong with either system, because they're both fairly similar in a lot of ways; for example, they both cost $12.95 per month. That said, there are some differences.

In terms of programming, XM is a little more adventurous with its music programming, while SIRIUS is a little more attuned to the news radio junkie—although that's probably a subjective evaluation. They're both good for sports, but in different ways; XM has deals to broadcast college football and basketball, major league baseball, and NASCAR races, while SIRIUS broadcasts NFL games and various college sports. SIRIUS has also signed shock jock Howard Stern to an exclusive contract starting later in 2005.

Audio-wise, both sound pretty good in the car—much better than regular FM radio. That said, XM sounds slightly better to perceptive ears; SIRIUS has some noticeable audio compression that bothers some listeners.

Between the two, XM is the most popular system, with twice as many subscribers as SIRIUS has. Does this mean XM is the better system? Not necessarily, but for what it's worth XM is what I have in my car, and I love it. Check out the programming on both systems, however, before you make your choice.

Video Killed the Radio Star

Between your CD player, AM radio, FM radio, and 130+ channels of satellite radio, you ought to be fully entertained while driving from point A to point B. But if you travel with kids, you know that's not enough. When they start getting wriggly and whiny in the back seat, you need something else to settle them down. And what's more engaging than watching a movie?

Movies in the car, you say? Yeah, it's possible—and becoming more and more common, thanks to the profusion of mobile video systems. These systems typically consist of a DVD player (which doubles as a CD player, of course), an LCD screen, and some sort of audio. Most video systems connect to and use your car's existing stereo system; some even have dual-zone operation, which lets you listen to the radio in the front seat while your kids listen to movie sound in the back. For more privacy, consider having your kids use headphones—maybe even a set of wireless phones, for best mobility.

When it comes to screen placement, you have some choices. Most in-car systems are dash-mounted, with the screen sliding out and flipping up for viewing. The only problem with this type of system is that rear-seat passengers have to view the screen from between the front seats, which can be problematic.

The other option is to mount one or more displays in the rear passenger compartment. You can find screens that mount on the roof and fold down for viewing, screens that attach to the rear of your car's front seats, and screens built in to the back of front-seat headrests. See your installer for additional options.

Now, back to the in-dash display, which you can use for more than DVD video. These touch-screen displays can show map and navigation data, be connected to a rear-firing video camera (great for when you're backing up), or be used to control your entire audio system. (That's why they have touch screens; you get an assortment of virtual controls on the screen that you can then press as needed.) Most systems also have input jacks that let your kids connect their favorite videogame systems—which is another great way to keep them happy during long trips.

Getting to Where You Want to Go

Driving is fun—when you know where your going. If you're on vacation or driving through a strange city, it's all too easy to get lost. And, if you're like me, you're loathe to stop and ask directions. (That's admitting defeat!)

So what do you do when you're not quite sure how to get to where you're going? Well, if you have a GPS navigation system in your car, you're in good shape; you'll not only be able to figure out where you are, but where you need to go.

If you're new to the technology, GPS stands for *global positioning system*, which is a way to determine location based on signals beamed from a network of 24 satellites positioned in six geosynchronized orbital paths around the Earth. A GPS unit receives signals from several of these satellites simultaneously, measures the speed of each satellite, and compares it relative to the unit's location—thus determining your latitude, longitude, and altitude. That is, it tells you where you're at. Precisely.

It's rather complicated technology, originally developed for military use, which has now filtered down to the consumer level. Automotive GPS units are remarkably easy to use; the gizmo can not only tell you where you are, but also show you where you're going. You punch in a location, and the GPS software maps out a route and displays it on an onscreen map. Your current position is marked on the map, and the map scrolls as you travel. Most units provide turn-by-turn directions; some even use a synthesized voice to tell you what to do next. The latter option is particularly useful when you're driving, so you don't have to take your eyes off the road.

Most automotive GPS systems come with either windshield or dashboard mounts and are typically battery powered, although some can also tap into your car's DC power. Most car GPS devices come specially configured for road travel, with a variety of points of interest—gas stations, restaurants, hotels, ATMs, and so on—preprogrammed into memory. You also get built-in road maps, of course, as well as those turn-by-turn driving instructions.

When shopping, compare the many different kinds of displays offered by various devices. You typically have your choice of traditional overhead-view road maps or text instructions; some devices even provide a 3D view of the road as you drive it. The bigger the display, the better.

The other big difference between devices is whether the maps and points of interest are preloaded onto the device's hard drive or have to be downloaded from your computer (typically via media cards) as you need them. The advantage of preloading is convenience, of course; the advantage of load-as-you-go systems is that you can download updated maps as they become available. In any case, make sure you get adequate map coverage for whatever regions you frequently travel.

You should also do a basic specs comparison. First, determine how many satellites a unit uses for navigation (sometimes described as the number of *channels*); most utilize 12 satellites, but others use more for higher accuracy. Second, examine the base maps that come with the unit; make sure your home area is fully covered. Third, see how many routes the unit can store in memory; the more, the merrier. Fourth, find out how many *waypoints* the device can store. (A waypoint is a place or attraction along a route—like a gas station or restaurant.) Fifth, look for the largest number of *track points*, which are locations you manually add to your route. Finally, examine the GPS-to-PC connection and the mapping software that comes with the unit.

Other features to look for are portability, which lets you take the unit with you when you change cars or use it in a rental car when you travel; audible alerts when you near turns; and the ability to quickly recalculate your route if you make a detour or take a wrong turn. Also make sure you're comfortable with the size and viewability of the display. Purchase the right unit, and you'll never get lost again!

IN-DASH AUDIO SYSTEMS

Sony MEX-R5

Leo's Pick

There are a lot of really cool car audio systems out there, but Sony's MEX-R5 takes the coolness to a new level. In addition to being a first-rate in-dash audio system, it also functions as a DVD player—but without a screen. Instead, the video signal is sent via 2.4GHz wireless signal to Sony's XVM-F65WL rear-seat video monitor ($400, optional, extra). No cables to run, everything happens wirelessly. See what I mean by cool?

Another cool thing about the MEX-R5 is that it handles just about any disc format you can throw at it. Audio CDs, CD-Rs, CD-RWs, MP3 discs, DVDs, DVD-Rs, DVD-RWs, DVD+Rs, DVD+RWs—you name it, the MEX-R5 can play it. And the unit features electronic shock protection with a 12-second memory buffer, so rough roads shouldn't interrupt your listening pleasure.

The MEX-R5 also delivers in the sound department. The amplifier delivers 52 watts per channel across four channels, and the Burr-Brown digital-to-analog converter (with full 24-bit resolution) provides superb CD playback. You can even tailor the sound to your personal liking via the built-in seven-band equalizer. And if you want to add satellite radio now or later, the unit is XM ready.

In terms of style, the MEX-R5 is somewhat minimalist. There are only a few buttons, with most of the space given over to the huge display (with removable anti-theft faceplate). That's okay, because the display makes it easy to read the ID3 tags on your MP3 discs. Operation is facilitated with the wireless remote (great for the folks in the rear seat), and the unit offers the now-obligatory dual-zone capability.

Bottom line, this is one fine-looking and fine-sounding audio system, with the added benefit of wireless DVD playback. As I said, pretty cool.

Model: MEX-R5 **Manufacturer:** Sony (www.sonystyle.com) **Power:** 52 watts × 4 **Size:** DIN **Price:** $450

Pioneer DEH-P80MP

Pioneer's DEH-P80MP sounds as good as it looks, which is saying a lot; the deep blue organic electro-luminescent display is pretty darned cool-looking—it can even display screensaver movies, animations, and pictures. The unit plays audio CDs, CD-Rs, CD-RWs, and MP3 and WMA discs, and displays disc ID3 tags. The seven-way Rotary Commander makes it easy to operate the thing, and the DEH-P80MP is both XM and SIRIUS satellite radio ready.

Model: DEH-P80MP **Manufacturer:** Pioneer (www.pioneerelectronics.com) **Power:** 27 watts × 4 **Price:** $440

Clarion ProAudio DXZ955MC

Here's an innocent-looking in-dash unit that delivers some nifty unexpected features—like a full-color touch-screen display and a built-in digital recorder, so you can record programs while you're driving. You also get Dolby Pro Logic II surround sound processing, a 3-band parametric equalizer, and remote control for and add-on DVD changer, TV tuner, or SIRIUS satellite radio receiver.

Model: DXZ955MC **Manufacturer:** Clarion (www.clarion.com) **Power:** 53 watts × 4 **Price:** $899.99

Dual XDV8125

Here's an in-dash audio system with a built-in TV tuner and 2.5" LCD monitor—something you definitely don't see every day. The monitor is on a two-step motorized face; one side is your normal CD and radio controls, the other is the TV display. Plus you get all the expected radio and CD playback options, including CD-R/RW compatibility, as well as an input for an add-on DVD player—all for under four hundred bucks.

Model: XDV8125 **Manufacturer:** dual (www.dualav.com) **Display:** 2.5" **Power:** 55 watts × 4 **Price:** $399.99

Panasonic CQ-CB8901U

This Panasonic unit is one of the first car audio systems to offer the new high-definition HD Radio technology. If you have an HD Radio station in your area, you get digital reception that makes AM stations sound like FM, and FM stations sound like CDs. HD Radio also displays artist name and song title, just like you get with satellite radio—but without the monthly service fee. And if HD Radio isn't enough for you, you can upgrade this unit with an optional XM satellite radio receiver—now that's a lot of radio options!

Model: CQ-CB8901U **Manufacturer:** Panasonic (www.panasonic.com) **Power:** 50 watts × 4 **Price:** $499.99

SATELLITE RADIO RECEIVERS

XM Commander

Leo's Pick

Chances are, your current car radio doesn't have XM or SIRIUS radio built in, which means you need some sort of add-on unit if you want to go the satellite radio route. That's why I like the XM Commander; it's a universal XM receiver that lets you add satellite radio to any vehicle.

The XM Commander is an all-in-one satellite receiver package. You get the XM Commander itself, which is the controller and display for the system; a separate remote control, for operating the system from the rear seat; a hide-away tuner box; a low-profile satellite micro-antenna; and all the cables and mounting accessories you need to complete the installation. The XM Commander installs in your dash, the tuner box can be put under a seat or in the trunk, and the antenna goes on the outside of your vehicle. It all integrates seamlessly into your car's current sound system, via either a direct line-in connection or transmitted to your radio over an unused FM channel.

The micro-antenna is a first, and very cool all by itself. Instead of the traditional long and pointy external antenna, this puppy looks like a small computer mouse; it's small enough to fit in the palm of your hand, and looks very inconspicuous when mounted on your vehicle. The last thing you need is another geegaw hanging off your car, which makes the XM Commander's micro-antenna very attractive, indeed.

The controller unit includes a dual-line display, so you can see song and artist info for the current programming. You get direct channel entry plus 30 presets for your favorite XM channels—although, I'll tell you from my experience, you'll probably find more than 30 stations that you like!

By the way, if you don't want to or simply can't mount the XM Commander control unit in your dash, check out The Bug, a cool mounting kit from ProFit (www.pro-fit-intl.com/bug/). For just

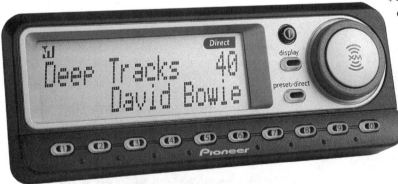

$19.95, this kit lets you put the controller just about anyplace in your car's cockpit; the base can sit on the floor or on an armrest console, affix to your windshield or dashboard, or hang from your rearview mirror. The controller then mounts on two small bug-like arms, which rotate and pivot for best position.

Model: XM Commander **Manufacturer:** XM Radio (www.xmradio.com/commander/) **Dimensions:** 3.75" (w) × 4.3: (h) × 1.25" (d) **Audio output:** 3.5mm mini-stereo jack **Price:** $169.95

Delphi XM SKYFi2

If you don't need a permanent satellite radio installation, check out Delphi's XM SKYFi2. This is a transportable receiver that you can carry between your car and your home or office. The SKYFi2 connects to your car radio via FM, and includes a 30-minute recording buffer so you won't miss any of your favorite XM programming. Car and home adapter kits are available, as is the tabletop SKYFi Audio System.

Model: SKYFi2 **Manufacturer:** Delphi (www.xmradio.com/skyfi2/) **Dimensions:** 4.65" (w) × 2.91" (h) × 1.26" (d) **Price:** $119.99

SIRIUS Sportster

If you prefer SIRIUS to XM, consider the Sportster, a transportable receiver similar to the XM Roady2. It connects to your car radio via FM, and includes its own wireless remote control. Car, home, and boombox kits are available.

Model: Sportster **Manufacturer:** SIRIUS (www.sirius.com) **Dimensions:** 4 3/8" (w) × 2 3/4" (h) × 1 1/8" (d) **Price:** $99.99

Delphi XM Roady 2

Delphi's XM Roady 2 is another transportable satellite receiver, this one a little smaller and without quite as many features—and, subsequently, priced a little cheaper. Like the SKYFi2, it connects to your existing car radio via FM, and includes its own micro-mini antenna. And, even better, you don't need an additional mounting kit; the Roady 2 comes with everything you need to connect inside your vehicle.

Model: Roady 2 **Manufacturer:** Delphi (www.xmradio.com/roady2/) **Dimensions:** 3.9" (w) × 2.4" (h) × 0.7" (d) **Price:** $99.99

Sanyo CRSR-10

Sanyo's CRSR-10 is another transportable SIRIUS receiver, this one with a very cool-looking design. The unit itself is a perfect square, with the control and preset buttons arranged in an arc below the six-line display. Also nice—it comes with its own car and home kits, no extra charge.

Model: CRSR-10 **Manufacturer:** Sanyo (www.sanyo.com) **Dimensions:** 3.97" (w) × 3.97" (h) × 1.26" (d) **Price:** $149.99

DVD ENTERTAINMENT SYSTEMS

Pioneer AVIC-N2

Leo's Pick

If all the AVIC-N2 did was play CDs and DVDs, it would still be one of my favorite in-dash entertainment systems. But what makes it stand out from the crowd is its built-in GPS navigation system. This one unit does it all—music, movies, and maps!

Let's talk about the navigation function first. The unit comes with two DVD-ROMs that contain a massive "Tele Atlas" database. Load in a disc and you can plot your route via multiple routes, with turn-by-turn directions displayed onscreen or given via voice prompts. The maps contain nearly 11 million points of interest throughout the United States and Canada, which makes it easy to find the nearest gas station, restaurant, or hotel.

In addition, the AVIC-N2 offers XM NavTraffic, a satellite-based service that offers up-to-the-minute traffic information—including road conditions, construction, and the like. If there's trouble up ahead, the system automatically alerts you and suggests alternate routes. And if you get into trouble on the road, the AVIC-N2 displays roadside assistance information, including emergency phone numbers and your current location (by street name and longitude/latitude!).

Maps and directions are displayed on the big 6.5" touch screen display, which also displays your DVD movies (when you're not driving, that is). Otherwise, the DVD playback is routed to your rear seat monitors (optional and extra, of course).

While the rear-seat passengers are watching movies, those of you in the front seat can listen to AM or FM radio, satellite radio, or your favorite audio CDs. Operation is via the touchsreen itself, or via optional voice command. And when the big display is folded up, you still have a smaller 10-character sub-display to use.

And here's another neat feature. Pioneer lets you add an optional rear-view camera, which you can display on the in-dash monitor. When using the camera, you get a split-screen display, with the rear view camera image on one side and the navigation map on the other. It's hard not to like this puppy!

Model: AVIC-N2 **Manufacturer:** Pioneer (www.pioneerelectronics.com) **Display:** 6.5" 16:9 ratio touch panel **Power:** 22 watts × 4 **Price:** $2,200

Alpine IVA-D901

Alpine's car systems are always top-notch, and the IVA-D300 is no exception. The motorized 7" touch panel display doubles as both video display and system controller; with 1.15 million pixel resolution, it's four times sharper than most competing units. The unit reads both CDs and DVDs, is upgradable for GPS navigation and XM satellite radio, and comes with its own wireless remote control for rear-seat operation.

Model: IVA-D901 **Manufacturer:** Alpine (www.alpine.com) **Display:** 7" touch panel **Power:** 50 watts × 4 **Price:** $2,400

Panasonic CQ-VD7001U

Here's a nice little in-dash DVD entertainment system with a big screen and a relatively small price. This Panasonic system gives you a 7" 16:9 ratio touch panel display, along with the normal complement of CD/DVD/AM/FM playback features and 5.1-channel surround sound. The unit can be upgraded for XM satellite radio.

Model: CQ-VD7001U **Manufacturer:** Panasonic (www.panasonic.com) **Display:** 7" touch panel **Power:** 50 watts × 4 **Price:** $1,199

Pioneer AVH-P5700DVD

Pioneer's AVH-P5700DVD is a good basic in-dash entertainment system, with a focus on great sound and lots of flexibility. The sound comes from a 50 watt × 4 channel amplifier; everything is operated via the 6.5" touch screen display. And if you want, you can expand the AVH-P5700DVD with an optional iPod interface adapter, XM or SIRIUS satellite radio receiver, TV tuner, or navigation system. Pick the features you want, and build it from there.

Model: AVH-P5700DVD **Manufacturer:** Pioneer (www.pioneerelectronics.com) **Display:** 6.5" 16:9 ratio touch panel **Power:** 50 watts × 4 **Price:** $1,100

JVC KD-AVX1

Who says mobile multimedia has to be expensive? If you don't mind going with a smaller monitor in the dash, you can save some bucks with this JVC system. It features a 3" in-dash monitor, but provides full CD and DVD playback functionality. It also gives you a wireless remote control, and is upgradable for SIRIUS satellite radio.

Model: KD-AVX1 **Manufacturer:** JVC (www.jvc.com) **Display:** 3" **Power:** 50 watts × 4 **Price:** $649.95

GPS NAVIGATION SYSTEMS

TomTom Go 700

Leo's Pick

There are lots of different in-car GPS navigation systems available, but I find the TomTom Go 700 to be my favorite. It's a little smoother and sleeker than the competition, and offers a few more features—which is why it earns my Leo's Pick designation.

Let's look at the features first. The unit is pretty much all screen, and that screen is an extra-sharp 3.5" touch screen LCD with 320 × 240 pixel resolution. The internal 2.5GB hard drive is large enough to store (and is preloaded with) maps for the entire United States and Canada, as well as millions of points of interest. You can get your directions onscreen or via voice command, in your choice of 30 different languages (and 50 different voices!). Operation is via the touch screen display—there are no buttons or knobs to deal with. There's also no external antenna, as the TomTom Go includes a built-in GPS antenna.

The TomTom Go 700 includes a 12-channel GPS receiver, as well as an Assisted Satellite Navigation (ASN) system. ASN ensures that you get continuous navigation, even when you're driving through tunnels or parking garages.

In addition, this is a fully portable unit—which means it's easy to take from car to car. This is especially nice if you travel and use a lot of local rent-a-car services; just carry your TomTom with you and use it in whatever car you're driving that day. Mount it to the windshield or dashboard with the supplied suction cradle, turn it on, and you're ready to go.

And here's the really neat part. The TomTom Go 700 features Bluetooth connectivity and functions as a wireless car phone kit. That's right, if you have a Bluetooth phone you can use

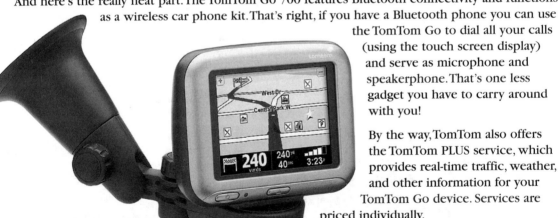

the TomTom Go to dial all your calls (using the touch screen display) and serve as microphone and speakerphone. That's one less gadget you have to carry around with you!

By the way, TomTom also offers the TomTom PLUS service, which provides real-time traffic, weather, and other information for your TomTom Go device. Services are priced individually.

Model: TomTom Go 700 **Manufacturer:** TomTom (www.tomtom.com) **Display:** 3.5" touch screen **Hard disk storage:** 2.5GB **Dimensions:** 4.5" (w) × 3.6" (h) × 2.3" (d) **Price:** $899.95

Garmin Streetpilot c330

Garmin's Streetpilot c330 is another small GPS unit that operates via touch screen controls. It offers a 3.5" 16-color display (320 × 240 resolution), and data is stored on a 128MB SD flash card. Navigation is either onscreen or via voice prompts, through the dual integrated speakers. Garmin's database includes more than 5 million points of interest, including hotels, restaurants, gas stations, and ATMs.

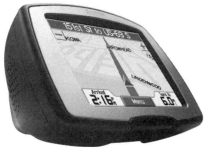

Model: Streetpilot c330 **Manufacturer:** Garmin (www.garmin.com) **Display:** 3.5" touch screen **Dimensions:** 4.4" (w) × 3.2" (h) × 2.8" (d) **Price:** $899.99

Magellan RoadMate 700

Magellan's RoadMate 700 is built on the same technologies used in Hertz's NeverLost system. The unit offers TrueView 3D navigation, for a heads-on view of your route; you control the unit via the front-panel rocker switch. The RoadMate 700 features pre-loaded maps for the United States and Canada, with more than 2 million points of interest.

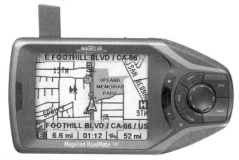

Model: RoadMate 700 **Manufacturer:** Magellan (www.magellangps.com) **Display:** 2.5" × 3" **Dimensions:** 3.25" (h) × 6.5" (w) × 2" (d) **Price:** $1,049.99

Navman iCN 510

Navman's iCN510 is a more affordable in-car navigation unit, with both touch-screen and rocker control operation. You get a 3.5" touch panel display (320 × 240 resolution), 32MB of internal memory, and additional map storage via SD or MMC flash cards.

Model: iCN 510 **Manufacturer:** Navman (www. navman.com) **Display:** 3.5" touch screen **Dimensions:** 4.75" (w) × 2.75" (h) × 1" (d) **Price:** $749.95

Lowrance iWAY 500C

What makes the iWAY 500C a little different is that it does double-duty as a portable MP3 player. It also has a larger display than other units, a 5" whopper with 320 × 240 resolution, as well as a 20GB internal hard drive for map and database storage. Navigation is either onscreen or via voice prompts.

Model: iWAY 500C **Manufacturer:** Lowrance (www.lowrance.com) **Display:** 5" touch screen **Dimensions:** 6.1" (w) × 4.5" (h) × 2.15" (d) **Price:** $649.99

MORE COOL CAR GADGETS

ScanGauge Automotive Computer

The ScanGauge is a multi-function diagnostic computer that works with any automobile. It can check for and interpret diagnostic trouble codes, turn off the check engine light, display a variety of digital gauges, and function as a trip computer for up to three trips at a time, tracking average speed, fuel economy, maximum RPM, and the like. This gadget, which hooks easily into a service connector found on most new cars, will tell you everything you ever wanted to know about your car!

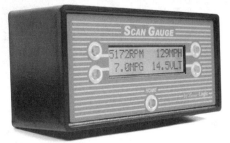

Model: ScanGauge **Manufacturer:** ScanGauge (www.scangauge.com) **Price:** $129.95

Road Safety Black Box Computer

The RS-1000 is a black box computer that helps you monitor your teen's driving—without you actually being in the car. The Road Safety system monitors vehicle speed, g-forces, and the like, and emits warnings when your teen is speeding or accelerating too fast. You can then download the data to your PC, and produce detailed driving reports. It connects to the standard Data Link Connector under your car's dash, and then to your PC (via USB).

Model: RS-1000 **Manufacturer:** Road Safety (www.roadsafety.com) **Price:** $280

TrimTrac GPS Security Locator

If your car ever gets stolen, you can find it fast with the TrimTrac security locator. It operates via GPS technology to fix its location, and then sends its location via SMS text messages over the GSM network. It's small and battery operated, so you can mount it out of sight anywhere in your vehicle.

Model: TrimTrac **Manufacturer:** Trimble (www.trimble.com) **Dimensions:** 5.78" × 2.99" × 1.44" **Price:** $499.99

ARKON Executive Laptop Steering Wheel Mount

Not that anyone recommends computing while driving, but it is possible to get some work done in the car while you're parked for lunch. To that end, use the ARKON Executive Laptop Steering Wheel Mount to fix your laptop to your car's steering wheel, then start typing away. The mount will hold all laptops up to 10 pounds in weight.

Model: CM175 **Manufacturer:** ARKON (www.arkon.com) **Price:** $49.95

SportVue MC1 Heads-Up Display

Now here's a cool use of new technology. The SportVue's MC1 adds a heads-up display to any motorcycle helmet, so you can see key readouts—speed, RPM, and gear—without taking your eyes off the road. The display is projected onto the helmet's windscreen via the MC1 device, which mounts onto the front of your helmet; it's the same technology used by fighter pilots. Cool!

Model: MC1 **Manufacturer:** SportVue (www.sportvue.net) **Price:** $329

MOMO Design Fighter Bluetooth Motorcycle Helmet

If you think heads-up displays are cool, take a look at what MOMO Design and Motorola have in store. The Fighter Bluetooth is a motorcycle helmet with built-in Bluetooth wireless connectivity; now you can listen to the radio or talk on the phone without running wires up to and under your helmet. It's a very cool and practical use of existing technologies.

Model: Fighter **Manufacturer:** MOMO Design (www.momodesign.com) **Price:** TBA

TracVision A5 Mobile Satellite TV

If satellite radio isn't entertaining enough on long trips, go the extra step and add satellite television to your car or van. The TracVision A5 system puts a thin (5" high) mobile satellite antenna on top of your vehicle, so you can receive DIRECTV service on the go. Just feed the signal from the TracVision satellite receiver to any in-car monitor, and you can watch DIRECTV MOBILE while you're driving.

Model: A5 **Manufacturer:** TracVision (www. tracvision.com) **System:** DIRECTV MOBILE **Price:** $2,295

Velox Coffeebreak Espresso Maker

If all the entertainment gadgets don't keep you awake, you definitely need some caffeine—which you can get thanks to Velox Coffeebreak in-car espresso maker. The Coffeebreak (designed by Bertone Design) connects to your car's cigarette lighter and brews up three ounces of coffee in less than five minutes. It has a built-in coffee screen, so no filters are necessary.

Model: Coffeebreak **Distributor:** Restaurantequipment. com (www.restaurantequipment.com/velox.html) **Price:** $49.95

5

The Ultimate High-Tech Adventurer

HOW TO BECOME THE ULTIMATE HIGH-TECH ADVENTURER

All About GPS

Back in Part 4, "The Ultimate High-Tech Car Owner," I first talked about GPS navigation systems. It's an especially useful technology for finding your way when driving, but it's also quite popular among outdoor adventurers. The technology is a tad complex, originally developed for military use, but it's definitely filtered down to the level of the average consumer—in terms of both usability and price. Today you can purchase a decent handheld GPS unit for less than $200 and get the same type of performance that our soldiers do in the field.

You can also spend a lot more than $200, especially if you like lots of gee-whiz features. Spend more money and you get a more compact unit (it costs big bucks to make things smaller), a color display, and more creature comforts, in the form of automatic route generation, more programmed points of interest, more storage capacity, and so on. Some higher-end units also claim increased accuracy, by using more satellites to gauge position. (The typical unit tracks up to 12 satellites at a time; some track a few more.) In any case, expect accuracy in the three-meter range, which isn't shabby.

As with in-car GPS units, there are certain features you want to look for when shopping for handheld units. In particular, you want to be sure the unit comes with the base maps you need for where you'll be using it. (In other words, don't buy a European unit if you're trekking in the Sierra Nevadas.) You also want to see how many different routes the unit can store in memory; the more stored routes, the better. In addition, check the number of waypoints it can store, both in total and per route; a unit that holds 50 waypoints per route is more versatile than one that holds only 25 waypoints per route.

While many adventurers are happy with general handheld GPS units that they can use across a number of different activities, you also have the choice of activity-specific units. That is, there are GPS units targeted specifically at campers and hikers, at hunters, at runners, at boaters, and so on. These sport-specific units typically come with customized maps and databases, and often offer other features of interest to a particular type of activity. For example, a GPS unit for hunters might include a built-in compass and onscreen icons to track hunting stands and such; a unit for runners might include a chronometer and lap counter. You get the picture.

Whichever type of unit you choose (general or sports-specific), make sure you like the look and feel of the device. Pay particular attention to the display; is it easily viewable in all weather conditions? Is the device light enough and compact enough to carry around all day? Does it feel good in your hand; does it come with a carrying case or strap? And, depending on your activity, is it water resistant or waterproof? All these things are important, as is battery life; you don't want your GPS device dying on you when you're out in the middle of nowhere!

Gadgets for Runners

Like all sports, running has become particularly high-tech in recent years. From the simple pedometer to the complete performance monitoring systems, computers are being put to good use to help you track and monitor your activities and performance.

At the high end, performance monitoring systems incorporate GPS receivers to help track your location, distance traveled, pace, speed, and so on. You'll also get separate heart monitors, which are typically worn around your chest; signals are transmitted from the heart monitor to the main unit via wireless technology. You can set a target heart rate and get an alert if you go beyond it.

Most high-end performance monitoring systems also let you transfer the collected data to your PC, either via USB, infrared, or RF signals. You can then upload the data to performance-tracking software and generate all manner of graphs and reports. It's a cool way to track and analyze your performance over time.

When shopping for a performance monitoring system of any sort, probably the most important factor is size. You don't want to be weighted down by a bulky monitor and display; you want something small and sleek and light-weight. Some systems are incorporated into sports watches, which is nice. Others come in separate units that you can clip to your belt or wear on an armband. Whichever type of system you choose, make sure it's something you'll be comfortable with during a long run.

Gadgets for Campers

Obviously, one of the most essential gadgets for campers is a handheld GPS device. You don't need anything fancy, just something to tell you where you are when all you can see are trees and rocks. That's not to say that extra features aren't useful; I particularly like those units with a built-in electronic compass, altimeter, and the like. The more info the better, I say!

Speaking of info, for those long hikes it's nice to know what to expect of the weather. To that end, consider a portable weather tracker. The best of these provide dozens (if not hundreds) of measurements, from temperature and humidity to wind chill and dew point. Most units come with built-in thermometers and barometers, as well as little fan-like thingies to measure wind speed. Make sure the unit is small enough to carry comfortably, of course.

Other useful gadgets for campers tend to fall into the creature comforts category. By this I mean backpacks, coolers, water carriers, and the like. There are even portable ice cream and espresso makers designed especially for use out in the wild. Heck, take along your cell phone, PDA, and portable video player, and it's like you've never left home!

Gadgets for Hunters

GPS devices are especially useful for hunters, considering their ability to store important track points. Once you locate a good location, just program it into the device, and you'll be able to find the spot again when you come back next year. (Plus, and this goes without saying, you stand a much lower chance of getting totally lost, which is always a major embarrassment.)

But that's not the only way that high-tech gadgets can improve your hunting experience. I especially like electronic viewing and listening aids, such as night-vision viewers and amplified headphones. I know it sounds a little *Six Million Dollar Man*-like, but augmenting your senses electronically makes a lot of sense when you're in a hostile environment. (Okay, so your local woods isn't all that hostile, but you know what I mean.) Plus, it's kind of cool to be able to see in the dark and hear raccoons whispering from a hundred yards away. (Do raccoons whisper? I don't know…)

Technology can also be used to attract your prey. I'm particularly intrigued by robotic decoys, like the RoboDuk, that are kind of creepy yet fascinating, all at the same time. Also interesting is the computerized take on the old-fashioned animal call, with dozens of different calls digitized for extremely accurate reproduction in the wild. It sure beats trying to do all those calls yourself!

Gadgets for Fishermen

Fishing used to be a relaxing sport. You bait your hook, drop your line, then settle back with a cold beer and a hat over your eyes. (The cold beer isn't over your eyes; the hat is.) Today, however, there are all sorts of high-tech devices that make fishing more like hunting, an active activity rather than a passive one.

First off, consider the concept of the fishfinder. This is a device that uses sonar technology to beam back electronic images of underwater life, so you can see onscreen whether there are any fish nearby. Extremely high-tech and extremely practical, a good fishfinder will keep you from wasting time fishing where the fishes aren't.

If sonar is good, why not utilize an underwater camera to actually see any fish that are nearby? It's doable, thanks to today's miniaturized and ruggedized video cameras. Just drop a special fishcam off the side of your boat, and watch the show on an attached LCD monitor. Low-light technology ensures that you can actually see through the murky depths—although not as far as you can with sonar. (That's why the best bet is to use a combination of video and sonar technology.)

Finally, we have the option of trying to attract the fish, not just look around and see if they're nearby. To that end, consider a submersible fish light, which uses a special colored bulb to make fish think that there's a full moon out. Fish are attracted to the light, which makes them easy prey. Once again, technology delivers!

Gadgets for Boaters

If you like fishing technology, you'll love boating technology. (Of course, for many adventurers fishing and boating go hand-in-hand.) For the high-tech boater there's no end of expensive gadgets to invest in.

First off is a GPS device specialized for boating use, called a chartplotter. A chartplotter is like a traditional GPS but with detailed maps of waterways rather than roadways. If you're navigating any large expanse of water—from the Great Lakes to the Atlantic ocean—one of these devices is essential for determining exactly where you are at any given point in time. As with any GPS device, you want to look for highly detailed maps and lots of storage for different routes and trackpoints.

What gets fun is combining a chartplotter with other technology. Here you have two different ways to go. The first combines the chartplotter with a sonar device, so you can track your progress underwater as well as on the waves. (It's also great for fishing!) The other option combines the chartplotter with a radar transmitter, so you can track oncoming weather while you're on the water. The best of these units function much like the professional units used by your local TV weatherperson, with color displays for various levels of precipitation and such.

If you go with one of these combo devices, pay particular attention to the display screen. The more data you display, the bigger the screen you want. Some of these displays go to 10" or more and are designed for use in both shade and direct sunlight. A bigger screen lets you display two types of info side-by-side—GPS chart and sonar map, for example, or GPS map and radar screen. Even better, some units let you superimpose one type of map on top of the other. Trust me, it's extremely useful to see your normal map with radar conditions overlaid on top.

The whole point of all these marine electronics is to keep you on course and away from dangerous conditions—on, under, or above the water. Sure, some of these gizmos are a little expensive, but you can't put a price tag on your safety, especially when you're out on the open water. When all you can see with the naked eye is a horizon full of wet, you need high-tech help to get to where you want to go, safely.

Gadgets for Scuba Divers

I'm not a scuba diver myself, but I know some guys who are, and I really think it's a fun sport—not just for what you do while underwater, but for all the cool gear you get to buy. Scuba diving has long been a high-tech sport, and it keeps getting more high-tech as time goes on.

The first high-tech device for any serious diver is the dive computer. This is a gizmo that measures depth, time, temperature, ascent/descent rate, and the like, and calculates how much time you have left on your oxygen tank, when you need to ascend (and how quickly), and so on. Newer technology is helping to miniaturize the traditional dive computer, to the point that you can now get a dive computer on a wrist watch. This tech is so cool it tempts me to take scuba lessons myself!

There's also the issue of how you get around while you're underwater. If you remember the James Bond movie *Thunderball*, you recall how 007 jetted from place to place using an underwater jetpack of sorts, which was extremely cool. Well, underwater jetpacks haven't quite come into the mainstream, but the concept of an underwater propulsion device has become viable. I'm talking about a small propeller-driven gadget that you hold onto with both hands and let it drag you behind it. You only go a couple of miles an hour, but that's a couple of miles an hour faster than you can manage with a pair of flippers. It's actually quite cool, and a lot of fun.

But these two types of gadgets just scratch the surface. There's a lot more out there for the high-tech diver, as well as for high-tech adventurers of all sorts. Read on to see some of the most useful and most fun gadgets available—and don't forget to check at your local sporting goods store for even more!

PORTABLE GPS DEVICES

Garmin eTrex Vista C

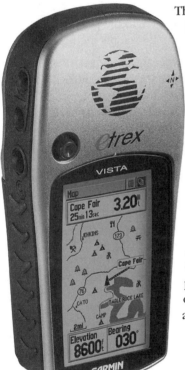

Leo's Pick

The hallmark of any high-tech outdoorsperson is a state-of-the-art portable GPS device. You can go with a device customized for specialized use (hunting, boating, etc.) or with one of the many general-purpose handheld devices.

My favorite general-purpose GPS device is Garmin's eTrex Vista C, primarily because it packs so many useful features into such a small package. This gizmo is small enough to fit in your shirt pocket, but offers a color display, automatic routing, and a whole bunch more. The whole thing is wrapped up in a waterproof case that you can use for boating, hiking, biking, or geocaching.

The 256-color display is easily readable in even the brightest sunlight, which is a necessity for outdoor use. Indoors, it connects to your PC via USB for downloading of map data from Garmin's library of MapSource CDs. You operate it all via a rocker switch on the front of the unit; it's easy to both input data and pan across a full map image.

As far as performance, you get automatic route generation, off-route recalculation, turn-by-turn directions (with alert tones!), an automatic track log with 20 saved tracks, and display of up to 500 waypoints. The built-in trip computer calculates current speed, average speed, time of sunrise/sunset, maximum speed, and trip time and distance. The 12-channel WAAS-enabled receiver uses up to 12 GPS satellites to compute and update your position. Accuracy is typically within 3 meters.

And here's something even neater. In addition to the standard GPS functions, the eTrex Vista C also includes an electronic compass and barometric altimeter with elevation computer. This is a one-stop-shop outdoors positioning device—and it's a good inch-and-a-half shorter than competing units!

Model: eTrex Vista C **Manufacturer:** Garmin (www.garmin.com) **Display:** 1.3" × 1.7" (176 × 220 pixels) **Dimensions:** 2.2" (w) × 4.2" (h) × 1.2" (d) **Weight:** 5.6 oz. **Price:** $428.56

Lowrance iFINDER

Lowrance's iFINDER is an affordable handheld GPS device with a 1.7" × 2.2" high-contrast monochrome display. It uses a 12-channel WAAS receiver and accepts both SD and MMC flash memory cards. You can save up to 100 plot trails with up to 10,000 points on any trail; you also get 1,000 waypoints and event markers. A nice bonus: You can customize your unit with interchangeable face plates. (The camouflage plate is great for hunting!)

Model: iFINDER **Manufacturer:** Lowrance (www.lowrance.com) **Dimensions:** 2.55" (w) × 5.59" (h) × 0.95" (d) **Weight:** 7.62 oz. **Price:** $159

Magellan eXplorist 500

If you want a color display without spending a bundle, check out Magellan's eXplorist 500. The 16-color display is very readable, and the 14-channel WAAS/EGNOS receiver is accurate up to 3 meters. The eXplorist 500 can store up to 5 track files, each with 2,000 track points. The unit itself is extremely compact and waterproof.

Model: eXplorist 500 **Manufacturer:** Magellan (www.magellangps.com) **Dimensions:** 2.2" (w) × 4.7" (h) × 1.3" (d) **Weight:** 5.4 oz. **Price:** $399.99

Garmin iQue M5

Garmin's iQue M5 isn't your standard handheld GPS handheld device. It's a PDA married to 12-channel GPS functionality, all in one compact device. The smallish GPS antenna folds out from the top of the case, and maps and directions are displayed on the 3.5" color screen. When you're not using it to find your way, you can use it as a standard Pocket PC device, with all the normal Windows Mobile 2003 applications.

Model: iQue M5 **Manufacturer:** Garmin (www.garmin.com) **Dimensions:** 2.8" (w) × 5" (h) × .8" (d) **Weight:** 5.8 oz. **Price:** $749.99

Suunto X9 GPS Watch

Here's another unique GPS device, this time in the form of a GPS wristwatch. Suunto's X9 is an electronic watch that incorporates a 12-channel GPS receiver, altimeter, barometer, thermometer, and compass; it works just like the larger handheld units but fits neatly on your wrist. Of course, you don't have a big display, but it does a good job of telling you precisely where you are and how far you have to go to get to where you going. The watch holds 50 routes in memory, with 50 waypoints per route.

Model: X9 **Manufacturer:** Suunto (www. suuntowatches.com) **Dimensions:** 2.2" × 2.3" (h) × 0.67" **Weight:** 2.68 oz. **Price:** $699.99

RUNNING GADGETS

Timex Bodylink System

Leo's Pick

Timex's Bodylink system is the ultimate performance-monitoring system for serious runners. It combines a sport watch, heart-rate monitor, and GPS device to track your performance in real time, as well as a data recorder that can upload your data to your PC for more detailed analysis.

Let's look at each component separately, starting with the Ironman Triathlon Bodylink Performance Monitor sport watch. In addition to normal watch functions (with INDIGLO night light), you get a 100-hour chronograph with lap/split, 100-lap memory, 100-hour countdown timer, and alerts for targeted heart rate zone, pace, speed, and distance. It's not a small watch, but then you need a little space for all these sensors and a big readout.

The Timex Speed + Distance Sensor is actually a GPS tracking device, using Navman II technology. It's small enough to clip on your belt or wear on the included arm strap, and uses GPS technology to track your position and pace. It measures real-time, average, and maximum speed; calculates pace, average pace, and best pace; and tracks total distance for a single workout or group of workouts.

The Timex Digital Heart Rate Sensor straps around your chest to provide continuous heart rate readings. It sends signals to the data recorder via FM signals and isn't affected by exercise equipment or other electronic devices.

All of this information comes together in the Timex Data Recorder. It not only tracks the recorded data in real-time, you can also connect it to your PC (via USB) to upload the data to the Timex Trainer software. The software creates a variety of reports and graphs to help you track your progress over time.

Bottom line, this is an extremely high-tech system for tracking your running and workout performance. Use the information gathered to help fine-tune your workouts and to improve your performance.

Model: 5E671 **Manufacturer:** Timex (www.timex.com/bodylink/) **Includes:** Ironman Triathlon Bodylink Performance Monitor sport watch, Timex Speed + Distance Sensor, Timex Digital Heart Rate Sensor, Timex Data Recorder, Timex Trainer software **Price:** $300

Garmin Forerunner 301

Garmin's Forerunner 301 is another performance monitoring system, this time in a single compact device (plus a separate chest-strap heart rate monitor, of course). You wear the Forerunner 301 on you wrist, and it monitors heart rate, speed, distance, pace, and calories burned. The embedded GPS sensor provides basic navigation capabilities, so you won't get lost on long runs. Recorded information is uploaded to your PC into Garmin's Training Center software, for further analysis.

Model: Forerunner 301 **Manufacturer:** Garmin (www.garmin.com) **Dimensions:** 3.3" × 1.7" × 0.7" **Weight:** 2.75 oz. **Price:** $324.98

Nike Triax Speed 100 Super Speedometer

Nike's Triax Speed 100 is a low-cost sport watch and performance monitor for runners. It lets you set target times then monitors your actual performance; you can then review how your performance compares to your goals. It includes a 100-lap chronograph and five-segment interval timer and tracks lap time, total time, best lap, average lap, and target time differentials.

Model: Triax Speed 100 **Manufacturer:** Nike (www.nike.com/nikerunning/) **Price:** $79

Navman Sport Tool R300

Navman's Sport Tool R300 is a neat-looking little triangle of a device that uses GPS technology to measure speed, distance, and pace. It also calculates current, maximum, and average speeds and offers target zone monitoring with an acoustic alarm. Best of all, the Sport Tool is small enough to fit on an arm strap.

Model: Sport Tool R300 **Manufacturer:** Navman (www.navman.com) **Dimensions:** 3.07" × 3.11" × 1.06" **Weight:** 4.23 oz. **Price:** TBA

Polar S625X Running Computer

The Polar S626X is a sport watch with built-in running computer. It includes automatic lap recording and monitors speed, pace, and distance. Even better, it includes a wireless heart rate monitor so you can track maximum, minimum, and average heart rate during your run—and for each individual lap. Information is transferred to your PC via an infrared connection.

Model: S625X **Manufacturer:** Polar (www.polar.fi) **Price:** $369.95

CAMPING GADGETS

Camelbak Hydration System Backpacks

Leo's Pick

When you're out camping and hiking, it's important to have plenty of fresh water. When there's no water on the way, take your own with Camelbak's hydration system backpacks.

A Camelbak backpack looks like a normal backpack, except it has a reservoir for H2O. It's more than a simple water bottle, as the reservoir is integrated into the body of the backpack itself. You access the water via a bite valve positioned at the end of a delivery tube, which means you can drink while you're hiking, without ever having to stop—or to reach for a squeeze bottle.

Obviously, a Camelbak backpack carries more than just water—it's also a fully functioning backpack, with lots of traditional storage space. The Camelbak design is such that the weight of the water is equally distributed, so it won't be too much of a load on your back.

Camelbak makes a variety of models in different capacities, capable of carrying from 1 to 3 liters of water. Smaller models are in a fannypack design; larger models use the backpack design. Prices range from $25 to $120, depending on capacity and design.

Model: Various **Manufacturer:** Camelbak (www.camelbak.com) **Capacity:** 1–3 liters **Price:** $25–$120

Flowlab Pack-n-Chair

A good chair is hard to find, especially when you're camping—so carry yours with you. Flowlab's unique Pack-n-Chair is a Transformers-like gizmo that morphs from a traditional backpack (with built-in cooler compartment on the bottom) into an aluminum folding chair. The system is designed so that the backpack can stay mounted on the back of the chair, even when you're sitting in it. And the chair is light enough to be barely noticeable when you're hiking along. Neat!

Model: Pack-n-Chair **Manufacturer:** Flowlab (www.flowlab.com) **Price:** $29

Kestrel 4000 Weather Tracker

Track the weather conditions while you're camping with the full-featured Kestrel 4000 portable weather tracker. This handheld device lets you track, recall, and graph up to 250 measurements, including temperature, barometric pressure, humidity, altitude, wind speed, wind chill, dew point, heat index, and more. It's small enough to carry in your pocket, and extremely accurate.

Model: Kestrel 4000 **Manufacturer:** Nielsen Kellerman (www.nkhome.com) **Dimensions:** 5" (h) × 1.8" (w) × 1.1" (d) **Weight:** 3.6 oz. **Price:** $329

REI Camper's Dream Ice Cream Maker

Feel a hankerin' for an ice cream cone at the end of a long hike? Well, the Camper's Dream Ice Cream Maker lets you make your own ice cream wherever you are, even at a remote campsite. Just add ice, rock salt, and the necessary ingredients into the ball-shaped device, then start rolling the thing around. After 20 minutes or so, you'll have a pint of delicious homemade ice cream!

Model: 709077 **Manufacturer:** REI (www.rei.com) **Dimensions:** 8" (diameter) **Price:** $29.95

GSI Mini-Expresso Maker

Coffee's important to manage those early-morning hikes—and why forsake your fancy espresso just because you're out camping? GSI's Mini-Expresso Maker (yes, they spell it *expresso*, not *espresso*) serves up your favorite brew in just minutes. Just fill the basket with ground coffee and add water, then screw the unit shut and place it over a low fire. Put your cup under the steam pipe, and you're ready to go.

Model: Mini-Expresso Maker **Manufacturer:** GSI (www.gsioutdoors.com) **Price:** $35.50 (1-cup), $44.95 (4-cup)

HUNTING GADGETS

Action Ear Sport Electronic Listening Device

Leo's Pick

Hunting is a lot more efficient when you can hear your prey. The Action Ear Sport is an amplified hearing enhancer built into a set of battery-operated headphones. With the Action Ear Sport, sounds are amplified by 40dB, so you can hear game up to 100 yards away.

The Action Ear Sport is a stereo device, so you get 360° awareness of sound direction. Independent volume controls let you compensate for hearing differences between your two ears, and the sculpted air/foam ear cushions provide hours of comfortable listening. There's even a collar-level tension band and Velcro head strap, so the headphones stay in place no matter how fast you move.

Noise-limiting technology works to amplify only soft sounds, so you don't get blasted out by louder sounds. In the LMT setting, loud sounds are heard at 70dB while soft sounds are continuously amplified; in the MAX setting, an automatic shut-off circuit shuts off all sounds over 95dB.

And here's a neat touch. These headphones include both an input jack (so you can listen to a radio while hunting) and an output jack, the latter to record what you hear. (Can you imagine a podcast of your amplified hunting experience?)

The Action Ear Sport is relatively lightweight and folds flat for easy storage. It comes in four different colors: tan camo, dark camo, tan, and black.

Model: Action Ear Sport **Manufacturer:** Silvercreek Industries (www.silvercreekindustries.com) **Weight:** 17.1 oz. **Price:** $159.99

Lowrance iFINDER Hunt

The iFINDER Hunt is a customized version of Lowrance's iFINDER GPS device, designed with the active hunter in mind. It's totally waterproof, ruggedized for hard use, and comes in a camouflage case. It also adds hunting-specific icons so you can mark your tree stands, game signs, and truck and ATV positions. Added bonus—built-in electronic compass and barometric altimeter.

Model: iFINDER Hunt **Manufacturer:** Lowrance (www.lowrance.com) **Dimensions:** 5.59" (h) × 2.55" (w) × 0.95" (d) **Weight:** 8.7 oz. **Price:** $299

Leupold Wind River Laser Range Finding Binocular

Here's a great tool for the high-tech hunter. The RB800 Range Finding binocular combines high-quality binocular optics with laser-precise measuring capability. Just sight your target and press a button, and the RB800 generates precise measurements, accurate to within one yard. It works up to 900 yards away, and you can perform continuous scanning to track animals in motion. The digital display shows distance in either yards or meters.

Model: RB800 **Manufacturer:** Leupold (www.leupold.com) **Magnification:** 8X **Weight:** 23 oz. **Price:** $699.99

RoboDuk Electronic Decoys

Okay, this one makes my list for the name alone. (I just love saying "robo-duck!") The RoboDuk is a state-of-the-art robotic decoy that simulates a duck in the landing position, complete with flapping (actually, spinning) wings. It runs on a quiet waterproof motor, powered by a rechargeable battery with 10-12 hours of run time. Models are available for drake and hen ducks, as well as Canadian and snow geese.

Manufacturer: RoboDuk (www.roboduk.com) **Weight:** 5.5 oz. **Price:** $119.95–$139.95

Compucaller II Digital Animal Caller

When you think animal calls, you probably envision one of those quacking pipes you blow into. Well, this isn't that. The Compucaller II is a two-piece electronic animal caller that works via RF remote control. The caller device itself has a built-in amplifier and is concealed in a water-resistant camo bag. You change calls by inserting new sound chips; chips are available for everything from quail and geese to feral hogs, coyotes, bobcats, and mountain lions—although why you'd actually want to call a bobcat or mountain lion is beyond me.

Model: Compucaller II **Manufacturer:** Burnham Brothers (www.burnhambrothers.com) **Weight:** 2.5 lbs. **Price:** $329.95

FISHING GADGETS

Aqua-Vu Underwater Video Camera

The high-tech fisherman has lots of cool gadgets at his disposal, from GPS devices to underwater sonar, but nothing beats actually seeing the fish you're angling for. To that end, Aqua-Vu's Spool SC-100 lets you see what's happening underneath the surface, via a specialized underwater video camera.

The camera itself looks like a little fish itself, so it won't disturb any curious fishies in the neighborhood. It connects to the viewing device via 80 feet of Kevlar-reinforced cable, which you can crank up or down. You view the images on a 4" color LCD monitor, in real time.

The SC-100's picture is surprisingly viewable, thanks to a combination of the built-in light and Spectral Response lighting technology that maximizes the amount of available light the camera can use while minimizing particle reflection. External ballast weights and a stabilizing fin help to keep the camera fish properly positioned underwater; the camera fish is painted in a patented "emerald shiner" finish, to better attract other fish. And, as an added bonus, the LCD display also shows the current water temperature. The whole thing is powered by a 12-volt battery, or your boat's external 12-volt power.

You know, it's really neat to be able to see what's going on under the surface. Not only can you see how many and what type of fish are swimming around, you can also use the camera to view bottom terrain, inspect brushpiles and stumps, locate prime weedline junctions, and peer beneath vegetation maps. If nothing else, the SC-100 will help you better understand the readings from your separate sonar device; the two different devices together provide a complete overview of the underwater world. Plus, need I say, it's just plain cool to have a James Bond-type fish camera. It makes even the most boring fishing trip pretty fun!

Model: SC-100 **Manufacturer:** Nature-Vision Inc. (www.aquavu.com) **Display:** 4" color LCD **Price:** $599.99

Navman TrackFish 6600 Chartfinder/Fishfinder

Now this is one full-featured fishfinder! Actually, the TrackFish 6600 is a combination chartfinder and fishfinder, with 7" color display (480 × 800 pixel resolution) with split-screen functionality. You get a 12-channel GPS receiver, 600-watt sonar (for readings up to 1,000 meters), C-MAP NT+ cartography, and built-in fuel computer. This one does practically everything!

Model: TrackFish 6600 **Manufacturer:** Navman (www.navman.com) **Display:** 7" color widescreen (480 × 800) **Dimensions:** 6.14" (w) × 9.29" (h) × 4.33" (d) **Price:** $249.95

Optronics Submersible Fish-N-Lite

When you're night fishing, nothing attracts the fish like an underwater light. So check out Optronics' Submersible Fish-N-Lite, which combines a halogen light with a green fluorescent bulb to attract both bait and game fish. (The soft green glow simulates a full moon and feeding pool.) The 20-foot cord gives you plenty of depth; the safety snap lets you pinpoint the desired level.

Model: UW-500G **Manufacturer:** Optronics (www.optronicsinc.com) **Price:** $29.99

Fishpond Swift Current Thermometer

When you're fresh water fishing, fluctuations in water temperature have a dramatic effect on fish feeding patterns. If you know the precise water temperature, you'll have a better gauge on where and when the fish are biting. To that end, pick up Fishpond's Swift Current Thermometer, which measures water temperatures from 20° to 120° Fahrenheit. It comes in a rugged aluminum case, but it's small enough to fit in your pocket or bait box.

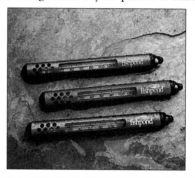

Model: SCT/F-AC **Manufacturer:** Fishpond (www.fishpondusa.com) **Price:** $18

Dakota Angler II

The Dakota Angler II is a unique little gadget. It combines a full-featured water-resistant watch with a hook sharpener, stainless steel nippers, compass, thermometer, and LED microlight (with visibility up to 1 kilometer!). It's everything the efficient fisherman needs, all in one relatively compact gadget.

Model: Angler II **Manufacturer:** Dakota Watch Company (www.dakotawatchco.com) **Price:** $79.95

BOATING GADGETS

Furuno NavNet Radar/Chartplotter

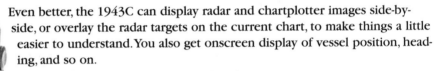

This is an expensive gadget for the serious boater. The 1943C is a combination radar/chartplotter with an extra-large 10.4" color LCD display. It's a rugged, waterproof unit with lots of pro-level features.

The color radar system is just like the kind your local TV weather guy uses, with six levels of target density to track storms and other weather conditions. The powerful X-Band radar transmitter cuts through all types of weather, thanks in part to the 4-foot open array antenna. It has a range of 64 nautical miles, with a horizontal beamwidth of 1.85°, and can display target or echo trails with selectable time intervals.

The chartplotter lets you use either Furuno CDC or Navionics mini-chart cards and offers a variety of display modes: north-up, course-up, automatic course-up, plotter, nav data, steering director, highway, and so on. The unit can track 1,000 waypoints and up to 200 routes, at 35 waypoints apiece.

Even better, the 1943C can display radar and chartplotter images side-by-side, or overlay the radar targets on the current chart, to make things a little easier to understand. You also get onscreen display of vessel position, heading, and so on.

Suffice it to say, with the 1943C you'll have to try really hard to get lost or caught in a storm. If the Skipper had one of these puppies on the S.S. Minnow, we'd never have heard of Gilligan's Island!

Model: 1943C NavNet **Manufacturer:** Furuno (www.furuno.com) **Display:** 10.4" color LCD
Dimensions: 15.1" (w) × 10.3" (h) × 7.1" (d) **Price:** $7,495

Lowrance LCX-111C HD GPS Mapper

The Lowrance LCX-111C HD combines sonar, GPS mapping, and a precision chartplotter. The display is a 800 × 600 pixel 10.4" color LCD, with multiple full- and split-screen sonar and GPS display options. The 20GB hard drive holds tons of electronic charts and lets you record sonar graph and GPS details. The sonar's depth range extends to 3,000 feet; the GPS unit lets you track 100 routes with 100 waypoints per route.

Model: LCX-111C **Manufacturer:** Lowrance (www.lowrance.com) **Price:** $2,449

Suunto M9 Sailing Watch

Not every boating gadget is big and bulky. Suunto's M9 sailing watch packs an electronic watch, compass, barometer, thermometer, altimeter, and GPS receiver (!) into one compact device. Thanks to the 12-channel GPS receiver (on the world's smallest GPS chip), the M9 can calculate line bias and distance to the starting line, detect changes in wind direction, suggest appropriate courses, and provide layline information. That's a lot of information to put on your wrist, but there you go.

Model: M9 **Manufacturer:** Suunto (www. suuntowatches.com) **Dimensions:** 2.2" × 2.2" × 0.67" **Weight:** 3.6 oz. **Price:** $699

Navman Tracker 5500i GPS Chartplotter

Navman's Tracker 5500i combines a chartplotter with a GPS receiver (no sonar, sorry). On the chartplotter side, you get C-MAP NT cartography with tide and port services data; the 12-channel GPS receiver lets you track up to 25 routes with 50 waypoints per route. The 5" color LCD display has 320 × 234 pixel resolution, with normal, night, and day viewing settings.

Model: Tracker 5500i **Manufacturer:** Navman (www.navman.com) **Display:** 5" color LCD **Dimensions:** 6.5" (w) × 6.5" (h) × 3.5" (d) **Price:** $679.95

Lotus Designs Critter Life Vest

Okay, this one is a little low-tech, but it's still fun and practical. The Critter is a personal flotation device (aka "life vest") for dogs. Now you can take Fido on the boat with you and make sure he won't drown if he goes overboard. It even has a sturdy handle on the back so you can haul the soggy mutt out of the water, if necessary. Available in five sizes and two colors (yellow and orange).

Model: Critter **Manufacturer:** Lotus Designs (www.lotusdesigns.com) **Sizes:** XS, S, M, L, XL **Price:** $65

SCUBA GADGETS

Sea Doo Sea Scooter

Leo's Pick

I really like this little gizmo. When paddling about underwater isn't fast enough for you, just fire up the Sea Doo sea scooter and hang on as it blasts you through the water. It runs at a top speed of 2 MPH with 11 pounds of thrust, at depths up to 65 feet. It's the only way to get from here to there when you're scuba diving—just make sure you hang on when you get up to speed!

The Sea Doo is powered by a rechargeable battery that lasts up to an hour per charge. To start it up, just press the finger-activated soft-start trigger; the propeller starts slowly for a moment, and then ramps up to full speed. Let go of the trigger and the Sea Doo shuts off automatically and floats to the surface. A safety grill keeps you from poking your fingers into the propeller.

Driving the Sea Doo is a simple matter of turning it on, pointing it where you want to go, and then hanging on for dear life. It pulls you along underneath the water, so you'll need a good grip and a bit of arm muscle. Steering it involves turning the device right or left; you change depth by pointing it up or down. There are no fancy navigational controls to learn; it really is a point-and-shoot type of device.

Speaking of depth, you can adjust the Sea Doo to have anywhere from 5 ounces to 2 pounds of buoyancy. You want more buoyancy for snorkeling, and less for diving. You make the appropriate adjustments via a built-in buoyancy chamber.

It's a pretty sleek looking device, very James Bond-like and lots of fun. The Sea Doo is small and lightweight and can be carried in a small duffle bag in the trunk of your car. Anybody can use it, no license required.

And here's a fun fact: The Sea Doo was engineered by the same guy who invented the first portable PC, Sir Clive Sinclair. (Remember the Timex Sinclair computer?) From computers to sea scooters—what a life!

Model: Sea Doo **Manufacturer:** Sea Doo (www.seascooter.net) **Dimensions:** 15" × 16" × 9" **Weight:** 11 lbs. **Price:** $399.95

Mares Nemo Dive Computer/Watch

The dive computer is an essential part of any diver's gear package, and many of them are fairly high-tech gadgets. But Mares takes the concept to a new level by packing dive computer technology into a water-proof wrist watch. You get all the standard dive computer functions (depth, dive time, temperature, ascent rate, and so on) combined with an elegant electronic watch. It's a way-cool alternative to the traditional dive computer—perfect for the scuba diving gadget hound!

Model: Nemo **Manufacturer:** Mares (www.mares.com) **Operating temperature:** 14°–122° Fahrenheit **Price:** $600

Dive Alert SubDuck Underwater Signaling Device

Don't confuse Dive Alert's SubDuck with the RoboDuk I discussed previously; this one has nothing to do with hunting ducks. Instead, the SubDuck is an air-powered underwater signaling device that connects between your low pressure hose and power inflator. It generates a loud signal that's audible up to 75 feet underwater—great for getting the attention of your fellow divers.

Model: SubDuck **Manufacturer:** Dive Alert (www.divealert.com) **Dimensions:** 2.5" × 3" **Price:** $59.95

JBL 38 Special SHD Speargun

What fun is scuba diving if you can't shoot anything? That's why every diver with a James Bond fantasy needs a JBL spear gun, like the 38 Special SHD. It shoots standard 3/8" diameter spears and feels real powerful in your hand. Heck, it's a fun gadget even if you don't dive—it's great for picking off geckos in the back yard!

Model: 38 Special SHD **Manufacturer:** JBL Spearguns (www.jblspearguns.com) **Length:** 42" **Range:** 17 feet **Price:** $219.95

SurfaceDive Deck Snorkel

Here's a diving gadget for non-divers. That is, the Deck Snorkel can turn anybody into a part-time diver, no oxygen tanks necessary. The Deck Snorkel is an air compressor unit that connects to your boat's battery and feeds you oxygen as you dive over the side. It comes with the compressor unit, one regulator with dive harness, and a 48 ft. hose. You can stay under as long as you like and never have to worry about running out of air!

Model: Deck Snorkel **Manufacturer:** SurfaceDive (www.surfacedive.com) **Dimensions (compressor unit):** 16" (l) × 10" (w) × 9" (h) **Price:** $1,080

MORE COOL ADVENTURER GADGETS

FreePlay Ranger Radio

FreePlay's Ranger is an AM/FM radio that works on your choice of AC/DC power, solar power, or crank. That is, you can power the thing by turning the hand crank, which makes it ideal for use when camping, or as an emergency radio. You can get about 35 minutes of use out of a 30-second crank.

Model: Ranger **Manufacturer:** FreePlay (www.freeplayenergy.com) **Dimensions:** 3.9" (h) × 8" (l) × 2.5" (w) **Price:** $49.95

Suunto n6HR SPOT Sports Watch

Suunto's n6HR is a wristwatch that combines a heart rate monitor with wireless SPOT technology. SPOT (with a Microsoft Direct subscription) offers real-time news, weather, sports, and stock information, while you keep fit by monitoring your heart rate while you exercise. It also features a stopwatch and interval timer; your training data can be uploaded to your PC via USB.

Model: n6HR **Manufacturer:** Suunto (www.suuntowatches.com) **Price:** $399.99

ATN Night Storm 2 Night Vision Monocular

Now you can see in the dark, just like the soldiers do, thanks to ATN's Night Storm 2 night vision monocular. Yeah, everything looks all greenish, just like you'd expect, but it lights things up as bright as day—no matter how dark the night. Its range extends to 150 meters, with 3.5X magnification. The Night Storm 2 even features an optional camera adapter, so you can connect your digital camera and take night vision photos!

Model: Night Storm 2 **Manufacturer:** ATN (www.atncorp.com) **Dimensions:** 6.7" × 2.28" × 3.7" **Weight:** 14.5 oz. **Price:** $1,395

Princeton Tec Corona Headlamp

If you don't mind seeing in the dark the old fashioned way—with a light—then check out the Corona headlamp form Princeton Tec. This gizmo fastens around your head, so you'll get light in whichever direction you happen to be looking, hands-free. Light is generated from eight super-bright wide-angle LEDs; you can switch on or off individual LEDS to generate more or less light. And it's all powered by three AA batteries!

Model: Corona **Manufacturer:** Princeton Tec (www.princetontec.com) **Price:** $49.95

Neoteric Hovercraft

When money is no object, go in style—over land or water. Neoteric offers a line of leisure hovercraft, powered by 55 hp engines. Because you're floating on a cushion of air, you can go wherever you want, no matter the terrain—fields, deserts, beaches, rivers, lakes, sea, even snow and ice. The craft hovers 8 inches off the ground and has a cruising speed of 35 MPH. Lots of fun—and no license required!

Model: 01990 **Manufacturer:** Neoteric (www. neoterichovercraft.com) **Dimensions:** 13' 8" (l) × 8' 4" (w) × 4' 5" (h) **Capacity:** 4 persons (600 lbs.) **Price:** $15,833

Survival Kit in a Sardine Can

This one is exactly as the name says—a survival kit crammed into a sardine can. You get 25 survival items, including a compass, hook and line, duct tape, matches, whistle, razor blade, fire-starter cube, signal mirror, safety pin, and the like. It's small enough to carry in your glove compartment or purse—just pop it open when an emergency arises!

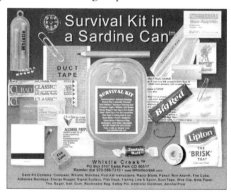

Model: Survival Kit in a Sardine Can **Manufacturer:** Whistle Creek (www.whistlecreek.com) **Price:** $12

Precision Shots Laser Slingshot

Combine stone-age weaponry with 21st-century technology and you get this fun little gizmo—a slingshot with a laser sight. The laser lets you accurately hit objects up to 150 feet away, which is pretty impressive. Buy the optional shotgun pouch and use it to shoot a spray of BBs!

Model: PS-55 **Manufacturer:** Precision Shots (www.catsdomain.com) **Price:** $69.95

ProAim Golfing Goggles

Better golfing through technology—thanks to ProAim's "virtual alignment trainer." This gizmo is actually a set of goggles that use night-vision technology to project a virtual alignment grid into your field of vision. Line up your shot with the grid, and your shots will be perfectly aligned with the hole.

Model: ProAim Virtual Alignment Trainer **Manufacturer:** ProAim (www.proaim.com) **Price:** $59.95

The Ultimate Digital Photographer

HOW TO BECOME THE ULTIMATE DIGITAL PHOTOGRAPHER

Photography has long been a great hobby for gadget lovers, even before it went all high-tech and digital. Today, digital photography affords one the opportunity to purchase all manner of fun gadgets, from the cameras themselves to a virtual plethora of add-ons and accessories—lenses, filters, battery chargers, cases, you name it.

Whether you're just starting out with digital photography or are an experienced shutterbug, the big question is where do you start—that is, what type of digital camera should you buy? There's no single answer to this question, because the type of camera you buy depends on how exactly you plan to use it. Let me explain.

Different Types of Digital Cameras

There's no such thing as a typical digital camera. While a $200 point-and-shoot model and a $1,000 digital SLR both take digital pictures, they're so different in look, feel, operation, and features that they may as well be creatures from two different planets. The key, then, is determining how you want to use a digital camera, then choosing the right type of camera to get that particular job done. You won't find a one-size-fits-all solution, I'm afraid.

That said, I think you can break down digital camera users into a handful of main groups:

- **The casual snapper**—This describes the bulk of the digital photography market, of course. You don't take a lot of photos, but when you do you want them to count. You're mainly shooting photos of family get-togethers, vacations, outdoors weekends, and the like—nothing too fancy, but important nonetheless. What you want is a camera that's fairly easy to use, without a lot of complicated features. You probably don't want something big and heavy; if you can slip the camera in your shirt pocket or in a purse, all the better. The right camera for you is a low-priced, compact, point-and-shoot model. You don't need to spend a lot of money on fancy features or lots of megapixels; something in the 3–5 megapixel range will do the trick.

- **The eBay seller**—This is a new category of photographer, a by-product of the eBay online auction revolution. What's important here isn't size or price (although you don't want to spend any more than you have to); instead, you want a camera that shoots quality pictures indoors and close up. Look for a point-and-shoot model that offers good low-light perform-ance and an easy-to-use macro mode. Again, you don't need to worry too much about the megapixels, as you can only upload low-resolution pictures for use in your auction listings.

- **The shoot-it-for-keeps**—If you want to create something more than simple snapshots—I'm talking high-quality photo prints, suitable for framing—you need more than just a point-and-shoot camera. The cameras you're interested in are called *prosumer* models, in that they offer a lot of professional-level features in a consumer-friendly package. These cameras let you shoot high-resolution pictures, in the 6–8 megapixel range, that can be blown up to 8 × 10 or larger print sizes. You'll also get a better-quality lens, typically with a longer zoom (6X–10X), as well as the ability to bypass the automatic shooting mode and shoot with either aperture- or shutter-priority modes. Most prosumer cameras also feature metal bodies (instead of the plastic bodies found in most point-and-shoot cameras), elec-tronic viewfinders (in addition to the standard large LCD monitor on the back), and intelli-gent hot shoes to which you can attach external flashes, strobe lights, and the like. Many of these cameras also let you save photos in the RAW file format, which is more versatile that JPEG or TIFF when it comes to post-photo processing in Adobe Photoshop or some similar program. Of course, you pay extra for all these features; a typical prosumer camera will cost you close to a thousand bucks, give or take.

- **The aspiring pro**—Now we're into the really good stuff, a category known as the digital single-lens reflex (D-SLR) camera. A D-SLR is the digital equivalent of a high-end SLR film camera and takes higher-quality pictures than even the prosumer digital models. You get lots of flexibility with a D-SLR, including the ability to use differ-ent types of lenses. (That's right, in a D-SLR the lenses are inter-changeable.) These cameras aren't cheap, although they're not that much more expensive than a good prosumer model; prices start at around a grand, and go up from there. I'll talk more about D-SLRs in a few pages, so read on if you want to learn more.

Sorting Through the Features

Whichever type of camera you settle on, there are some key features that you need to be aware of. Here's a short list:

- **Picture resolution**—This is measured in megapixels. (One megapixel equals a million pixels, natch.) The more megapixels, the sharper your pictures will be. Most decent point-and-shoot cameras today have a resolution in the range of 3–5 megapixels; prosumer and D-SLR models go up to 8 megapixel resolution. Why do you need more megapixels? It's simple, really. If you want to create large-size prints, you have to fill up all that space with picture information. The more pixels, the more picture information—and the bigger the prints you can make. With an 8-megapixel camera, you should be able to make prints up to 14" × 17"; lower-resolution point-and-shoot cameras can only make prints half that size.

- **Zoom lens**—This helps you get up close to distant subjects. Ignore the *digital* zoom specs (that's an electronic zooming effect that creates blocky-looking results) and focus on the *optical* zoom. Most low-end cameras have a 3X zoom; prosumer models go up to a 10X zoom. When you buy a D-SLR, you can choose lenses with all manner of zoom ranges. As you might expect, the bigger the zoom, the better.

- **Size and weight**—Many point-and-shoot cameras are little bigger than a credit card and weigh less than half a pound. Prosumer models are bigger and heavier, and D-SLRs even more so. Photo pros actually like the heft of a "real" camera, although most casual snappers prefer something smaller and lighter. This is definitely a personal choice.

- **Video capabilities**—Believe it or not, most digital cameras (except D-SLRS) also let you shoot short video+sound movies. I suppose there's some value to this feature for some people, although it escapes me. (If I want to shoot movies, I'll buy a bloody camcorder!)

- **Operating speed**—That is, how long it takes to power up and shoot a picture after you've pressed the auto focus button. Many low-end cameras have a noticeable shutter lag that makes it difficult to take pictures of fast-moving subjects—like kids at sporting events. Prosumer cameras are a little better at this, but the best performance in this regard comes from D-SLRs. Most D-SLRs turn on practically instantly and can shoot multiple pictures in a single second, without pausing in between. They're the best bet if you shoot a lot of sports photos.

- **Battery life**—Digital cameras eat batteries. Lots of them. Go ahead and check the battery specs, but if you're choosing a point-and-shoot or prosumer camera, set aside a few extra bucks for a set of rechargeable batteries and an external battery charger. D-SLRs, on the other hand, use proprietary internal rechargeable batteries and have extremely long battery life. (Since you set up your shot through the lens itself, a D-SLR doesn't have to constantly power the power-draining back-of-camera LCD display.)

- **Storage capacity**—All digital cameras store their photos on a flash memory card of some sort. Most cameras come with a blank memory card, typically a low-capacity model. Which means you'll probably want to spring for a higher-capacity card—or even two, if you plan on shooting a lot of photos all at once. And remember, the higher the resolution of your photos, the more storage space they take. (That's why I have a 1GB card in my D-SLR!)

By the way, when you're comparing features, check out Digital Photography Review (www.dpreview.com) and Steve's Digicams (www.steves-digicams.com), two websites that feature a ton of extremely comprehensive digital camera reviews. These sites will give you the real scoop!

Pro-Level Performance for the Masses: Digital SLRs

As you probably gathered, point-and-shoot and prosumer digital cameras all use pretty much the same technology, although to different degrees. It's when you get to a D-SLR that the technology changes; they differ significantly from point-and-shoot and prosumer digital cameras in both operation and performance.

Let's take the typical point-and-shoot or prosumer digital camera. These cameras have their lenses permanently attached and require you to view what you're shooting via either an electronic viewfinder or LCD monitor screen. They typically have small image sensors (less than an inch across) that produce good, but not great, pictures, and they don't offer a lot of operating flexibility.

D-SLR cameras use a reflex mirror apparatus so that, when you look through the optical viewfinder, you're actually viewing through the lens itself. That helps you take better pictures, and it also helps battery life—because you're not powering the LCD display every time you take a picture. (In fact, you can't use the LCD display as a viewfinder; it's only there when you need to make a selection from the camera's menu system or review the photos you've taken.)

You also get the ability to use interchangeable lenses and larger image sensors, often as big as 35mm film, which provide better results in low-light conditions. In addition, these cameras are usually designed by the companies' 35mm camera divisions (instead of their consumer electronics divisions) and provide all the operating flexibility you need to make great photos, fast.

D-SLR cameras have been around since the early 1990s, when they used to cost $20,000 or more. Fortunately for us, the price has come down over the years; today's most affordable D-SLRs cost around the same price as high-end prosumer cameras.

Bottom line, a D-SLR camera delivers a better picture (no matter what the megapixel rating), lets you use interchangeable lenses, and has more operating flexibility. So, if all you want to do is take quick snapshots, stick with a point-and-shoot or prosumer digital camera. But if you want pro-level performance and flexibility, check out a D-SLR. You'll notice the difference as soon as you pick it up; a D-SLR just *feels* like a real camera.

Getting the Most Out of Your Digital Camera

To get the most use out of your digital camera, it pays to fill up your camera bag with a variety of useful accessories. This is maybe less true if you have a low-price point-and-shoot camera, but accessorizing is definitely a good idea if you've spent north of five bills for a more fully featured model.

How will camera accessories help you take better pictures? Here are some examples:

- **Rechargeable batteries**—As I mentioned, digital cameras go through batteries like babies go through diapers. You can use standard-grade batteries, and lots of them, or invest in a set of rechargeable batteries and accompanying battery recharger. When I'm on vacation, I take two sets of rechargeable batteries—one in the camera, the other in the recharger, so I'm prepared when the batteries run down.

- **Memory card**—The more (and higher-resolution) pictures you take, the more storage space you need. Pictures are stored on flash memory cards, so investing in a higher-capacity card for your camera is always a good idea.

- **Digital photo vault**—An alternative to hoarding multiple memory cards is to offload your photos to a photo vault. This is a portable device that combines hard disk storage with a color LCD viewing screen. Actually, most photo vaults double for portable video players; the technology is the same, in any case. As prices for these devices drop, this is becoming an increasingly attractive option for the active digital photographer.

- **Lens filters**—Most digital camera lenses accept screw-on lens filters, which is a great option that too few casual photographers avail themselves of. Lens filters can reduce glare and improve color rendition in all your photos—at the very least, you should invest in a UV or polarizing filter.

- **External flash kit**—The more light, the better—and the built-in flash in the typical consumer-grade digital camera is barely adequate, at best. An external flash kit will provide much better fill lighting for both indoor and outdoor shots, trust me.

- **Lighting kit**—When you're shooting indoors, flash isn't always the best way to go. A set of freestanding photo floods will help you shoot more detailed portraits and indoor still-life photos—it's especially useful when shooting eBay product photos.

- **Tripod**—This is another necessity for shooting eBay product photos. A tripod will hold your camera steady and help to eliminate blurry shots, especially when you're shooting in low light.

- **LCD hood**—Ever have trouble seeing what you're shooting (or just shot), especially outdoors? Then you need a hood for your camera's LCD display; this makes it easier to view your camera's monitor, especially in bright sunlight.

- **Cleaning kit**—An ounce of prevention is worth a couple of hundred bucks of cure, or something like that. That's why you should invest a few bucks to keep your camera free of dust and dirt and extend its working life.

Professional photographers spend a lot of money on accessories like these, and for good reason. When it comes to taking good pictures, they appreciate all the help they can get—as should you. It's amazing how a small investment in an accessory or two can make your life so much easier.

And here's something else to keep in mind. With the exception of memory cards and digital photo vaults, these accessories aren't specific to digital cameras. That is, you can use most film camera accessories with your digital camera, and vice versa; you don't have to buy special digital accessories. A tripod is a tripod, no matter what kind of camera you put on top. So, head down to your local camera store and see what they have to offer!

And Don't Forget the Software!

Your digital photos don't stay in your camera for long; sooner or later, you transfer your photos to your PC for long-term storage, editing, and printing. After all, a digital picture file is just like any computer file, which means you can copy it, move it, delete it, or whatever. You can also use special photo editing software to manipulate your photos—to touch up bad spots and red eye, crop the edges, and apply all sorts of special effects.

When it comes time to touch up your digital photos, you need a photo-editing program. You can choose a low-priced, consumer-oriented program or a high-priced program targeted at professional photographers. For most of us, the consumer-oriented programs are more than adequate—and, in fact, you might have received one bundled with your new PC or digital camera.

If you're in the market for a low-priced photo-editing program, here are the most popular programs in use today:

- Adobe Photoshop CS (www.adobe.com)
- Adobe Photoshop Elements (www.adobe.com)
- IrfanView (www.irfanview.com)
- Microsoft Picture It! Photo (www.microsoft.com/products/imaging/)
- Paint Shop Pro (www.corel.com)
- Picasa (www.picasa.com)
- Roxio PhotoSuite (www.roxio.com)

For the casual photographer, I heartily recommend Adobe Photoshop Elements. This is a lower-priced and easier-to-use version of the Adobe Photoshop CS program, which happens to be the software I recommend for professional photographers and serious hobbyists. For the non-pros among us, Elements offers about 85% of Photoshop CS's features, but with a lot faster learning curve. Elements is extremely easy to use, with one-button operation for most common photo editing tasks. I especially like Elements' quick and easy red eye removal tool, and the new healing brush and spot healing brush tools, which help you patch over flaws in a picture. (Photoshop CS offers the same tools, of course.)

All of these programs will also help you manage your digital photos. If all you want is photo management, without a lot of editing capability, then check out Picasa, which you can download for free. Picasa is a Windows program, very similar to Apple's iPhoto, which is another one of my favorite programs. (Hey, I'm a fool for full-featured, easy-to-use programs that also happen to be free!)

Whichever program you end up using, prepare to spend a lot of time in front of your PC screen, touching up your photos. It gets addictive after awhile, to be honest. If you do a lot of photo editing, consider upgrading your PC with a bigger monitor and more hard disk space. (More memory and a faster processor won't hurt, either—especially if you're using Photoshop CS.) That's what I like about digital photography—it's the gift that keeps on giving!

DIGITAL SLR CAMERAS

Nikon D70s

Leo's Pick

Nikon's D70 has long been my favorite digital camera, D-SLR or otherwise, and the D70s is the updated version of this old favorite. The D70s is a little faster than the D70, has a bit longer battery life, and a slightly larger LCD display. In short, it's more of a very good thing.

With the D70s, you get high-end D-SLR performance at a relatively affordable price. This camera is fast (operation is virtually instant-on, and you can shoot up to 3 frames per second—up to 144 consecutive shots in a row), rugged (black metal case), and versatile. You can shoot in a variety of preprogrammed modes, as well as aperture priority, shutter priority, or manual mode; you can also override the auto focus just by touching the manual focus ring on the lens. The D70s delivers shutter speeds from 30 to 1/8000 seconds, and flash-synchronized shutter speeds up to 1/500 seconds.

Image-wise, the D70s's performance is exemplary. Images are sharp and clean, with a remarkable depth of field. (Resolution is 6.1 megapixels.) Of course, some of that depends on which lens you use, and the D70s works with any Nikkor lens—even those you use with your 35mm camera. You can buy the D70s body-only or in a package with an 18–70mm zoom lens; I recommend the package, which is surprisingly affordable.

Digital SLRs offer more versatility than a standard digital camera, and not just in lens choice. For example, the D70s gives you three types of auto focus: single area AF, dynamic area AF, and closest subject priority dynamic area AF. It shoots in either JPEG or RAW (NEF) format, with ISO settings of 200–1600. Buy a big CompactFlash card (I or II) to hold all those big images!

One nice improvement of the D70s over the original D70 is the improved autofocus system. The D70s uses a new five-area AF with a cross-type sensor in the center and broad frame coverage; refinements to the original system provide more consistent subject acquisition and improved focus tracking. I'll admit, wonky autofocus was one of the few drawbacks to the original unit; improving the AF system fixes the only thing I griped about.

Model: D70s **Manufacturer:** Nikon (www.nikonusa.com) **Resolution:** 6.1 MP **Power-up time:** 0.2 seconds **LCD screen:** 2" **Shutter speed:** 30–1/8000 sec. **Dimensions (body):** 5.5" × 4.4" × 3.1" **Weight:** 20.8 oz. **Package lens:** Nikkor 18–70mm **Price:** $899 (body only), $1,199 (w/lens)

Nikon D50

Nikon's D50 is the kid brother to the bigger D70s; this camera is just a little smaller and lighter than the D70s, and a tad bit easier to use. While the image quality is nearly identical between the two cameras, there are a few fewer adjustments to make, which the average photographer probably won't notice. Like the D70s, the D50 can use any Nikkor lens; the basic package includes an 18–55mm zoom lens (a tad shorter than the D70s' 18–70mm package lens). All-in-all, you get a ton of camera for about $300 less than the D70s (in kit form)—what's not to like?

Model: D50 **Manufacturer:** Nikon (www.nikonusa.com) **Resolution:** 6.1 MP **Dimensions (body):** 5.2" × 4" × 3" **Weight:** 19.2 oz. **Package lens:** Nikkor 18–55mm **Price:** $749 (body only), $899 (w/lens)

Canon EOS Digital Rebel XT

Nikon's chief competitor in the D-SLR market is Canon, which actually beat Nikon to market with the original EOS Digital Rebel. Now Canon ups the ante with the replacement EOS Digital Rebel XT, which delivers improved performance in a slightly smaller, slightly lighter body. The big news here is the 8 megapixel sensor; it's a nice addition to a very popular performer. Like the original, the Digital Rebel XT is compatible with more than 50 of Canon's EF lenses.

Model: EOS Digital Rebel XT **Manufacturer:** Canon (www.usa.canon.com) **Resolution:** 8 MP **Dimensions:** 5" × 3.7" × 2.5" **Weight:** 17.6 oz. **Package lens:** 18–55mm **Price:** $899 (body only), $999 (w/lens)

Olympus EVOLT E-300

Olympus joins the D-SLR fray with one of the first Four Thirds System cameras, which uses a 4/3-size CCD and more compact lenses than competing D-SLRs. Unique to the E-300 is the Supersonic Wave Filter, which "shakes" dust off the CCD sensor, which has long been a problem with removable-lens cameras. It's a very good performer (with 8 megapixel resolution), and the sensor-cleaning thing is a very nice feature. Definitely worth your consideration.

Model: EVOLT E-300 **Manufacturer:** Olympus (www.olympusamerica.com) **Resolution:** 8 MP **Dimensions (body):** 5.77" × 3.35" × 2.52" **Weight:** 20.5 oz. **Package lens:** 14–45mm **Price:** $999 (w/lens)

Pentax *ist DS

As long as I don't have to pronounce "*ist" (I have no idea...), I'll put this camera on my list of favorite D-SLRs. I've always been a Pentax fan, primarily because of their lenses, and this camera doesn't disappoint; you can use it with just about any Pentax K-mount lens. This is one of the smallest and lightest D-SLRs available and it's quite easy to operate—both of which make it an ideal pro-level camera for anyone upgrading from the point-and-shoot world.

Model: *ist DS **Manufacturer:** Pentax (www.pentaximaging.com) **Resolution:** 6.1 MP **Dimensions (body):** 4.9" × 3.6" × 2.6" **Weight:** 17.8 oz. **Package lens:** 18–55mm **Price:** $799.95 (body only), $899.95 (w/lens)

PROSUMER DIGITAL CAMERAS

Sony Cybershot DSC-F828

Leo's Pick

Pocket-sized snapshot digital cameras are fine, but when you want really good pictures, you want a camera with a little beef between the bun—what the industry calls *prosumer* digital cameras. Most of these cameras have similar specs and performance, and look and feel similar, too.

There are differences, however, which is why my favorite prosumer camera is the Sony Cyber-shot DSC-828. Why? For me, it's the lens. Sony uses a Carl Zeiss Vario Sonnar lens with T* coating, which translates into an extremely sharp picture under even the most demanding conditions. Sony's cameras are known for their fine lenses, and this one sets a new standard of quality. (It's a 7X zoom, the equivalent of a 28–200mm traditional zoom.)

Performance-wise, you get an 8 megapixel sensor, so you know you'll get high-resolution pictures, even when you blow them up or crop them. In fact, if you're thinking of creating poster-sized prints, it's hard to recommend anything less than an 8 megapixel photo.

I also like the color this camera delivers. That's because of Sony's unique four-color filter CCD. That extra color (RGB + Emerald) produces photo colors that are closer to human color perception, especially with blue, blue-green, and red hues.

And here's something else neat about this camera: It can shoot in the dark. Sony's NightShot system captures infrared images in total darkness, up to 10 feet away. I dare you to find another consumer-level camera that does that!

What else do you get on this puppy? Well, a Real Imaging Processor delivers increased speed with lower power consumption; you also get the ability to shoot in automatic, aperture priority, shutter priority, or manual mode; manual zoom and manual focus rings; the expected eye-level electronic viewfinder and 1.8" LCD monitor; the ability to save in JPEG, TIFF, or RAW format; and the ability to write to Memory Stick, Memory Stick PRO, CompactFlash I and II, or IBM Microdrive media.

All these features add up, however; this is a big camera, weighing in at a hefty two pounds. So, buy yourself a strong strap!

Model: DSC-F828 **Manufacturer:** Sony (www.sonystyle.com) **Resolution:** 8 MP
Lens: 7X (28–200mm) **Dimensions:** 5.3" × 3.6" × 6.1" **Weight:** 32 oz. **Price:** $999

Nikon Coolpix 8800

Nikon ups the ante with this 8-megapixel camera with a 10X zoom lens—just a tinch longer than competitors. This is a nice, solid-feeling camera, thanks to the magnesium alloy body and a sturdy construction. I particularly like the 1.8" LCD on a snap-out, tilting connector; this lets you shoot at just about any angle. A special noise reduction mode minimizes digital artifacts in long nighttime exposures. You can save to RAW or JPEG format and to CompactFlash or Microdrive media.

Model: Coolpix 8800 **Manufacturer:** Nikon (www.nikonusa.com) **Resolution:** 8 MP **Lens:** 10X zoom (35–350mm) **Dimensions:** 4.6" × 3.3" × 4.8" **Weight:** 24 oz. **Price:** $999

Canon Powershot Pro 1

Canon's offering in the prosumer camera market comes in a professional black finish and features a large 2" LCD monitor. You get 8-megapixel resolution (of course) and a 7X zoom lens. The Pro 1 features 12 EOS-based shooting modes—Portrait, Landscape, Night Scene, and so on. There's also an enhanced Super Macro mode for really close-up photography. And, like other Canon cameras, you get a Direct Print mode for one-button printing to select Canon printers, as well as one-touch file transfer to your Windows PC.

Model: PowerShot Pro 1 **Manufacturer:** Canon (www.powershot.com) **Resolution:** 8 MP **Lens:** 7X zoom (28–200mm) **Dimensions:** 4.6" × 2.8" × 3.5" **Weight:** 19.2 oz. **Price:** $999

Konica Minolta DiMAGE A2

Minolta's DiMAGE A2 has two unique things going for it. First, its proprietary anti-shake technology results in better stability, especially when using the zoom. Second, a tiltable LCD monitor (up by 90° or down by 20°) provides positioning flexibility. Beyond those features, the DiMAGE A2 has the expected 8-megapixel resolution, the expected 7X zoom lens (28–200mm), and all the other expected bells and whistles. It's a solid performer, no matter how you look at it.

Model: DiMAGE A2 **Manufacturer:** Minolta (www.dimage.minolta.com) **Resolution:** 8 MP **Dimensions:** 4.6" × 3.4" × 4.5" **Weight:** 19.2 oz. **Lens:** 7X zoom (28–200mm) **Price:** $999

Olympus Camedia C-8080 Wide Zoom

I've always like Olympus's digital cameras, especially their zoom lenses. The C-8080 Wide Zoom has a 5X wide-angle zoom (28–40mm) which, while good, isn't quite as long as some of the other prosumer cameras. That aside, this is a very fast camera, thanks to the TruePic TURBO image processor. This technology decreases the camera's start-up and camera lag time and lets you shoot 1.6 frames per second. You can save your pictures in JPEG or TIFF formats and to xD or CompactFlash cards.

Model: C-8080 Wide Zoom **Manufacturer:** Olympus (www.olympusamerica.com) **Resolution:** 8 MP **Lens:** 5X zoom (28–140mm) **Dimensions:** 4.9" × 3.3" × 3.9" **Weight:** 24 oz. **Price:** $999

SPECIALTY DIGITAL CAMERAS

Bonica Sea-Pix Underwater Camera

Leo's Pick

Put a normal digital camera underwater, and the electronics fizzle out. Even if the electronics could be protected, the case would soon implode from the pressure as you take it to greater depths. How, then, do scuba diving photographers take all those cool underwater pictures you see in magazines and such?

Underwater photography is possible thanks to specially designed underwater cameras, such as Bonica's Sea-Pix. The Sea-Pix is designed with a waterproof housing that also protects against high levels of water pressure. It also has special larger controls that are easier for a diver to operate underwater. (Just imagine twiddling the knobs and switches on a typical point-and-shoot camera while you're in the water—not bloody likely!)

The Sea-Pix uses a Sony 5.25 megapixel CCD processor, for large, high-resolution photos. You view your shot on a 1.5" LCD panel, large enough and bright enough to see in murky water. The camera itself has a 3X optical zoom lens so you can get up close to your subject; there's also a macro setting for close-ups of sea life away to just 4 inches away. The lens has a 67mm threaded lens ring that can accept add-on filters, diopters, and wide-angle lenses. Focusing is automatic, which is a necessity when you're diving. Photos are stored on SD cards, and there's even a video mode for recording short underwater movies.

The camera's housing is made of extremely tough polycarbonate, and it lets you take the Sea-Pix as deep as 160 feet. When the camera is in the housing, you have access to just six controls (including zoom in, zoom out, macro, and flash) for easier operation. The control seals are protected by quad rings, and all hardware on the unit is either marine-grade stainless steel, nickel-plated brass, or anodized aluminum. There's also an internal trim ballast, which makes the camera lighter or heavier in the water.

For best pictures, use the Sea-Pix with Bonica's Neon Strobe III ($299). This is a powerful underwater strobe light that helps to enhance picture quality in deep or murky water. The strobe has a fully adjustable arm and a flash head that swivels 360°, so you can flash your subject from just about any angle. The Neon Strobe III fires simultaneously with the camera's built-in flash for best results.

Model: Sea-Pix **Manufacturer:** Bonica (www.bonicadive.com) **Resolution:** 5.25 MP **Lens:** 3X zoom (37–111mm) **Shutter speed:** 8-1/2000 second **Dimensions:** 6.25" × 6" × 6" **Weight:** 17.25 oz. **Price:** $519.95

Pentax Optio33WR Water-Resistant Camera

If you don't plan to dive with your camera but you still want to take it with you on the water, consider Pentax's water-resistant Optio33WR. As Pentax says, you can splash it, dunk it, or take pictures in the rain—or on your boat. You get decent 3.2 megapixel resolution, a 2.8X zoom lens, 1.6" LCD display, and all manner of auto picture modes—and it's all packed inside a small, hard-plastic, water-resistant case.

Model: Optio33WR **Manufacturer:** Pentax (www. pentaximaging.com) **Resolution:** 3.2 MP **Lens:** 2.8X zoom (37–104mm) **Dimensions:** 3.2" × 3" × 1.2" **Weight:** 5.6 oz. **Price:** $349

JB1 James Bond 007 Spy Camera

The JB1 is the kind of gadget you'd expect Agent 007 to carry—a digital camera built in to a cigarette lighter case. It's small enough to fit in any pocket and inconspicuous enough not to draw attention if Blofeld's around. The camera's a quick shot—flip the top, click the button, and close the top again. There's no switching on required. Even cooler, the camera offers a surveillance mode that lets you record images at preset time intervals of up to 90 minutes. It takes pictures at either 640 × 480 or 320 × 240 resolution; the internal memory holds up to 150 of the higher-resolution pictures.

Model: JB1 **Manufacturer:** Digital Dream (www. jbcamera.com) **Resolution:** 0.3 MP **Price:** $99.99

Photo3-D Kit

Remember 3D movies? Now you can take 3D pictures from any digital camera, thanks to the Photo3-D 303 Kit. Attach your camera to the hand-held Photo3-D device and snap a picture; then slide the camera to the second position and take a second picture. This creates a *stereo pair* of images; use the included Photo3-D Mixer software to combine the images into a single 3D image, which you can view with special 3D glasses.

Model: Photo3-D 303 Kit **Manufacturer:** Photo3-D (www.photo3-d.com) **Price:** $129

MagPix SX3 Digital Camera/Binocular

Here's a neat idea: Combine a quality pair of binoculars with a digital camera, so you can shoot what you see. That's what you get with MagPix's SX3, which combines a 3.1 megapixel digital camera with 10×25mm ruby-coated binoculars. It's great for any outdoor activity, from bird watching to watching NASCAR races. There's even a TV-out jack, so you can feed what you see through the binocs to a video display. All these neat features and you only have two buttons to worry about—power and shutter!

Model: SX3 **Manufacturer:** MagPix (www.magpix.com) **Camera resolution:** 3.1 MP **Binoculars:** 10×25mm **Dimensions:** 5" × 4" × 2" **Weight:** 9.6 oz. **Price:** $149.99

DIGITAL PHOTO VAULTS

Epson P-2000

Leo's Pick

A photo vault is a portable device that lets you offload digital photos from your digital camera (either via memory card or USB transfer), and then view those pictures when you're on the go. You get the advantage of freeing up storage space on your camera to take more pictures, as well as easily sharing your photos with others via the photo vault's LCD screen.

For all practical purposes, just about any portable video player can be used as a photo vault, as can some portable audio players (those with bigger screens, anyway, such as the iPod Photo). But the best photo vaults are those dedicated to the task, such as my favorite device, Epson's P-2000.

The P-2000 comes with a 40GB hard drive, which is as big as the drives in some desktop PCs; it'll hold a ton of photos, even at high resolution. You view the photos on a big 3.8" color LCD, which is a lot easier than staring at the smaller display on the back of your camera. The display has a zoom feature, so you can zoom into just part of a picture to see more detail. You can also connect the P-2000 to a television or projector by connecting a standard video cable.

You transfer photo files from your camera to the P-2000 via USB 2.0, or just by inserting the camera's flash card. (The P-2000 accepts both CompactFlash I/II and SD memory cards.) And here's an added bonus: You can print directly from the P-2000 to selected Epson printers, no computer required.

Aside from storing photos, the P-2000 can also function has a portable video and audio player. That's right, you can use the P-2000 to view photos, play movies, and listen to music—and with that 40GB drive, you can store lots of each type of file.

Model: Epson P-2000 **Manufacturer:** Epson (www.epson.com) **Storage capacity:** 40GB **Display:** 3.8" (640 × 480) **Dimensions:** 5.8" (w) × 3.3" (h) × 1.2" (d) **Weight:** 1 lb. **Price:** $499.99

Archos AV420

Remember when I said that any portable video player can double as a photo vault? Case in point is Archos' AV420, which has 20GB of hard drive storage and a 3.5" LCD display—perfect for storing and viewing digital photos. You can transfer files via USB 2.0 or CompactFlash cards (or, with an optional adapter, SD, SM, MMC, and MS cards). The AV420 is also a full function video recorder and player that can hold 80 hours of television programs.

Model: AV420 **Manufacturer:** Archos (www.archos.com) **Storage capacity:** 20GB **Display:** 3.5" **Dimensions:** 4.9" (w) × 3.1" (h) × 0.8" (d) **Weight:** 9.88 oz. **Price:** $499.95

SmartDisk FlashTrax XT

SmartDisk's FlashTrax XT is an affordable photo vault with a cool flip-up 3.6" LCD screen. File transfer is via USB 2.0 or CompactFlash cards. The FlashTrax XT has a 40GB hard disk and can display photos in JPEG, GIF, BMP, and RAW formats. (It also functions as a portable video player.)

Model: FlashTrax XT **Manufacturer:** SmartDisk (www.smartdisk.com) **Storage capacity:** 40GB **Display:** 2.6" **Dimensions:** 3.82" × 6.22" × 1.38" **Weight:** 15 oz. **Price:** $399.99

Jobo GIGA Vu PRO

Jobo's GIGA Vu PRO is one monster photo viewer, available in both 40GB and extra-large 60GB models. Whatever size hard disk you choose, you get a really large 3.8" touch screen LCD display that doubles as both viewer and controller. Add an optional WiFi card and you can exchange and view photos over any wireless network; otherwise, you can transfer photos via USB 2.0 or CompactFlash cards.

Model: GVP040/GVP060 **Manufacturer:** Jobo (www.jobodigital.com) **Storage capacity:** 40GB or 60GB **Display:** 3.8" **Dimensions:** 5.7" (w) × 4.2" (h) × 1.5" (d) **Weight:** 14.8 oz. **Price:** $549.95 (40GB), $599.95 (60GB)

Sony MCS1 PhotoVault

Our final photo vault is Sony's MCS-1. What's unique about this gizmo is that it lets you transfer photos directly from your camera to mini CD-R discs, instead of to hard disk. Once you burn a mini-disc, you can play it in any computer CD drive. File transfer is via USB 2.0 or Sony MemoryStick media (no CompactFlash reader, sorry); while you do get a video-out jack to display pictures on any TV, there's no built-in LCD display.

Model: MCS-1 **Manufacturer:** Sony (www.sonystyle. com) **Storage media:** Mini CD-R discs **Dimensions:** 4.5" × 3.5" × 1" **Weight:** 7 oz. **Price:** $199.99

LIGHTING AND FLASH KITS

AlienBees DigiBee Lighting Kit

Leo's Pick

Every serious photographer needs a lighting kit—whether you're shooting portraits or eBay product shots. The key is to get a lighting kit that combines versatility, portability, and adequate lighting power without breaking the bank.

Those parameters describe exactly what you get in AlienBees' DigiBee lighting kit. This is a lighting kit designed with the digital photographer in mind, and it gives you just what you need at an affordable price. The DigiBee is a two-light setup that's ideal for both home studio and location photography.

What you get are two B400 flash units, two 10-foot stands, one reflector umbrella and one shoot-through umbrella, and two carrying bags, all for under $600. It's a lot of lighting for the money, providing the option of high-contrast silver bounce lighting, a softer white bounce, or a really soft diffused glow.

At the heart of the DigiBee kit is AlienBees' B400 flash unit. This is a self-contained studio flash that produces 400 effective wattseconds of power, with 7,000 lumenseconds of output. You can adjust the lighting power over a stepless five f-stop range, from full all the way down to 1/32nd total power. You control the flash level with a slide fader on the back of each unit.

The two 48" umbrellas help make this kit unique. One umbrella is a combination silver and white reflector; use the silver side for a high-contrast bounce and the white side for a software white bounce. The other umbrella offers shoot-through diffusion for the softest light possible. Use them separately or in combination with each other.

And when you want to take your show on the road, pack everything up into the two carrying bags. The stands telescope down, the umbrellas fold up, and the lights and everything else (including power cords) pack right into the compact bags. Each bag measures 13.5" tall × 9" diameter.

Model: DigiBee **Manufacturer:** AlienBees (www.alienbees.com) **Components:** B400 flash units (2), LS 3050 light stands (2), U48TWB translucent umbrella (1), U48SW silver/white umbrella (1), CB1 carrying bag (2) **Price:** $599

Smith-Victor KT500 Lighting Kit

If you don't want to fork over six bills for the AlienBees kit, consider the much lower-priced (but still quite effective) Smith-Victor KT500 kit. This is a two-light photoflood kit that delivers a total of 500 watts of lighting. The kit includes two 10" reflectors, two sockets and cords, two 6-foot telescoping stands, and two 250-watt photoflood bulbs. Just set them up and turn them on, and see for yourself how much better your photos look.

Model: KT500 **Manufacturer:** Smith-Victor Corporation (www.smithvictor.com) **Price:** $135

Photoflex Basic Starlite Lighting Kit

Here's another way to go, a single-light photoflood kit with softbox that's great for shooting small products like ceramics, jewelry, crystal, and arts and crafts items. The Basic Starlite kit comes with a 500-watt Starlite lamp, stand, and SilverDome Softbox; if one isn't enough, buy two.

Model: Basic Starlite **Manufacturer:** Photoflex (www.photoflex.com) **Price:** $399.95

Metz Mecablitz Digital Flash Kits

Using an external flash produces much better results than most cameras' built-in flash units, because the light is generally more powerful and offset slightly to the side of the camera, which reduces both glare and red eye. Metz produces dozens of different flash models for different uses. Most flashes attach to your camera's hot shoe; if your digital camera doesn't have a hot shoe, try Metz's 34-CS-2 Digital model, which incorporates a slave trigger unit and automatic flash mode.

Model: Various **Manufacturer:** Metz (www.metz.de) **Price:** $50–$400

Sunpak Digital Camera Flash Enhancement Kit

Here's another flash unit designed for digital camera use. Sunpak's Digital Camera Flash Enhancement Kit works with any digital camera that has a built-in flash or hot shoe, and works to supplement the built-in flash. It sits on its own tripod stand and has a 200 millisecond delay for optimum flash synch. It's also quite affordable, at around $30.

Model: 018ST **Manufacturer:** Sunpak (www.sunpak.com) **Dimensions:** 2.5" × 2" × 3.75" **Weight:** 3.4 oz. **Price:** $30

MORE COOL DIGITAL PHOTOGRAPHY GADGETS

Tiffen Digital Camera Lens Filters

You'd be surprised how big a difference a little filter can make on the pictures you take. If your camera accepts lens filters (and most do), check out Tiffen's offerings. Tiffen manufactures a wide range of filters for use on both consumer and pro-level digital cameras, including ultraviolet, polarizing, light-balancing, color graduated, color conversion, color compensating, and special effects filters. Tiffen also makes a number of adapter rings and other camera accessories. See the company's website for the full range of products.

Model: Various **Manufacturer:** Tiffen (www.tiffen.com) **Price:** $25–$150

VidPro TT-800 Tripod

Every serious photographer needs a tripod for his or her camera, to keep low-light pictures from jittering. VidPro makes a full line of camera tripods, and my favorite is the TT-800. It extends to 55" in height and has a three-way pan head with a large quick-release platform. For even steadier pictures, the TT-800 has a built-in center column stabilizer and lock, along with flip-lock legs with rubber nonskid feet.

Model: TT-800 **Manufacturer:** VidPro (www.vidprousa.com) **Price:** $49.99

Minolta Auto Meter VF

Minolta's Auto Meter VF is a multifunction light meter with simple operation and exceptional accuracy. It has a large, easy-to-read LCD display; recommended shutter speed appears on the left, aperture on the right. It even has an analyze function, which displays the flash/ambient lighting ratio. Hold it out, press a button, and let it tell you what settings to use.

Model: Auto Meter VF **Manufacturer:** Minolta (www.minoltausa.com) **Price:** $229.99

Hoodman LCD Hoods

Seeing your camera's LCD screen is a particular problem outdoors on a sunny day, which is why you might want to consider using an LCD hood. Hoodman sells a variety of rubber hoods that fit over any LCD screen and turn your open-to-the-elements monitor into a hooded viewfinder. Each Hoodman hood incorporates a 2X magnifier to allow close focus on the LCD screen and provides glare-free viewing; they're also good for use with camcorders.

Model: Various **Manufacturer:** Hoodman (www.hoodmanusa.com) **Price:** $9.95–$19.95

Epson Perfection 4180 Photo Scanner

A digital camera isn't the only way to create digital photos; you can also scan in photo prints and slides via a photo scanner. One of the best mid-price photo scanners out there is the Epson 4180, which offers 4800 × 9600 resolution, as well as a built-in adapter for scanning 35mm negatives, slides, and medium-format transparencies. Connection is via USB, and the one-step photo restoration feature helps you quickly restore faded prints when you scan.

Model: Perfection 4180 **Manufacturer:** Epson (www.epson.com) **Resolution:** 4800 × 9600 dpi **Color depth:** 48 bit **Maximum scan area:** 8.5" × 11.7" **Price:** $199.99

SanDisk Photo Album Viewer

SanDisk's Photo Album lets you easily view your digital photos on any TV. Just connect the Photo Album to your TV, insert a memory card or USB flash drive, and settle back for a digital slideshow—no computer necessary. Press the store button and the Photo Album automatically creates an onscreen photo album, complete with background music. The enter operation is controlled by the included remote control unit.

Model: Photo Album **Manufacturer:** SanDisk (www.sandisk.com) **Price:** $49.99

Norazza Digital Cleaning Kits

Norazza's cleaning kits contain everything you need to keep your camera's body, lens, and monitor clean and free of dust and dirt. Each kit includes one microfiber cleaning cloth, a nylon brush, five cotton swabs, five wet/dry wipes, a carrying case, and an instruction booklet. The kits also come with two cleaning cards for cleaning inside your camera's media card slot; separate kits are sold for CompactFlash, Memory Stick, SD/MMC, SmartMedia, and xD Picture Card products.

Model: Digital Cleaning Kits **Manufacturer:** Norazza (www.norazza.com) **Price:** $19.99

Leupold LensPen

Leupold's LensPen is the ideal accessory for cleaning digital camera lenses, as well as binoculars, rifle scopes, and the like. The LensPen is a compact lens cleaning system in the shape of an ink pen that uses a two-stage process to remove dust, grit, and fingerprints from most lens surfaces—even those of coated lenses. The LensPen uses a state-of-the-art non-liquid cleaning compound and a combination of soft wicking brush (on one end) and impregnated microfiber chamois cleaning tip (on the other). A few swipes, and your lens is clean and clear!

Model: 48807 **Manufacturer:** Leupold (www.leupold.com) **Price:** $12.95

7

The Ultimate Digital Movie Maker

HOW TO BECOME THE ULTIMATE DIGITAL MOVIE MAKER

When I was a kid, my dad shot home movies using a Super 8 film camera. The movies themselves were about what you would expect—cute little Leo mugging about in a dark, shaky, poorly focused little film.

Well, all that's changed. Thanks to today's digital video technology, you can now shoot your movies in high-resolution home video and edit them on your home computer. The result? A cute little kid mugging about in a dark, shaky, poorly focused little film—but now it's all digital!

In other words, all the high-tech gadgets in the world won't make you a better movie maker. You can add all the glitzy digital special effects you want, but if you shoot in a dark room and can't hold the camera steady, it'll still look like a bad Super 8 film. Sorry about that.

Choosing the Right Format

Digital video recording lets you use your PC as a movie editing studio to create sophisticated home movies you can distribute on DVDs. The key to successful digital movie making—whether you're making independent films or movies of your kids' birthday parties—is to start with a digital camcorder.

You don't have to spend a lot of money to get a digital camcorder. Now that analog VHS camcorders have been relegated to the garbage bin (or to eBay—kind of the same thing), virtually every camcorder sold today records in a digital format. But which format is the right one for you?

Here's a short list of the digital camcorder formats you'll find in today's camcorders:

- **MiniDV**—This is the most popular and most common digital camcorder format. It records broadcast-quality video (500+ lines of resolution) on small, low-priced cassettes, about 1/12 the size of a standard VHS tape. Use MiniDV for optimal compatibility with video editing programs and other equipment.

- **HDV**—This is a high-definition version of the MiniDV format, found on only a few high-priced high definition camcorders. HDV uses standard MiniDV cassettes but produces either 720p or 1080i resolution, along with Dolby Digital surround sound.

- **DVD**—DVD camcorders don't use tape at all; they record directly to recordable (R) or rewritable (RW) DVDs. You can get up to 120 minutes on a blank DVD.

- **Digital8**—This is an older, and generally lower-priced, digital format. For compatibility with older analog recorders, Digital8 camcorders can view 8mm or Hi-8 tapes. Digital8 camcorders tend to be a bit larger in size and weight than MiniDV models.

Most camcorders today are in the MiniDV format, although some low-priced Digital8 models are still floating around. MiniDV camcorders are also the most affordable models to operate; a 60-minute MiniDV tape costs $5 or less. Look for a model that feels good in your hand, offers a wide zoom range, and delivers a good picture under all lighting conditions.

By the way, if you want to do some online research on camcorders, check out Camcorderinfo.com (www.camcorderinfo.com). It's a great place for news, information, and reviews about all the latest camcorders.

Sorting Through the Features

Even the lowest-priced MiniDV recorders will take surprisingly good pictures; most of the picture quality is in the format itself, rather than in additional features, which means many people can get by with a simple $500 camcorder, no problem. But higher-priced models are available, and worthy of your consideration—especially if you're a high-tech gadget hound, like me.

The more money you spend on a camcorder, the more bells and whistles you get. In particular, a bigger budget buys you one or more of the following three things: smallness (thanks to the compact MicroMV cassette format), ease of use (thanks to direct-to-DVD recording), or pro-level performance. And when I say pro-level performance, I mean pro-level performance; the very best consumer camcorders deliver digital pictures good enough for television or film use.

These pro-level camcorders look, feel, and perform just like the type of camcorder you see TV news crews or independent filmmakers lugging around. They're big and bulky, often let you use interchangeable lenses, and shoot in the 16:9 widescreen format. More important, they come with a bevy of automatic recording modes and manual adjustments that let you custom-tailor your movies to a variety of shooting styles and situations. Plus, picture quality is second to none, especially under difficult lighting conditions. Lots of technospeak, I know, but it all translates into lots of flexibility to deliver eye-popping widescreen pictures.

Even if you don't pop for one of these uber-expensive pro-level camcorders, you should still expect pro-level performance and features when you spend more than $600 or so on a camcorder. Any camcorder selling in this range should have a good-quality zoom lens, an image stabilization system (to keep your pictures steady even if your hands aren't), a variety of automatic exposure modes, and some sort of video editing built in. This last feature lets you perform in-camera edits between scenes, including audio dubbing, fade in and out, and other special effects.

You should also pay particular attention to the camcorder's image sensing system. Most lower-priced camcorders use a single CCD to capture the video image; higher-priced models use a 3-CCD system that splits the image optically and feeds color-filtered versions of the scene to three CCD sensors, one for each color—red, green, and blue. (All TV and film production is done with 3-CCD cameras, BTW.) The bigger the CCDs, the better; 1/3" CCDs are better than 1/6" ones. And, for even better picture quality, look for a camcorder with progressive scan technology and true 16:9 framing for film-like results.

Shooting in High Definition

The best camcorders today, however, move beyond the traditional standard definition format to record movies in true high definition video (HDV). Today, HDV camcorders are few and far between (and priced like small cars), but expect more (and lower-priced) models to hit the market over the next year or two.

An HDV camcorder offers all the features of a pro-level standard definition, but with the capability of recording high-definition signals onto a MiniDV tape. Depending on the camera, you're looking at recording in either the 720p or 1080i format, both of which should be playable on any HDTV-capable television. The 720p format uses progressive scanning for better reproduction of fast-moving action; the 1080i format offers the highest-resolution picture available today, especially noticeable when shooting nature videos. Either format is head and shoulders better than 480-line standard definition video, though a MiniDV tape's recording capacity is reduced in recording in HD.

Naturally, an HDV camcorder will shoot in the 16:9 aspect ratio, which is part of the high-definition format. (Some HDV cameras let you switch to the 4:3 ratio, and to standard definition recording, if you like.) You can also record Dolby Digital surround sound, although you'll probably need an external surround sound microphone for this. (Don't worry, Sony makes a nifty little surround sound mic' that mounts right on top of your camcorder; I talk about it later in this section.)

Should you spring for a HDV camcorder? Well, the high-definition picture is definitely nice—better than nice, actually. But, for now anyway, you're limited in how you can distribute your high-definition videos. That's because we don't yet have a high-definition DVD format, so you can't burn your HDV video to DVD. You're pretty much limited to connecting your HDV camcorder to your HDTV set and playing back right from the camcorder. That's great for playback in your living room, but leaves something to be desired if you want to send a tape to Grandma in Des Moines—unless Grandma has an HDV camcorder, too. (And she probably doesn't.)

Another option, of course, is to copy your HDV video to your computer's hard disk. You'll need to do this anyway, of course, if you want to engage in any fancy video editing. But most newer PCs (especially Media Center PC models) let you play back high-definition videos, so if you have a Media Center PC hooked up to your home theater system, this may be the way to go.

Beefing Up Your PC for Video Editing

The topic of editing your videos warrants a bit of further discussion. Just what do you need to do your own home movie editing?

The short answer is, lots of horsepower. That's because video editing is the second-most demanding operation you can do on your PC. (The most-demanding activity is playing games, believe it or not.) It takes a lot of processing power, memory, and hard disk storage to edit and process full-motion video on your PC, and most older and lower-priced PCs simply aren't up to the task. Which means, of course, that you now have a new reason for upgrading your personal computer. (As if you needed an excuse…)

So, what kind of PC do you need for video editing?

First off, let me make yet another case for going the Apple route. There's no better computer for video editing than a Power Mac G5, period; it has all the horsepower and all the features you need to do all sorts of fancy video editing, without even breaking a sweat.

But let's assume that you're a Windows type of person, which you probably are. (I shall think no less of you for this.) To start with, you want to go with the fastest, most powerful processor you can afford. The AMD Athlon FX 64 is the fastest single processor out there today, and is always a good choice. On the Intel side of things, look for a fast P4 with Hyper-Threading Technology—at least 3.2GHz, faster if you can get it. In fact, look back at the gaming PCs I talked about in Chapter 2, "The Ultimate Gamer"; if a PC is fast enough to play Doom 3, it's fast enough for video editing.

Memory is an important part of the equation, too. I'd recommend no less than 1GB of fast RAM, and go for 2GB or more if you can.

You'll also need lots of hard disk space, with a fairly fast hard disk. My recommendation here is to go with a dedicated hard disk just for your video editing, maybe an external model with FireWire connection. (FireWire is faster for this type of data transfer than even USB 2.0.) The bigger the better, of course, especially if you're editing high-definition video—although even standard definition video is a real space hog. For example, if you shoot a standard definition video with a 16:9 aspect ratio at 5:1 compression, you'll need 3.6MB for every second of video you shoot. That's almost 13GB for a full hour of video. As you can see, get a few videos on your hard disk (or even a few differently edited versions of the same video) and the space used starts getting pretty big. For this reason, I like big 300GB and 400GB drives for video storage. You can't have too much hard disk space.

Naturally, your PC needs to have a FireWire connection, since that's how most digital camcorders connect. (Your camcorder manufacturer might use the consumer electronics term *iLink*, or the more technical IEEE 1394, but it's still FireWire.) If your computer doesn't have a FireWire port, you can add one via PCI card, no problem.

As for video editing software, there are a few different ways to go. If you're editing on a Mac, you have Final Cut Pro available, which is a very good program to use. On a Windows XP computer, you have Windows Movie Maker included for free; it's okay for basic editing, but you probably want something just a tad more full featured. To this end I recommend Adobe Premiere Elements (www.adobe.com), which will do all sorts of whiz-bang transitions and special effects. Then, of course, you can use any DVD authoring software to burn your movie to DVD; one is as good as another, in my experience.

Other Accessories for Video Movie Making

If you're just shooting movies of your kid's birthday party, you probably don't need any fancy accessories. If you plan on becoming the next Quentin Tarantino, however, you can make your movies more professional by using the appropriate camcorder accessories.

For example, you get a better-quality picture when you put more light in the lens, so using auxiliary lighting makes a lot of sense—via either a single camera-mounted light or a full multiple-flood setup. You can also enhance your shoots by using a better microphone than the one in the camcorder; you can choose from boom mics (for picking up sounds from a distance), stereo mics, surround sound mics, and even wireless mics—just like the pros use.

And let's not forget stability. Only amateur movies (and professional movies trying for an artsy "shaky cam" effect) bounce around like a monkey on caffeine. You need a way to steady your camera when you shoot, which can be as simple as a monopod or tripod, or a fancy shoulder mount with some sort of motion-stabilization rig.

Put it all together, and you end up with a steady, well-lit movie with legible sound. That's a far cry from the dark, shaky Super 8 movies of my youth—and a good reason to invest in all these fun little gadgets.

PRO-LEVEL CAMCORDERS

Sony HDR-FX1

Leo's Pick

Today's state-of-the-art moviemaker records with high-definition television in mind. Of course, to record in high-def you need a high-def camcorder, like Sony's HDR-FX1. This is the dean of all HD camcorders, the first to market and still the best available.

The HDR-FX1 records in the HDV format, with 1080i resolution at a 16:9 aspect ratio. (That's 1080 × 1440 pixels, for those of you out there measuring.) This is true professional-quality video, of the same resolution as you'll find broadcast on your nearest HDTV station. You have the option of recording at either 24 or 30 frames per second; the former creates a more film-like picture.

The camera's innards contain three 1/3" 16:9 Advanced HAD CCD imaging chips for just about the best picture available. The digital recording incorporates professional-level MPEG2 video compression, using a real-time HD codec engine and 14-bit HD Digital Extended Processor (DXP) for faster processing speed. You can switch back and forth between HD and standard DV recording as necessary.

Lens-wise, we're looking at a Carl Zeiss Vario-Sonnar T* lens with 12X optical zoom. Sony's Super SteadyShot image stabilization system takes the jitters out of the picture, without noticeable video degradation. You can view your recording-in-progress on a 3.5" 16:9 LCD display that swivels out from the body of the camera.

That's not all, of course; the HDR-FX1 contains all the bells and whistles you'd expect of a camcorder in this class. That means you get automatic scene transitions, the ability to smoothly shift the focus from the front of the screen to a deeper area of the picture, and both manual and automatic control over zoom, focus, and iris. Sony's Picture Profile feature lets you create up to six preset video modes, each containing a variety of shooting settings.

Bottom line, this is the premier camcorder to buy if you want to create high-definition movies. For the time being at least, it just doesn't get any better than this.

Model: HDR-FX1 **Manufacturer:** Sony (www.sonystyle.com) **Format:** HDV (1080i) **Lens:** 12X zoom
Dimensions: 6" × 7 1/8" × 14 3/8" **Weight:** 4.25 lbs. **Price:** $3,699.99

JVC GR-HD1

Sony isn't the only player in the high-definition camcorder game, as witnessed by JVC's GR-HD1. This pro-level camcorder records in 720p (720 × 1280) HDV format with 16:9 aspect ratio; it can upconvert its signals to 1080i if you want, or switch to standard definition DV mode. Recording is via 1/3" CCD; the lens is a 10X zoom. Naturally, you get all the requisite bells and whistles, all in a very solid-feeling design.

Model: GR-HD1 **Manufacturer:** JVC (www.jvc.com) **Format:** HDV (720p) **Lens:** 10X zoom **Dimensions:** 4.56" × 3.94" × 10.75" **Weight:** 2.8 lbs. **Price:** $3,499.95

Sony HDR-HC1

If you want to go high-def without springing for a bulky pro-level camera, check out Sony's new HDR-HC1. In addition to your choice of HDV (1080i)/DV recording and 16:9/4:3 aspect ratios, you also get a Carl Zeiss Vario-Sonnar T* 10X zoom lens and a 2.7" touch-panel LCD display that does double-duty as a menu controller. Sony keeps the size (and cost) down by using a one-chip CMOS design.

Model: HDR-HC1 **Manufacturer:** Sony (www.sonystyle.com) **Format:** HDV (1080i) **Lens:** 10X zoom **Dimensions:** 2.8" × 3.7" × 7.4" **Weight:** 1.5 lbs. **Price:** $1,699.99

Sony DCR-VX2100

Not all pro-level camcorders are high-definition; there are plenty of standard definition models around, such as Sony's DCR-VX2100. This MiniDV model uses HAD progressive-scan technology with three 1/3" CCDs; recording is in the 16:9 widescreen format, with sound in 16-bit digital PCM stereo. Lens-wise, you get a 58mm aspherical lens with 12X optical zoom, and Sony's Super SteadyShot optical stabilization system uses motion sensors to deliver super-steady pictures under a variety of conditions.

Model: DCR-VX2100 **Manufacturer:** Sony (www.sonystyle.com) **Format:** MiniDV **Lens:** 12X zoom **Dimensions:** 4.75" × 6.365" × 15.5" **Weight:** 3.4 lbs. **Price:** $2,999.99

Canon XL2

Even though it's not high definition, the Canon XL2 is the uber-camera of choice for many independent filmmakers; what the pros especially like is the interchangeable lens system that lets you use any of Canon's XL and EF 35mm camera lenses. The XL2 incorporates professional styling and a rugged magnesium body, uses a 3-CCD imaging system, and shoots in the 16:9 widescreen aspect ratio. It's a true pro-level camera—used by real pros!

Model: XL2 **Manufacturer:** Canon (www.usa.canon.com) **Format:** MiniDV **Lens:** 20X zoom **Dimensions:** 8.9" × 8.7" × 19.5" **Weight:** 5.3 lbs. **Price:** $6,499.99

CONSUMER-LEVEL CAMCORDERS

Panasonic PV-GS65

Leo's Pick

With so many good consumer-level camcorders out there, it's hard to pick just one favorite. But, heck, it's my book, so I get to choose—and the model I choose is the Panasonic PV-GS65, one of the most affordable 3-CCD camcorders on the market today.

What makes the PV-GS65 such a good camera is its three 1/6" CCDs—one each for red, green, and blue. It's the same technology used in pro-level cameras, and it creates videos with 540 lines of resolution. Not quite high-def, but as sharp as you'll get on non-HD equipment. (And extremely high-quality for the price!)

The camera uses a 10X zoom lens, which is the equivalent of a 42–420mm film lens. A special Digital Electronics Image Stabilizer (D-EIS) compensates for shaky movement, virtually eliminating blurry pictures.

And here's something else. Want to shoot close-ups without capturing too many unflattering facial details? Then turn on the PV-GS65's Soft-Skin mode, which automatically detects skin tones and then softens the focus in that area of the picture. The result is the kind of soft-focus effect that you see in the movies—very complimentary for your subjects.

The PV-GS65 offers lots of other bells and whistles, of course. You get three white balance settings, macro zooming, and a 2.5" swing-out LCD. You can even use this camcorder to shoot 1.2 megapixel still digital photos—at the same time you're shooting movies. The still photos are recorded onto SD memory cards.

Outside of the outstanding picture, the thing I really like about this camcorder is its ease of use. Most operations are controlled via a small joystick, which you can operate with one finger. Instructions appear on the LCD screen, which means you don't have to take your eye off the action to adjust the controls. And, as an added bonus, you can also operate the camera via wireless remote control—a good way to put yourself in the picture!

Model: PV-GS65 **Manufacturer:** Panasonic (www.panasonic.com) **Format:** MiniDV **Lens:** 10X zoom
Dimensions: 3" × 3" × 4.75" **Weight:** 15 oz. **Price:** $599.95

Canon ZR100

Canon's ZR100 is my pick for best entry-level camcorder. You get a number of pre-programmed shooting modes, various gee-whiz visual effects (fades, wipes, sepia tone, and so on), and a special Night shooting mode. You have your choice of 4:3 or 16:9 aspect ratios, and there's a very cool Multi Image Screen, which divides the picture into four, nine, or sixteen separate pictures—great for capturing sports or other fast-moving images. Not bad for the price!

Model: ZR100 **Manufacturer:** Canon (www.usa.canon.com) **Format:** MiniDV **Lens:** 20X zoom **Dimensions:** 2" × 3.7" × 5.1" **Weight:** 15.2 oz. **Price:** $349.99

Panasonic VDR-M53

What's unique about this camcorder is that it doesn't record to tape—it records directly to DVD-R or DVD-RAM discs. You get all the standard features, of course, including image stabilization, but it's that DVD recording that sets this camera apart from the rest. Shoot direct to disc, then watch that disc immediately in the nearest DVD player. Cool!

Model: VDR-M53 **Manufacturer:** Panasonic (www.panasonic.com) **Format:** Direct-to-DVD **Lens:** 24X zoom **Dimensions:** 3.5" × 2" × 5.3" **Weight:** 15.5 oz. **Price:** $599.95

Sony DCR-HC42

Sony's DCR-HC42 is a compact MiniDV camcorder with a very nice Carl Zeiss Vario-Tessar 12X zoom lens. The neat thing about the DCR-HC42 is the Handycam Station—a convenient docking device that provides a quick and easy connection to your TV or PC—no need for connecting messy cables.

Model: DCR-HC42 **Manufacturer:** Sony (www.sonystyle.com) **Format:** MiniDV **Lens:** 12X zoom **Dimensions:** 2.25" × 3.625" × 4.5" **Weight:** 14.5 oz. **Price:** $599.99

JVC GZ-MC200

JVC's GZ-MC200 is a cube-shaped camcorder that doesn't use any removable media—no tapes or discs. Instead, it records directly (in MPEG-2 format) to a 4GB hard disk. The MicroDrive holds 60 minutes of video, which you can then transfer (via USB 2.0) to your computer for editing. It's an interesting approach, and makes for a much lighter unit than you're used to.

Model: GZ-MC200 **Manufacturer:** JVC (www.jvc.com) **Format:** Direct-to-MicroDrive **Dimensions:** 2.3" × 3" × 3.8" **Weight:** 12.3 oz. **Price:** $1,299.99

MICROPHONES

Sony ECM-HQP1 Surround-Sound Microphone

Leo's Pick

The built-in microphone in most camcorders is functional at best. If you want to pick up more and better sound when you're shooting, you need an auxiliary microphone, like Sony's ECM-HQP1.

Now, there are lots of different types of auxiliary mics, from simple shotgun mics to fancy wireless models. What makes the ECM-HQP1 unique is that it's a surround sound microphone—it records more than just mono or stereo sound, which makes an ideal match for your HDV or 16:9 ratio recordings. Now you can shoot your movies in true surround sound and play them back on your surround-sound home theater system.

What's amazing is that all this multiple-channel recording is done with a single microphone casing. The ECM-HQP1 captures four distinct channels of high-quality audio; just point it toward the front, and you get automatic four-channel surround with proper channel positioning.

The microphone easily attaches to your camcorder's hot shoe; it's not big or bulky at all. It has three distinct recording modes, which you can use for different shooting situations.

The ECM-HQP1 works with compatible Sony camcorders, and may work with other brands, as well; check first before you buy. (One advantage of using this mic with a Sony camcorder is that you can control the various recording modes from the camcorder's touch screen control.)

Model: ECM-HQP1 **Manufacturer:** Sony (www.sonystyle.com) **Microphone type:** Electret condenser **Directivity:** Unidirectional **Dimensions:** 1 5/16" × 3" × 2 5/8" **Weight:** 1.8 oz. **Price:** $149.99

Sony ECM-S930C Stereo Microphone

Sony's ECM-S930C is an affordable add-on stereo microphone for your camcorder. It utilizes left- and right-side microphone capsules, as well as a directional switch, to record real-world stereo sound. And it's a high-quality microphone, as well, with a wide frequency response and low noise level. It's also very small and light, with a universal mount to fit on top of almost any camcorder.

Model: ECM-S930C **Manufacturer:** Sony (www.sonystyle.com) **Dimensions:** 2 1/16" × 1 3/8" × 1 5/8" **Weight:** 14.4 oz. **Price:** $159.99

Audio Technica ATR55 Shotgun Microphone

When you want to record someone from across the room, you need a shotgun microphone—like the ATR55. This is a unidirectional condenser mic that works for close-, medium-, and long-distance pickup. In its long-distance mode, it effectively picks up dialogue and sound effects while bypassing unwanted ambient noise.

Model: ATR55 **Manufacturer:** Audio Technica (www.audio-technica.com) **Price:** $99.95

Audio Technica ATR35s Lavaliere Microphone

The ATR35s is an omnidirectional condenser microphone designed for accurate voice reproduction. It's a newscaster-style lavalier mic that easily clips onto the subject's tie or shirt; it comes with a 20-foot cable, tie clip, and foam windscreen.

Model: ATR35s **Manufacturer:** Audio Technica (www.audio-technica.com) **Price:** $39.95

Audio Technica PRO 88W Wireless Microphone

Audio Technica's PRO 88W is a wireless microphone system just like the pros use. Clip the lavalier microphone onto the subject, tuck the transmitter pack in a back pocket, and connect the receiver unit to your camcorder. The transmitter and receiver each operate on a single 9-volt battery; the system works up to 300 feet distance.

Model: PRO 88W-829 **Manufacturer:** Audio Technica (www.audio-technica.com) **Price:** $199

MORE COOL DIGITAL VIDEO GADGETS

HP dc5000 Movie Writer

HP's dc5000 is an external DVD burner with built-in analog video capture. Just connect your VCR or camcorder to the dc5000, insert a blank DVD, and activate the Video Transfer Wizard for automated and unattended conversion of your home movies to DVD. The dc5000 burns to both DVD+R/RW and DVD-R/RW discs. If you want, you can use the included software to edit your movies (on PC) before you burn them.

Model: DC5000 Manufacturer: HP (www.hp.com)
Dimensions: 2.9" × 7.1" × 10" Price: $249.95

Dazzle Digital Video Creator

The Dazzle Digital Video Creator converts analog video from any camcorder, VCR, or TV. It connects to your PC via a fast USB 2.0 interface. The unit itself has S-Video and composite video inputs/outputs, along with RCA stereo audio inputs/outputs. It comes with Pinnacle Studio QuickStart software for editing your movies and burning to DVD or video CD.

Model: DVC-150 Manufacturer: Pinnacle Systems
(www.pinnaclesys.com) Price: $149.99

Sunpak Readylight 20

The quickest way to improve the picture quality of your home movies is to better light the scenes you shoot. To that end, check out the Sunpak Readylight 20, a video light that can attach to any camcorder. The Readylight 20 is cordless (with 17 minutes of operation on the rechargeable NiCd battery), so it doesn't even have to be attached to your camcorder; you can set it up to provide side lighting or back lighting, whatever is best. If you do mount it on your camera, it's compact enough not to get in the way while you're shooting.

Model: Readylight 20 Manufacturer: Sunpak
(www.sunpak.com) Weight: 7 oz. Price: $39.99

Sunpak Camcorder Lens Filters

Most camcorders let you attach various lens filters, which help you make better movies. Sunpak's PicturesPlus filters are available in a variety of models, including polarizer, ultraviolet, color enhancing and correcting, special effects (diffusion, fog, etc.), and close-up filters.

Model: Various Manufacturer: Sunpak
(www.sunpak.com) Price: $8.95–$32.99

SIMA VideoProp Camera Support

Add more support to you camcorder with SIMA's low-priced VideoProp. This is a brace that attaches to a strap that hangs around your neck; by letting the camcorder rest against the bottom of the neckstrap, you get better support and less-shaky pictures.

Model: SVP-3 Manufacturer: SIMA (www.simacorp.com) Price: $29.95

SIMA SMP-1 Monopod

Sometimes all you need is an extra leg to stand on—which is where SIMA's SMP-1 monopod comes in. Let your camcorder rest on the monopod for added support and to relieve arm fatigue. The collapsible monopod adjusts from 16.5" to 60.5" and features a quick-release mount.

Model: SMP-1 Manufacturer: SIMA (www.simacorp.com) Price: $39.95

VariZoom VZ-LSP Shoulder Support System

When you need even more support for your video camera, check out VariZoom's VZ-LSP. This is a light-weight system that provides three-point support for your camcorder via a shoulder brace, abdomen brace, and hand grip. It's even designed for hands-free operation!

Model: VZ-LSP Manufacturer: VariZoom (www.varizoom.com) Price: $429

VariZoom DV Sportster Stabilizer System

Now here's a motion stabilizing system just like the pros use. The DV Sportster consists of an articulating arm connected to a support vest; the whole rig helps to provide stability and eliminate arm fatigue during long shoots. (You can also use the Sportster with other VariZoom stabilization products, such as the FlowPod and Glidecam.)

Model: DV Sportster Manufacturer: VariZoom (www.varizoom.com) Price: $1,199

8

The Ultimate Portable Music Fan

HOW TO BECOME THE ULTIMATE PORTABLE MUSIC FAN

In the 1960s, it was the transistor AM radio. In the 1970s, it was the portable AM/FM radio. In the 1980s, it was the Sony Walkman, the revolutionary portable cassette player that went hand-in-hand with leg warmers and pastel-colored terrycloth headbands. In the 1990s, the Walkman gave way to the portable CD player. (And those legwarmers and headbands just went away, thankfully.) Now, a decade later, we're getting our portable music another way—via portable digital audio players.

Today's portable audio players—sometimes mistakenly called MP3 players—are small gadgets that hold large libraries of songs in digital fashion. These players let you download music from the web or rip songs from CDs, storing all that music in digital audio files. Even the smallest portable players hold hundreds of songs, and the largest devices can archive your entire music collection. And, best of all, these gadgets fit in the palm of your hand; no more carrying around bulky portable CD players.

Another advantage to these digital music players is that you can program them to play back your own personalized music mix, in the form of customized playlists. Put together one mix for your drive to work, another mix for your drive home, and a third to listen to on weekends. It's normally as simple as dragging and dropping specific songs in a PC- or Mac-based music player program and then transferring the songs—and the playlist—to your portable device.

Portable Music Players—Choose Your Poison

There are three types of digital music players available today, defined by their type and quantity of storage. Which type of player you choose depends on how you plan to use it, how many songs you need to store, and how big your budget is.

The smallest (and lowest priced) digital players are so-called *flash players*. These devices, such as the iPod Shuffle, store their digital music in flash memory, and offer anywhere from 64MB to 1GB of storage capacity. These miniature units are small enough to fit in any pocket, are relatively inexpensive (as low as $100 or so), and won't skip if you're jogging.

The biggest (and highest-priced) digital players are *hard drive players*. These devices, like Apple's iPod, use 1.8" hard disks that provide up to 40GB of storage capacity. These units let you store literally thousands of individual songs, and can even double as file and digital photo storage devices. The downside is size and weight, and they can cost anywhere from $250–$400. They can also skip if you jostle them around; they're not ideal for runners.

Occupying the middle ground are *MicroDrive players*, such as the Apple iPod Mini and Creative Zen Micro. These units use smaller hard drives—called MicroDrives—that offer a decent compromise between size, storage, and price. You'll get storage in the 1.5GB–4GB range, in a fairly compact form factor. Price is typically in the $200–$250 range, and they suffer from the same skipping tendency as the larger hard drive players.

So, which type of player should you choose? As with most gadgets, it depends on how you'll be using it. If you're a runner or jogger, skip the hard drive players (that skip when you run) and stick with a flash player that won't skip at all. If, on the other hand, you're relatively sedentary and want to put your entire CD collection in the palm of your hand, then go with a big-capacity hard drive player. If you want more storage capacity than you get with a flash player but still want a somewhat-small form factor, make the compromise and choose a MicroDrive player.

Know Your File Formats!

Another factor when choosing a portable audio player is where you're going to get your songs from, and what file format you're going to use. Different players are compatible with different file formats; choose the wrong player, and you might not be able to download songs from your online music store of choice.

While there are literally a dozen or more file formats used to store digital music, you're really only going to run into three formats that are best-suited for storing lots of files on portable devices:

- **MP3**—Short for MPEG-1 Level 3, the MP3 format remains the most widely used digital audio format today, with a decent compromise between small file size and sound quality. The primary advantage of MP3 is its universality; unlike most other file formats, just about every digital music player and player program can handle MP3-format music.

- **AAC**—Short for Advanced Audio Coding (and also known as MPEG-4 AAC), this is the proprietary audio format used by Apple's iPod and iTunes Music Store. AAC offers slightly better sound quality than MP3 files, along with strong digital rights management, to prevent unauthorized use. Unfortunately, most non-Apple music players won't play AAC-format songs—but if you're an iPod user, this is the format you'll be using.

- **WMA**—Short for Windows Media Audio, Microsoft's digital audio format is promoted as an MP3 alternative with similar audio quality at half the file size. That may be stretching it a bit, but WMA does typically offer a slightly better compromise between compression and quality than you find with MP3 files. It also provides strong digital rights management.

So which audio format should you use? It depends on your portable audio player, and the site you use to download your music. For example, the most popular music store is, far and away, Apple's iTunes Music Store. When you download a song from iTunes, it's in Apple's proprietary AAC file format. Unfortunately, the only music players that are compatible with the AAC format are (surprise!) Apple's iPod, iPod Mini, and iPod Shuffle. You can't play AAC-format files on any other player. So if you like iTunes, you need to buy an iPod—and if you own an iPod, you have to use the iTunes Music Store.

Similarly, the iPod cannot play back files recorded in Microsoft's popular WMA format. So if you download music from Napster, let's say (which uses the WMA format), you can't play them back on your iPod. Similarly, if you own a Creative Zen Micro, which plays both MP3 and WMA formats (but not AAC), you can use it with any other music store *except* iTunes. You get the picture.

So here's the important thing to know. Apart from iTunes, most online music stores and services, including Napster, download files in the WMA format. Almost all music players—except the iPod, of course—are compatible with the WMA format. So if you buy an iPod, you're going to become a customer of the iTunes Music Store, whether you like it or not. If you buy any other type of player, you won't be downloading from iTunes, even if you want to. Such are the joys of incompatible formats.

And Now for the Obligatory Section on the Apple iPod

Okay, it goes without saying (although I'm going to say it anyway) that the most popular portable music player today is the Apple iPod. Apple moves a million or so of these puppies every month; for many teenagers, an iPod is a required accessory—even more than the latest camera phone. You gotta hand it to Steve Jobs, he's done a good job of marketing this little white slab of plastic.

Apple sells several different versions of the iPod. The big daddy of the iPod line is, quite simply, the hard-disk iPod. Add a bigger hard disk and a color display and you get the iPod Photo. Shrink the case and use a smaller MicroDrive, and you get the iPod Mini. Go with an even smaller case and flash memory instead of a hard drive (and remove the display, for some unknown reason), and you get the iPod Shuffle. The iPod, iPod Photo, and iPod Shuffle are all in Apple-white cases; the iPod Mini comes in a variety of groovy colors.

Probably the best thing about the iPod (and the iPod Mini) is its Control Wheel. This is one area where Apple got it right, and competitors still haven't come close. Operating an iPod is as easy as moving your thumb around the outside of the wheel to scroll through the menu system, and then clicking the center button to select a menu item. It does exactly what you expect it to, no surprises.

Portable Video Players—Movies to Go

Now that you know all about portable audio players, how about portable *video* players? Well, there's nothing surprising or complex here; a portable video player is a portable device that plays back video (as well as audio) files on a built-in LCD screen.

That said, this is a relatively new consumer electronics category, and there aren't a lot of devices on the market yet. That's beginning to change, of course, as more and more consumers discover the benefits of watching movies on a handheld device that looks like a portable game machine.

Most portable video players have at least a 20GB hard disk. Movies are recorded in MPEG-4 format, which is the visual equivalent of audio MP3 files; you get 4 hours of programming per gigabyte. Picture quality is typically around 300 × 225 pixels, which is okay for watching on a small screen. Most units play back movies using Microsoft's Windows Media Center software.

All portable video players also function as portable music players, so you don't have to carry two devices around. Some also let you view digital photographs on the built-in screen, thus doing additional duty as digital photo vaults. There are even a few units that function as pure hard disk storage, for any type of PC file. The more options the merrier, is what I say.

Getting movies onto the portable device can be a bit of a challenge, considering that Hollywood insists on strong copy protection. Some players, like the Archos models, ignore the copy protection and let you record video from your VCR or DVD player. Other players, like the RCA Lyra, enable the copy protection, which limits what you can copy to and watch on the portable device. Before you buy, find out the type of programming you can copy to the portable device, and how.

It's All About the Accessories

A gadget wouldn't be any fun if it didn't provide the opportunity for you to accessorize—and to purchase even more stuff. To that end, there's no more accessorizable gadget than the Apple iPod, which has spawned an entire sub-industry in iPod-compatible accessories.

What types of accessories are we talking about? A short list includes cables and docking units, FM transmitters, car kits, media readers, voice recorders, remote controls, external speakers, and cases of all sorts and colors. A number of companies, including Belkin (www.belkin.com) and Griffin Technology (www.griffintechnology.com), manufacture a variety of iPod accessories. Belkin in particular has a large number of useful and stylish iPod accessories available; its catalog is definitely worth checking out.

Of course, because the iPod is Apple's baby, you can find a ton of iPod accessories on the Apple site (www.apple.com/ipod/accessories.html). Also good are sites such as iPodlounge (www.ipodlounge.com), We Love Macs (www.welovemacs.com), and XtremeMac (www.xtrememac.com), which offer accessories from a variety of manufacturers.

The Sound Is Only as Good as the Earphones

You'd be surprised at the difference a good set of headphones or earbuds can make. Most portable music players deliver pretty good sound, but you need a good set of phones to hear it. Even the standard iPod earphones, which are better than some, still kind of suck in my personal opinion. The very first thing I do when I buy a new portable player is to throw away the stock earphones and replace them with something that sounds a lot better.

Headphones come in two types—open-air and closed-ear. Open-air headphones sit lightly on top of your ears; this type of phone is lightweight and very comfortable to wear, even for extended periods. The downside—which might not be a downside, depending—is that they're not well isolated from ambient noise. That is, you can still hear what's going on around you. So you'll hear your music, but still know if the telephone is ringing.

Closed-ear headphones are often called *sealed* phones because the heavily padded ear cups completely cover your ears. This results in excellent sound quality and good isolation from external noises. The downside is that these phones are heavy and cumbersome and become uncomfortable in long listening sessions. They're better for use in your living room (or in the recording studio) than with a portable device.

And don't forget earbuds, which are like headphones without the phones. Instead of bulky foam cups that enclose your entire ear, earbuds are tiny earphones that fit inside your ear. The advantage of in-ear devices is that they do a better job of blocking background noise than standard over-the-ear headphones. Plus, they're small and light, perfect for portable use.

You might think that earbuds, because of their small size, wouldn't sound as good as full-size headphones. You'd be wrong. Most earbuds sound very good, and the best deliver even better sound than similarly priced headphones. That's because the tiny transducers fit right inside your ear, with nothing to interfere with the sound; the better the fit, the better the sound quality.

Interestingly, most earbuds sound better after a little use than straight out of the box. That's because the buds have to be broken in a bit to loosen the transducers; they might sound a little rough initially but will smooth out after a few weeks of listening. You can also improve the sound by letting the earbuds shape themselves to the contour of your ears. To that end, many high-end earbuds come with a number of tips or sleeves, typically in different sizes. You'll need to experiment with different sleeves to find the one that fits you best. The sleeves also improve the bass response, so they're definitely worth using.

By the way, one variation on the common earbud is the canal phone, which looks like an earbud but fits deeper into the ear canal, rather than just resting in the outer ear. This provides an air-tight seal and super-good sound isolation. Canal phones are at the high-end of the price spectrum but are good if you want professional sound reproduction. For the best sound, you can purchase custom-fitted canal stems that are made from molds of your ears.

Whether you opt for a set of headphones or earbuds, you need to evaluate two things—sound and comfort. Look for a unit that delivers a clear sound with no distortion; a deep and controlled bass without a lot of boominess; a smooth, even frequency response without bright or tinny highs; and good positioning of the sound image between the right and left channels. And be sure you like the way the phones or buds fit and feel. Imagine using the earphones for a couple of hours and determine how you'll like them after that kind of use. If the phones or buds start to feel a little uncomfortable in the store, think how much you'll hate them after a few hours of steady use!

HARD DRIVE AUDIO PLAYERS

Apple iPod

Leo's Pick

Imitators come and imitators go, but the coolest portable music player remains Apple's trendsetting iPod. The iPod is that rare gadget that's both stylish and popular with the masses; it's the best-selling portable music player in history, with more than six million units sold to date.

The fourth generation iPod is the best yet, now incorporating the touch-sensitive Click Wheel first introduced on the iPod Mini. You get a 20GB hard disk that can hold up to 5,000 songs; you can also use your iPod to store regular computer data, including digital photos and the like.

Even though the iPod is Apple's baby (and the styling definitely reminds you of the family connection), it's that rare Apple product that's compatible with both Apple and Windows computers. It stores and plays back music in the AAC, MP3, WAV, and AIFF formats.

Cool features (besides the trendy looks) include a high-resolution backlist display, dual USB 2.0 and FireWire compatibility, and the seamless interface to Apple's top-notch iTunes Music Store. And if you use the FireWire connection, you can recharge your iPod directly from your PC or Mac; FireWire doubles as a power connection for the portable device.

Weaknesses include a relatively short battery life (up to 12 hours with the fourth-generation unit—double that of earlier units, but still kind of puny compared to the competition), no built-in FM radio or CompactFlash slot, and incompatibility with Microsoft's WMA file format. This last weakness is the biggest because you can't use your iPod to download songs from Napster, Yahoo! Music Unlimited, or any non-Apple online music service.

Still, you can't go wrong with an iPod. It's slick, it's trendy, and it's well designed. If other players offer more capacity or longer battery life—well, they're still not iPods. Apple's got a good thing going here.

Model: iPod **Manufacturer:** Apple (www.apple.com) **Capacity:** 20GB **Dimensions:** 4.1" × 2.4" × 0.57" **Weight:** 5.6 oz. **Price:** $299

Creative Zen

The Creative Zen gives the iPod a run for its money; if only the controller was more like Apple's Click Wheel! What you do get is a 20GB capacity, big 1.65" LCD display, and 11 hours of battery life. It's all wrapped up in attractive case in a variety of colors—a good alternative for those of you who want WMA (and MP3) compatibility in your portable audio player.

Model: Zen **Manufacturer:** Creative (www.creative.com) **Price:** $249.95

Olympus m:robe 500i

Olympus makes only a couple of portable audio players, but they both hit my list. The m:robe 500i has a 20GB hard disk and a huge 3.7" high-resolution color screen that helps the player do double duty as a photo vault. The battery lasts anywhere from 8–12 hours, depending on how you're using it. It's a little higher-priced than the competition, but you gotta love that display!

Model: m:robe 500i **Manufacturer:** Olympus (www.olympusgroove.com) **Capacity:** 20GB **Dimensions:** 4 3/8" × 3" × 7/8" **Weight:** 7.4 oz. **Price:** $399.99

Archos Gmini XS200

The Gmini XS200 is a tiny hard-drive player with a big 2" screen. You get 20GB capacity with 10 hours of battery life, all in a package that looks and feels more like a mini than a maxi player. And here's something unique—you can use the XS200 to store data files from your PC, via USB connection. It has a very easy-to-use file management system!

Model: Gmini XS200 **Manufacturer:** Archos (www.archos.com) **Capacity:** 20GB **Dimensions:** 2.9" × 2.3" × 0.7" **Weight:** 4.3 oz. **Price:** $249.95

iRiver H340

iRiver's H340 offers huge storage capacity (40GB) and a really nice 2" color LCD display. You also get a built-in FM tuner and voice recorder, as well as ability to store and view digital photos; battery life is an astounding 16 hours. Also available is the sibling model H320, with 20GB storage for $299.99.

Model: H340 **Manufacturer:** iRiver (www.iriveramerica.com) **Capacity:** 40GB **Dimensions:** 2.4" × 4" × 0.9" **Weight:** 6.9 oz. **Price:** $399.99

MICRODRIVE AUDIO PLAYERS

Creative Zen Micro

Leo's Pick

Finally, a portable audio category that isn't completely dominated by Apple! I really like Creative's products, especially this compelling competitor to the iPod Mini.

The Zen Micro is a MicroDrive player that's available in three capacities (4GB, 5GB, and 6GB) and ten colors (red, purple, pink, orange, green, dark blue, light blue, white, silver, and black). The 4GB version will hold up to 2,000 songs (in 64kbps WMA format); the 5GB and 6GB versions hold 2,500 and 3,000 songs, respectively. Whichever color you choose, the Zen Micro has a luminescent blue glow and back-lit buttons, which actually out-cools the uber-cool iPod Mini.

I especially like the Zen Micro's control pad, which is almost as good as the iPod Mini's Click Wheel. What you get instead of a wheel is a vertical touch pad, combined with touch-sensitive dedicated controls. Play, pause, forward, and rewind are on the touch buttons; you scroll through your playlists with the vertical touch pad.

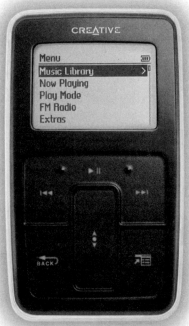

In terms of operation, you get 12 hours of playback on a single charge, and the Zen Micro's battery is removable—which means you can buy a spare and swap them in and out, as necessary. The Zen Micro connects to your PC or Mac via USB 2.0.

Now let's talk about the Zen Micro's cool extra features. I'm talking about things like a built-in FM radio, voice recorder (with microphone), sleep timer, and alarm. That's right, you can use the Zen Micro as a portable alarm clock—and wake to either digital music or FM radio. Nice!

As an aside, Creative also offers a variation on the basic Zen Micro called the Zen Micro Photo. As you can probably guess from the name, the Zen Micro Photo offers a 1.5" color screen and the ability to store and display digital photos. It's an interesting alternative if you're looking for a combination portable music player and photo vault. It's available in 5GB ($299) and 6GB ($349) versions, in a variety of colors.

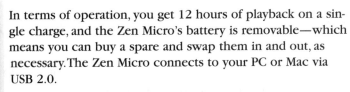

Model: Zen Micro **Manufacturer:** Creative (www.creative.com) **Capacity:** 4GB, 5GB, or 6GB
Dimensions: 3.3" × 2" × 0.7" **Weight:** 3.8 oz. **Price:** $179.99 (4GB), $199.99 (5GB), $229.99 (6GB)

iPod Mini

This is one category where Apple doesn't win the day. The iPod Mini is a very good player, but it doesn't deliver quite the bang for the buck that you get with competing players. What you do get is either 4GB or 6GB capacity, your choice of four colors (blue, pink, green, or silver), and Apple's well-designed Click Wheel operation. Battery life has been extended to 18 hours on the latest generation.

Model: iPod Mini **Manufacturer:** Apple (www.apple.com) **Capacity:** 4GB or 6GB
Dimensions: 3.6" × 2" × 0.5" **Weight:** 3.6 oz.
Price: $199 (4GB), $249 (6GB)

Rio Carbon Player

The Rio Carbon a nice little (and I mean little) MicroDrive player. You get your choice of 5GB or 6GB drives, 20-hour battery life, a big LCD display, and a built-in microphone and voice recorder. It's also one of the coolest-looking players around, with its thin teardrop-like shape.

Model: Rio Carbon **Manufacturer:** Rio (www.digitalnetworksna.com/rioaudio/) **Capacity:** 5GB and 6GB **Dimensions:** 2.5" × 3.3" × 0.6" **Weight:** 3.2 oz.
Price: $199.99 (5GB), $229.99 (6GB)

Olympus m:robe 100

Here's Olympus' other portable audio player, the m:robe 100. This is a 5GB player with a black faceplate with red lighting. Navigation is via a nifty touch panel; the LCD display is red, like the other controls. Battery life runs from 8–12 hours, but the real appeal of this one is its design. It looks different from—and a lot more stylish than—all the iPod-white players out there.

Model: m:robe 100 **Manufacturer:** Olympus (www.olympusgroove.com) **Capacity:** 5GB
Dimensions: 2" × 3.5" × 0.5" **Weight:** 3.5 oz.
Price: $199.99

iRiver H10

What makes iRiver's H10 unique is its 1.5" color LCD display; all the other mini players are just black and white. You also get a built-in FM radio and voice recorder, along with 12-hour battery life. It's the only mini player that can be used for both music playback and digital photo storage/viewing.

Model: H10 **Manufacturer:** iRiver (www.iriveramerica.com) **Capacity:** 5GB or 6GB
Dimensions: 3.8" × 2.1" × 0.6" **Weight:** 3.4 oz.
Price: $249.99 (5GB), $279.99 (6GB)

FLASH AUDIO PLAYERS

iPod Shuffle

Leo's Pick

Okay, here I am recommending a gadget that doesn't offer near the features of its competition, and isn't bargain-priced. What the iPod Shuffle is, however, is eminently cool, despite its shortcomings.

First, let's look at the good. The iPod Shuffle is a flash memory player that comes in 512MB and 1GB capacities. Battery life is an okay-but-not-great 12 hours, and it's small and lightweight. In fact, the form factor helps Apple to hit this one out of the ballpark; it's no bigger than a pack of gum, and operation is via a miniaturized variation of their larger Click Wheel controller. The iPod Shuffle looks and feels cool—which counts for a lot.

Now for the negatives, chief of which is the unit's display—or lack of. That's right, the iPod Shuffle doesn't have any sort of display, so there' no way for you to see what song is currently playing, or to queue up music in a playlist. You're totally at the mercy of the Shuffle's randomness—hence the unit's name. It's all shuffle all the time, which Apple uses as a selling point. Me, I'd like at least a little bit of control over what I'm listening to, but I understand the appeal. (And, to be fair, you can create playlists in iTunes, transfer them to the Shuffle, and choose to play the songs in order, which makes things just a little less random.)

The 512MB model can hold 120 songs or so, the 1GB model twice that. It connects directly to your PC or Mac by plugging into an open USB port, no cable necessary. (After all, it is the same size and shape of a USB flash drive.) It operates on two AAA batteries.

Can you find more features in other players? Most definitely. Can you find a better deal elsewhere? Maybe. But can you find a cooler flash memory player, or one in more demand? The answer is no; in this category, the Apple Shuffle is in a class by itself.

Model: iPod Shuffle **Manufacturer:** Apple (www.apple.com) **Capacity:** 512MB or 1GB
Dimensions: 3.3" × 0.98" × 0.33" **Weight:** 0.78 oz. **Price:** $99 (512MB), $149 (1GB)

Creative Zen Nano Plus

If you want more control over your music than the iPod Shuffle offers (and a display, too), then consider the Creative Zen Nano Plus. This is a flash player with reversible LCD display (for right- or left-handed operation), 18-hour battery life, and built-in FM radio and recorder. The Zen Nano Plus comes in 512MB and 1GB capacities, and in ten different colors. And, also unlike the iPod Shuffle, it plays WMA-format files, in addition to MP3 files.

Model: Zen Nano Plus **Manufacturer:** Creative (www.creative.com) **Capacity:** 512MB or 1GB **Dimensions:** 1.32" × 2.58" × 0.51" **Weight:** 0.8 oz. **Price:** $129 (512MB), $169 (1GB)

Rio Forge Sport Player

The Rio Forge Sport is a neat little player designed for on-the-go action. You get an extremely compact, extremely rugged player with pretty good sound, long battery life (20 hours), a big display, and (as an added bonus) a built-in FM radio. It comes in 128MB, 256MB, and 512MB models; the unique shape is actually easy to hold when you're running.

Model: Rio Forge Sport Player **Manufacturer:** Rio (www.digitalnetworksna.com/rioaudio/) **Capacity:** 128MB, 256MB, 512MB **Dimensions:** 2.6" × 2.4" × 0.7" **Weight:** 2.3 oz. **Price:** $129.99 (128MB), $159.99 (256MB), $219.99 (512MB)

iRiver iFP-900 Series

iRiver's iFP-900 series players are compact, squarish units that fit well in any pocket. All models offer 40 hours of battery life, a cool color display, and built-in FM tuner and voice recorder. You get your choice of 256MB, 512MB, and 1GB capacity.

Model: iFP-990 (256MB), iFP-995 (512MB), iFP-999 (1GB) **Manufacturer:** iRiver (www.iriveramerica.com) **Dimensions:** 2.5" × 2" × 0.75" **Weight:** 2.2 oz. **Price:** $199.99 (256MB), $249.99 (512MB), $299.99 (1GB)

AudioTronic iCool Scented MP3 Players

Technically, there's nothing outstanding about these AudioTronic MP3 players. What *is* cool about the iCool mini-players is that they smell—in a good way. All iCool players have changeable embossed faceplates, and selected faceplates come with an aroma smell. You have your choice of lemon, strawberry, cherry, blueberry, rose, chocolate, cookie, coffee, and even marijuana scents. Odd, but true!

Model: iCool (various models) **Manufacturer:** AudioTronic (www.audiotronic.com) **Capacity:** 128MB **Dimensions:** 2.6" × 2" × 0.67" **Weight:** 1.2 oz. **Price:** $65

SPECIALTY AUDIO PLAYERS

Delphi XM MyFi

Leo's Pick

This is one of my favorite portable audio players, period. Of course, I'm a big fan of XM satellite radio, so it's no surprise that I'd really like a portable player that lets me receive XM broadcasts on the go, which is exactly what the MyFi does.

The MyFi is, simply put, a portable XM radio receiver. As long as you're outdoors (or near a window), you should be able to pick up signals from one of the orbiting XM satellites. When you're indoors or in a car, attach the included satellite antenna to improve your reception.

And here's the neat part—as if satellite radio on the go wasn't neat enough. The MyFi includes a built-in audio recorder that can store up to 5 hours of XM programming. So you can record talk or music when you're in signal range, and play it back when you're indoors or out of range. Not a bad idea, all in all.

In addition to the portable MyFi unit itself, you get a home accessory kit (with antenna), vehicle accessory kit (with car antenna), headphones, and a remote control unit (great for listening at home.) The MyFi receiver has its own portable antenna built-in, of course, as well as a built-in wireless FM transmitter that lets you transmit MyFi programming to any home or car FM radio. The MyFi also has an illuminated six-line LCD display; it not only displays channel, song, and artist info, but also personalized stock tickers, sports score tickers, and so on.

I'm not sure the MyFi can totally replace an iPod; it doesn't let you download and store your own music, after all. But if you're an XM junkie, it's great to be able to get your XM programming wherever you go—and not just in your car.

Model: MyFi **Manufacturer:** Delphi (www.xmradio.com/myfi/) **Dimensions:** 4.5" × 2.8" × 1.2" **Weight:** 7.2 oz. **Price:** $299.99

Apple iPod Photo

I put the iPod Photo in the specialty category because it's a regular iPod with specialty functions—in this case, the ability to store and display digital photos. The normal iPod display has been replaced by a 2" color LCD, and you have a choice of 30GB or 60GB capacity. Naturally, the iPod Photo still works like a normal iPod music player—so much so that Apple has now dropped the iPod Photo designation. From now on, any large-capacity iPod with a color screen is simply a big iPod with a color screen!

Model: iPod Photo Manufacturer: Apple (www.apple.com) Capacity: 30GB or 60GB Dimensions: 4.1" × 2.4" × 0.63" (0.75" for 60GB model) Weight: 5.9 oz. (30GB), 6.4 oz. (60GB) Price: $349 (30GB), $449 (60GB)

Mobiblu DAH-220

Mobiblu's DAH-200 is an MP3 player shaped like a cassette tape. It actually works like a cassette tape when you insert it into a cassette deck; press your cassette player's play button and the MP3 player starts playing. Kind of old school, but clever. (At present the DAH-220 is only shipping in Europe; check with the company for U.S. availability.)

Model: DAH-220 Manufacturer: Mobiblu (www.mobibluamerica.com) Capacity: 128MB Price: ~$200

GPX SportX

GPX's SportX is a pair of backstrap-style headphones with a built-in flash audio player. The audio player has 128MB of storage, as well as its own FM radio. It's nice to combine a portable audio player and headphones in a single unit—it's one less gadget you have to lose!

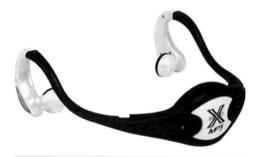

Model: HW6805DT Manufacturer: GPX (www.gpx.com) Capacity: 128MB Price: $99.95

Oakley THUMP

Here's another wearable MP3 player, this time built into a pair of stylish sunglasses. The Oakley THUMP grafts a flash player and pair of integrated earphones onto some tres cool Oakley shades. You get your choice of 128MB or 256MB models; the 256MB model has polarized lenses.

Model: THUMP Manufacturer: Oakley (www.oakley.com/thump/) Capacity: 128MB and 256MB Weight: 1.8 oz. Price: $395 (128MB), $495 (256MB)

PORTABLE VIDEO PLAYERS

Archos PMA400

Leo's Pick

Archos is the dean of portable video players; any one of the players they sell gets by heartfelt recommendation. But of all the Archos video players, my Leo's Pick award goes to the PMA400—and here's why.

The PMA400 is a relatively compact Linux-based device that functions as an audio/video player, PDA, and wireless web browser. (Don't let the Linux thing throw you; the PMA400 works with either Windows or Apple computers, no problem.) The main thing is, this one device does everything you could ever want it to do, and more. You can record directly from TV, watch recorded videos, listen to music, store and view digital photos, browse the Internet, play video games, store and transfer PC data files, and on and on and on. It can even function as a personal information manager; WiFi wireless connectivity is built-in.

In terms of specs, you get a 30GB hard disk and a nice 3.5" color LCD display Battery life is 4 hours for video playback or 9.5 hours for music playback, good enough for most uses. You get both a built-in speaker and microphone, so you're set for listening and recording at will.

Optional accessories include a USB-to-Ethernet cable (for connecting the PMA400 to your office network) and a USB foldable keyboard (for faster data entry). The PMA400 comes with its own docking cradle to connect to your TV; the cradle connects via either composite video or S-video,

and comes with an IR blaster for controlling a cable or satellite box—which means you can use the PMA400 as a TiVo-like mini-PVR to record all manner of television programming.

Yeah, the price on this puppy is a tad stratospheric; it costs twice as much as a PDA and almost as much as an entry-level laptop computer. But you get so much in such a small package, it's hard to complain.

Model: PMA400 **Manufacturer:** Archos (www.archos.com) **Capacity:** 30GB **Display:** 3.5" (320 × 240) **Dimensions:** 4.9" × 3.1" × 0.8" **Weight:** 9.9 oz. **Price:** $799.95

Archos Gmini 400

If the PMA400 is out of your price range, consider Archos' Gmini 400 instead. This is a small and thin portable media player, designed for both audio and video playback. The 20GB hard drive stores up to 80 hours of MPEG-4 videos, and playback is sweet (if a tad small) on the 2.2" color LCD display. The battery is good for 5 hours of video or 10 hours of music playback.

Model: Gmini 400 **Manufacturer:** Archos (www.archos.com) **Capacity:** 20GB **Display:** 2.2" (220 × 176) **Dimensions:** 4.17" × 2.37" × 0.69" **Weight:** 5.64 oz. **Price:** $349.95

Creative Zen Portable Media Player

This one almost made it as a Leo's Pick; it's a pretty cool little player. You get 20GB hard drive capacity (holds up to 85 hours of video), a big 3.8" color LCD display, built-in speakers, and easy-to-use thumbpad operation. It's good for MPEG, WMV, WMA, MP3, and JPG files; the display provides 320 × 240 resolution.

Model: Zen Portable Media Player **Manufacturer:** Creative (www.creative.com) **Capacity:** 20GB **Display:** 3.8" (320 × 240) **Dimensions:** 5.67" × 3.18" × 1.06" **Weight:** 12 oz. **Price:** $499.99

RCA Lyra 2780

RCA's Lyra was one of the first portable video players on the market, and the latest version is much better than the early models. The Lyra 2780 has a 20GB hard drive and a fairly nice 3.5" color LCD display. It can play back MPEG-4 video and WMA and MP3 audio files, and can also function as a photo vault for JPG digital photos.

Model: RD2780 **Manufacturer:** RCA (www.rcaaudiovideo.com) **Capacity:** 20GB **Display:** 3.5" (320 × 240) **Dimensions:** 5.37" × 3.13" × 0.95" **Weight:** 10.5 oz. **Price:** $399.99

Hasbro VideoNow Color

Hasbro's VideoNow Color is a portable video player for kids. Movies come on mini 4.25" DVD discs which hold up to 25 minutes of programming, and are displayed on the unit's color LCD screen. The device is small enough to fit in a six-year-old's hands, comes in a variety of attractive colors, and runs off of three AA batteries. And, for what it's worth, the VideoNow Color is a much more substantial device than Mattel's competing Juice Box—and the picture's a lot better, too!

Model: VideoNow Color **Manufacturer:** Hasbro (www.hasbro.com/videonow/) **Display:** 1.85" × 1.45" color LCD **Dimensions:** 4.75" × 5.75" × 1.25" **Price:** $59.99

HEADPHONES AND EARPHONES

Shure E5c Earphones

Leo's Pick

Shure's top-of-the-line E5c earphones—actually canal phones—provide a true audiophile listening experience. These are high-end earphones with high-end performance, priced at the high end of the scale.

Why spend this amount of money for a set of earphones? Simple—for the sound. The E5c delivers the type of studio-quality sound you expect from Shure products. The unit's high-energy micro-speakers are made of studio-grade components (hence the unit's high price) and deliver an extended frequency response. The result is heavenly.

The E5c's earbuds fit securely in your ears, and flexible sleeves produce great sound isolation. You get one pair of disposable foam sleeves, three pairs (small, medium, and large) of flex sleeves, and three pairs (small, medium, and large) of ultra-soft flex sleeves. For the best fit, however, consider having an audiologist make custom-fit ear molds; it'll cost you but will give you huge bragging rights among your friends.

Whichever earbud you use, the E5c weighs next to nothing—only 1.1 oz. It comes with its own carrying case, as well as an in-line level attenuator, to adjust for varying volume levels from different devices.

Bottom line, if you want the same earphones used by professional musicians, buy the E5c. You'll never go back to traditional models.

Model: E5c **Manufacturer:** Shure (www.shure.com) **Weight:** 1.1 oz. **Price:** $499

Etymotic ER-6 Isolator Earphones

Etymotic's ER-6 earphones deliver quiet sound at a surprisingly affordable price. Like the Shure model, these deliver pro-quality results—truly tremendous sound. (Use the foam eartips for best bass.) You get all sorts of eartips and filters as included accessories, as well as a nice zippered pouch to carry it all around in. You can also fit the ER-6 with a special Musicians Earplug (optional, extra) for an even tighter fit.

Model: ER-6 **Manufacturer:** Etymotic (www.etymotic.com) **Weight:** <1 oz. **Price:** $139

Sony MDR-EX81 Earphones

These are particularly stylish and comfortable earphones. It's a closed-type in-the-ear design equipped with 9mm drivers for deep bass and clear treble. It comes with two sizes of soft silicon earbuds for extra comfort.

Model: MDR-EX81 **Manufacturer:** Sony (www.sonystyle.com) **Weight:** 0.35 oz. **Price:** $49.99

Sony Street Style MDR-G74 Headphones

These are hip and happenin' headphones. The behind-your-neck design makes for comfortable (and non-slip) wear, while you get 30mm drivers for big sound. There's even a turbo duct for enhanced bass. Nice sound at a nice price.

Model: MDR-G74 **Manufacturer:** Sony (www.sonystyle.com) **Weight:** 2 oz. **Price:** $39.99

Stanton DJ Pro 3000 Headphones

These are serious headphones for serious listening—none of that wimpy earbud nonsense. You get a closed ear-cup design for maximum sound isolation, 50mm drivers for full-range reproduction, and an impressive 16–22kHz frequency range. And, in the totally gratuitous feature department, you get a set of blue LEDs that blink to the music!

Model: DJ Pro 3000 **Manufacturer:** Stanton (www.stantondj.com) **Weight:** 15.1 oz. **Price:** $129.99

IPOD ACCESSORIES

Belkin TunePower Battery Pack

When your iPod runs out of power in the middle of a playlist, turn to Belkin's TunePower for more power. The TunePower is a rechargeable external battery pack that fastens to the back of your iPod and connects to the dock connector. It gives you 8–10 hours of extra play time, and recharges via your iPod's FireWire recharger cable.

Model: F8E490 **Manufacturer:** Belkin (www.belkin.com) **Price:** $99.99

Solio Solar Charger

Solio is an add-on battery pack for your iPod or other portable audio player. It recharges via three solar panels or via standard AC power. Fold it up and it's small enough to fit in your shirt pocket; unfold it, and you get a neat three-petal shape. Solios are available for all iPod models, as well as most popular cell phones and PDAs.

Model: Solio **Manufacturer:** Better Energy Systems (www.solio.com) **Price:** $89.99

Griffin TuneJuice Battery Backup

Here's another external battery solution for drained iPods. The TuneJuice connects via a short cable to your iPod's dock connector, and provides up to 8 hours of additional play time. It works off a 9-volt battery, so when your 8 hours are up, just plug in a new battery to keep on playing!

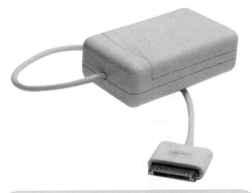

Model: TuneJuice **Manufacturer:** Griffin Technology (www.griffintechnology.com) **Price:** $19.99

Griffin PowerPod

Griffin's PowerPod lets you run your iPod off your car's cigarette lighter or AC power adapter. Just plug the PowerPod into the cigarette lighter, then connect the supplied 4-foot cable to your iPod's dock connector. It's great for listening to your iPod during long car trips!

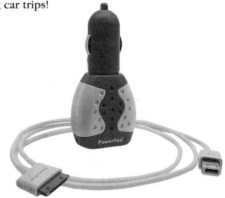

Model: PowerPod **Manufacturer:** Griffin Technology (www.griffintechnology.com) **Price:** $24.99

XtremeMac AirPlay FM Transmitter

Here's a neat little FM transmitter that works across the full FM frequency band, with no need to install special software; just press the up or down buttons to scan through all available frequencies. The AirPlay is powered by your iPod, no batteries necessary, and lets you play iPod music through any FM radio.

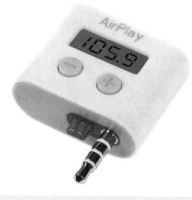

Model: AirPlay **Manufacturer:** XtremeMac (www.xtrememac.com) **Price:** $39.95

Griffin iTrip FM Transmitter

Griffin's iTrip lets you listen to your iPod music through any FM radio—in your car, in your home, wherever. The iTrip is a miniature FM station that transmits music from your iPod to any nearby FM radio; just tune in the radio to listen to your iPod tunes. After you install the iTrip software, you can transmit through any radio frequency by entering special station codes directly from your iPod.

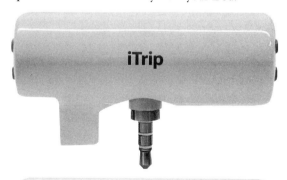

Model: iTrip **Manufacturer:** Griffin Technology (www.griffintechnology.com) **Price:** $39.99

DLO TransPod FM

Here's another iPod FM transmitter, this time built into a docking station and power adapter. Just plug the TransPod FM into your car's cigarette lighter, insert your iPod into the dock, dial in an open FM frequency on the digital tuner, and you're all set for in-car listening.

Model: DLO Transpod FM **Manufacturer:** Netalog (www.everythingipod.com) **Price:** $99.99

Denision ice>Link Plus Car Kit

The ice>Link Plus kit lets you connect your iPod to your car's existing CD changer port—no FM transmitter needed. The sound is better than you get with an FM kit, plus you can control your iPod from your car radio controls. You'll even get iPod's song and artist info on your car radio's display—a very cool solution! Adapters are available for most vehicle models.

Model: ice>Link Plus **Manufacturer:** Denision (icelink.denisionusa.com) **Price:** $199

Cube Travel Speakers

The Cube is a fold-up speaker system, ideal for travel use. It's powered by four AAA batteries; just unfold the cube, dock your iPod between the left and right speakers, and you're ready to go!

Model: Cube **Manufacturer:** Pacific Rim Technologies (www.pacrimtechnologies.com) **Price:** $39.99

Macally PodWave Mini-Speaker

The PodWave is a mini-speaker that attaches to the top of your iPod. It's battery powered, so it won't drain your iPod's battery. Just flip the on/off switch, and you can easily share your music with anyone in the room.

Model: PodWave **Manufacturer:** Macally (www.macally.com) **Price:** $39

JBL OnStage Speaker System

JBL's OnStage is an AC-powered speaker system just for iPods. Insert your iPod into the center cradle, and you get room-filling sound from the four built-in drivers. Even better, it looks kind of like a flying saucer!

Model: OnStage **Manufacturer:** JBL (www.jbl.com) **Price:** $159.95

Bose SoundDock Speaker System

Even better sound can be had from Bose's SoundDock. The shielded speakers deliver big Bose sound; all you have to do is dock your iPod at the front of the unit, then you can control the whole shebang with the included wireless infrared remote control. It's a tad expensive, but I gotta admit—the sound is impressive!

Model: SoundDock **Manufacturer:** Bose (www.bose.com) **Price:** $299

Altec Lansing inMotion Speaker System

Here's another iPod speaker system, completely battery powered. The base of the unit incorporates a highly efficient Class D power amplifier and two 1" microdrivers; just slip the iPod into the dock to start rocking. An auxiliary input jack on the back lets you connect a CD player or other device, if you want.

Model: inMotion **Manufacturer:** Altec Lansing (www.alteclansing.com) **Price:** $149.95

SavitMicro TriPod Speakers

This iPod speaker system is unique in its styling. The three legs (two with built-in speakers) fold out into a tripod base; connect your iPod (or any other portable audio player) to the top, and you have a nice combination stand and speaker system. Actually, the iPod connects *upside down*, but that's Korean engineering for you.

Model: TriPod **Manufacturer:** SavitMicro (www.savitmicro.co.kr) **Price:** TBA

JBL Creature II Speakers

JBL's Creature II speakers aren't iPod-specific speakers per se, but they do look very cool when connected to an iPod. The two satellite speakers and large subwoofer look very creature-like; they're powered speakers, so connect your iPod (or any portable audio player) and you're ready to party.

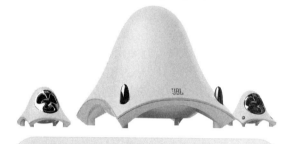

Model: Creature II **Manufacturer:** JBL (www.jbl.com) **Price:** $99.95

Griffin BlueTrip Audio Hub

Griffin's BlueTrip lets you connect your iPod to your home audio system, using Bluetooth wireless technology. The BlueTrip connects to your audio receiver via standard R/L RCA jacks or optical digital connection; it can transmit up to 30 feet away.

Model: BlueTrip **Manufacturer:** Griffin Technology (www.griffintechnology.com) **Price:** $149.99

iDirect Remote Control

The iDirect is a remote control for your iPod. Connect the receiver to the top of your iPod, then control volume, track selection, and so on from the wireless remote unit. It's simple to install and even simpler to use.

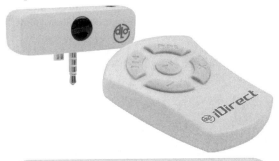

Model: iDirect Manufacturer: Digital Lifestyle Outfitters (www.dlodirect.com) Price: $49.99

Griffin iTalk Microphone

Plug Griffin's iTalk into the top of your iPod and you turn your iPod into a portable voice recorder. The iTalk includes a built-in microphone with automatic gain control, as well as a built-in speaker for play-back purposes—for music as well as voice.

Model: iTalk Manufacturer: Griffin Technology (www.griffintechnology.com) Price: $39.99

naviPlay Wireless Remote System

The naviPlay is another remote control system for your iPod, this time using Bluetooth wireless technology. The remote unit includes a headphone jack; tuck the remote somewhere on your person and hide your iPod (with the receiver unit attached) up to 30 feet away.

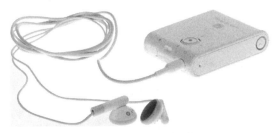

Model: naviPlay Manufacturer: TEN Technology (www.tentechnology.com) Price: $199

Belkin iPod Voice Recorder

Belkin's iPod Voice Recorder lets your iPod double as a digital audio recorder. It features a built-in micro-phone and plugs directly in to your iPod. You can record hundreds of hours of conversations in mono WAV format. The Voice Recorder even has a built-in speaker, so you can listen to what you've recorded without headphones. And here's something extra neat—thanks to the built-in speaker, you can use the Voice Recorder as a travel alarm clock!

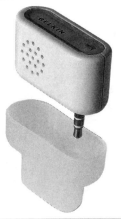

Model: F8E462 Manufacturer: Belkin (www.belkin.com) Price: $30

Griffin iBeam Flashlight/Pointer

Now this is a cool little gadget. Griffin's iBeam is a small laser light that snaps onto the top of your iPod. You get two different attachments; one functions as a flashlight, the other as a red laser pointer (with a Class IIIA laser).

Model: iBeam **Manufacturer:** Griffin Technology (www.griffintechnology.com) **Price:** $19.99

H2O Audio Underwater iPod Housing

Want to take your iPod boating—or swimming? Then tuck it into H2O Audio's waterproof housing, and you won't do any damage. The housing is submersible up to 10 feet, and lets you control your iPod from the outside. You can even buy armbands and swimbelts to fit the housing—even better for on-the-water use.

Model: SV-iP4G **Manufacturer:** H2O Audio (www.h2oaudio.com) **Price:** $149.95

Belkin Digital Camera Link

With Belkin's Digital Camera Link, you can use your iPod or iPod Photo to store hundreds of digital photos, transferred directly from your digital camera. All you have to do is connect your digital camera (via USB) to the Digital Camera Link and then connect the Digital Camera Link to your iPod. Transfer the pictures from your camera to your iPod; later, when you dock your iPod to your PC, you can download the pictures to your computer's hard disk. It's a great way to free up space in your digital camera without having to lug your PC around!

Model: F8E477 **Manufacturer:** Belkin (www.belkin.com) **Price:** $79.99

Belkin iPod Media Reader

Want to transfer digital photos and other files you have stored on a digital media card to your iPod? Then plug in Belkin's Media Reader and start transferring. The Media Reader connects directly to your iPod and reads the following digital media formats: CompactFlash I, CompactFlash II, SmartMedia, Secure Digital, Memory Stick, and MultiMediaCard. Use the software built in to your iPod to transfer the files, and store them on the iPod's hard disk.

Model: F8E461 **Manufacturer:** Belkin (www.belkin.com) **Price:** $99.99

MORE COOL PORTABLE AUDIO GADGETS

StikAx Music Mixer

Leo's Pick

Okay, so this gizmo isn't technically a portable audio gadget. It is, most definitely, an audio gadget, and it works with any PC to help you mix your music on the go.

The StikAx is a handheld device that you use to mix sound and images on your PC or Mac. It works with accompanying TrakAx software and a sample loop CD to let you create your own audio and video mixes—without touching a computer or musical keyboard.

This is a great gizmo for wannabe DJs who don't want to learn how to use complicated mixing software. You use the joystick-like device to drag, drop, clip, and merge sound and image files via the TrakAx software. The handheld unit has a bunch of dedicated thumb buttons that let you do the job one-handed, if you want.

Of course, a big part of this product is the TrakAx editing software, which works on any Windows XP computer. TrakAx lets you create mixes one event at a time; you can then edit your final mix using a variety of professional effects and transitions. All this is facilitated by the sample CD, which contains 450 prerecorded loops and beats in a range of different styles. (And each loop is pre-cleared for commercial use!) You can add your own sounds and music via USB microphone, keyboard, or synthesizer.

It's all surprisingly easy and extremely neat, thanks to the gun-like StikAx controller. The result is a type of point-and-shoot audio/video editing that anyone can master, at a price that's definitely affordable.

(As I write this, the StikAx is being sold exclusively in the U.K.; contact the company for details about U.S. availability.)

Model: StikAx **Manufacturer:** Ministry of Sound (www.stikax.com) **Minimum hardware requirements:** 1.3GHz Pentium 4, 256MB RAM, Windows XP, USB connection **Price:** ~$90

Edirol R-1 Portable Music Recorder

So far I've talked a lot about portable audio players; now it's time to talk about a portable audio *recorder*. The R-1 is a high-quality handheld audio recorder that records and plays back at any of nine quality levels, ranging from 64kbps compressed MP3 format to uncompressed 24-bit linear WAV. Maximum recording time is 137 minutes (in 64kbps MP3 mode), using the included 64MB memory card. You can record via built-in microphone, external mic, or line inputs.

Model: R-1 **Manufacturer:** Edirol (www.edirol.com)
Dimensions: 3 15/16" × 5 5/16" × 1 3/16"
Weight: 8 oz. **Price:** $450

Monster iSpeaker Portable

This is an odd little portable speaker system. The speaker folds up into a double-CD-sized case, then opens up for listening. Connect any portable audio player via the supplied 3-foot cable; the whole thing is powered by four AA batteries.

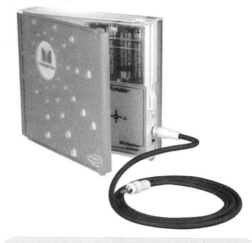

Model: iSpeaker Portable **Manufacturer:** Monster Cable (www.monstercable.com) **Price:** $59.95

SoundSak SonicBoom

The SonicBoom is a backpack with built-in speakers and power amplifier—ideal for jamming on the go. The whole thing is powered by six AA batteries, and the 4" speakers are powered by a 5 watt/channel amplifier. You can even get it with an optional hydration reservoir, in case you get dry mouth while grooving on the trail!

Model: SonicBoom **Manufacturer:** Sound Kase (www.soundkase.com) **Price:** $149.99

i-glasses Wearable Video Display

I would be remiss if I didn't mention at least one heads-up video display. The i-glasses system is a head-mounted video display that connects to any portable video player or gaming system. Flip down the visor and you have your own personal video display, with 800 × 600 resolution. It's like watching a 70-inch screen from 13 feet away, sort of.

Model: i-glasses VIDEO **Manufacturer:** i-O Display Systems (www.i-glasses.com) **Price:** $899

9

The Ultimate Home Theater Enthusiast

HOW TO BECOME THE ULTIMATE HOME THEATER ENTHUSIAST

When you're assembling a $10,000 or $20,000 home theater system, it's tough to think of all these expensive components as "gadgets," yet gadgets they are—just very expensive ones. To my mind, there's nothing more gadgety than home theater components, with all their fancy inputs and outputs, knobs and pushbuttons, and lights and displays. And then there's the most fun gadget of all, the remote control unit. Hey, a home theater system is a gadget lover's dream!

It All Starts with the (Big) Screen

Putting together the ultimate home theater system starts with the big thing right in the middle of your front wall—the video display. Let's face it, there's nothing more important than a big television screen to impress your friends and family. (Don't bother trying to impress your spouse; a giant TV will only become a point of conflict, so you might as well prepare yourself for it.) The better—and bigger—your video display, the more realistic your home theater experience.

Today's state-of-the-art video displays are much, much different from the simple television sets of yesteryear. Not only are they bigger and shaped differently (widescreen vs. squarish), they're also capable of reproducing high resolution programming broadcast in the new HDTV format. If you're purchasing a new home theater system, plan on allocating at least a quarter of your budget to the video display.

Also unlike the past, today you can choose from four different types of displays—and various technologies behind each display type. Which technology and type of display you choose depends on your budget, the demands of your room, and your personal preferences. Here's what you have to choose from:

- **Direct view**—Direct view displays are the traditional type of television sets you've always had in your living room. A direct view television utilizes a picture tube—also called a cathode ray tube, or CRT—as its video display. Direct view sets typically have the brightest picture of any display type, and generally cost less than similar-sized projection or flat panel sets. Their main limitation is size; with a maximum screen size of 40" (and most being smaller than this) if your viewing distance is 10 feet or more, a direct view set may be inadequate for your needs. In addition, direct view sets are bigger (front to back) and heavier than other displays, so factor that into your decision.

- **Rear projection**—Rear projection televisions (RPTVs) are ideal for viewers who have a bigger room and need a bigger screen than what you can get in a direct view set—but don't want to totally break the bank. Today's lowest-priced RPTV models use older CRT technology, where the picture is produced by three small, internal picture tubes; they're somewhat big, and bulky, however. Newer RPTVs use various microdisplay technologies, such as digital light projection (DLP) and liquid crystal display (LCD) to create a picture from a much smaller internal light engine. The result is a brighter picture than a CRT-based RPTV, but in a smaller, lighter cabinet. The only downside is price; microdisplay sets typically cost up to twice as much as similar-sized CRT-based units.

- **Front projection**—Front projection televisions (FPTVs) are used in most larger and professional home theater installations. The advantage of an FPTV is that you can project a *really* large picture—up to 20 feet diagonal in some super installations. An FPTV system works similar to an RPTV system, except the internal light engine (CRT, LCD, or DLP) sits in front of the screen, typically behind the audience, and projects the picture across the room directly onto the screen. This type of system is inherently less bright than any other type of display, and also has a somewhat narrow viewing angle. This means that the room has to be dark and narrow for a FPTV system to work—although the room can be very large, of course. While some FPTV systems cost as much as a car, decent FP units are comparable in price to a good RPTV.

- **Flat panel**—The newest type of display is very thin—and very expensive. These displays are thin and light enough to hang on a wall. While flat panel displays are attractive from an interior design standpoint, they're typically more expensive than similar RPTV displays. Note that there are actually two types of flat panel displays available today. Plasma displays are typically larger (42"-60"), while LCD displays are typically smaller (13"-45"), although they're starting to meet in the middle ground. While plasma is extremely popular, it's not a good choice if you're worried about screen burn-in; static images (such as network logos or letterbox bars) leave a ghost image if displayed for too long. LCD displays have no burn-in problems, but aren't quite as good at displaying deep blacks. Either type of display is attractive from a design standpoint, although somewhat expensive.

With all these different display technologies crowding your brain, how do you choose the right display for your own home theater system? As you can tell, it's definitely not a one-size-fits-all world. In general, each of the display technologies is best for specific uses.

For example, direct view is good for smaller rooms, when you want the brightest possible picture and a wide viewing angle, or if you're on a tight budget. On the other hand, rear projection is good if you have a larger room but want to make as few compromises as possible in terms of room lighting or viewing angle. Rear projection is also a good choice if you prefer to watch movies in their original aspect ratio without worrying about screen burn-in.

Then there's front projection, which is the best choice if you want the largest, most theater-like picture possible and don't mind restricting both viewing angle and room lighting—and if price isn't an object. Finally, a flat panel display is good if you have little or no floor space for a television set or projector—or if you just want to show off the neat technology. Plasma flat panels are especially popular when you want a larger picture, but present somewhat of a burn-in problem.

Whichever display technology you choose, you should also consider the number and types of video inputs on the back, the usability of the remote control, and any additional features offered, such as picture-in-picture and onscreen program guides. You should definitely go with a set that's ready for HDTV broadcasts, and that offers a 16:9 aspect ratio screen.

The Brains and the Power: The A/V Receiver

To many know-nothing consumers, the phrase "home theater system" really means "widescreen television." While a big TV (with HDTV capability) is certainly the visual center-piece of a home theater, true techies know that the full theater experience depends as much on sound as it does on picture—which is why the audio components in your system are every bit as important as the video display.

Home theater sound all starts with the audio/video receiver, to which you connect all your audio and video components and then switch between inputs with a single remote control. Connect your DVD player, digital video recorder, cable/satellite box, and Media Center PC to the inputs of your A/V receiver, then connect the output of the A/V receiver to your video display. Whatever you select on the receiver's remote appears on the television screen.

The A/V receiver also serves as the main processor/amplifier for your system's audio. Surround sound sources (either broadcast or DVD) are fed into the receiver, which decodes the surround sound signal using the appropriate technology. Most soundtracks today are encoded with Dolby Digital surround sound, which feeds the audio to six separate speakers—three in the front of the room, two in the back, and a final subwoofer for the deep bass signals. Pop in a DVD or tune to an HDTV broadcast with a Dolby Digital soundtrack, and your A/V receiver will create room-filling sound.

A/V receivers are available at a variety of price points, and if you can't tell the difference between a $200 and a $6,000 receiver, you need an ear exam. It's all about the sound—and, of course, the control. While all A/V receivers perform similar functions, the higher-priced models simply provide better quality sound and more flexibility in terms of control and component switching. Consider the following variables:

- **Power**—In general, you're better off getting as much power as you can afford, within limits. Don't sweat 10–20 watt per channel differences between models, as the difference won't likely be noticeable. (A 200 watt/channel receiver will sound a bunch better than a 100 watt/channel model, however.) You should look beyond simple power ratings and compare total harmonic distortion and signal-to-noise ratio—both of which typically have more effect on the actual sound than do power ratings.

- **Inputs and outputs**—This is key. Make sure there are enough—and the right kinds of—input and output jacks to connect all your different components. Higher-end receivers will provide a variety of composite (single-connector) video, S-Video, component (three-connector) video, and either DVI or HDMI digital video connectors; naturally, you should get a slew of optical and coaxial digital audio connections, as well. Also look for at least one front-panel audio/video connection, for camcorder and videogame use.

- **Control**—You operate an A/V receiver with its remote control unit—and there are big differences in remote controls. Look for a unit that feels right to you and is easy for others to figure out and use. Also look for a universal or learning remote that can be programmed to control all the components in your home theater system. If you get a good remote with your receiver, you won't have to buy a third-party remote later on.

- **Surround processing**—Almost all A/V receivers today decode all the current surround sound formats—Dolby Digital, DTS, Dolby Pro Logic IIx, and Neo:6 (DTS's Pro Logic equivalent). If you want a system with both surround and back speakers, make sure that the receiver includes a Dolby Digital EX/DTS ES 6.1/7.1 decoder and the requisite number of amplifiers.

- **Sound quality**—Before you buy, listen. Does this model sound noticeably different or better than comparable models? Is the sound loud enough, clean enough, and smooth enough? Make sure you bring your own source material when comparing units—and compare different types of sources, both movies and music.

And here's a little tip. When you can't tell one spec from another, go with the heavier unit. Yeah, it's simplistic, but it works; nine times out of ten, the heavier unit is better constructed and will probably sound better, too.

Speakers, Speakers, Everywhere

You can have the best surround-sound processor in the world and run through the cleanest and most powerful amplifier, but your system will sound horrible if you use the wrong or poor-quality speakers. Choosing the right speakers is essential to creating the best possible home theater experience; if you have any spare money in your home theater budget, there's no better place to spend the bucks than in upgrading your system's speakers!

While all speakers contain some type and combination of woofer and tweeter, there are several different types of speaker enclosure. Which type of enclosure you choose depends on your room, the space you have, and your personal tastes.

The three primary types of home theater speakers are

- **Floor-standing speakers**—These are speakers that are big enough to stand on the floor (either on their own, or with the help of speaker stands). Floor-standing speakers typically are larger than other types of speakers, reproduce a wider range of frequencies (including deep bass), and are quite efficient, producing more volume per watt. They're the best type of speakers for pure music reproduction. The downside of floor-standing speakers, of course, is that they take up valuable floor space, which may or may not be important to you.

- **Bookshelf speakers**—If you're working with limited space (including space within an audio/video cabinet), bookshelf speakers can be a more attractive alternative to floor-standing models. With bookshelf speakers, you get smaller speakers that take up less space (and can be mounted on stands or on shelves), good performance, and (in most instances) a smaller price tag. Some bookshelf speakers don't have a lot of oomph on the low end, and benefit from being paired with a powered subwoofer.

- **Satellite speakers**—Thanks to advances in speaker design, several manufacturers produce individual speakers that are small enough to fit in the palm of your hand. Think of these as mini-bookshelf speakers, if you like; they're small enough to be mounted or placed just about anywhere in the room. Despite the small size, some of these satellite speakers deliver surprisingly good performance. Any noticeable lack of bass inherent in the design is made up for by use of a separate subwoofer.

If you're using bookshelf or satellite speakers (or even some floor-standing speakers), you'll want to include a separate subwoofer in your system. The subwoofer is a powered speaker (it contains its own power amplifier) that reproduces the very lowest bass frequencies. In a Dolby Digital or DTS soundtrack, the subwoofer is the .1 of the 5.1-channel system and is fed a separate low frequency effects (LFE) audio channel.

Oh, about that 5.1 business. The 5 represents the five main audio channels: front left, front center, front left, surround left, and surround right. The .1 is the subwoofer. If you want a 6.1- or 7.1-channel system, the extra speakers go behind you, with the standard surround speakers to either side of the room.

Whichever type of speaker system you go with, make sure you listen to it before you buy—using a variety of different programming, both audio and video. Make sure that your speakers sound as good with music as they do with movies, which not all speakers do. (Music is harder to reproduce than even the loudest action film soundtrack.)

Also, for those speakers near your television—definitely your center speaker, and perhaps your front left and right speakers—make sure you're looking at models that are shielded. This shielding is actually for the benefit of your television, which can be effected by the impulses from the speaker magnets. If you put an unshielded speaker too close to a CRT, the tube's colors can be distorted.

Everybody Needs a Good DVD Player

The DVD player is an essential component of any home theater system.
Whether you choose a basic sub-$100
player or an uber-expensive $3,500 one
(yes, they exist—and one is my Leo's
Pick in this category!), you want a progressive scan player that can handle
both DVD movies and CD audio discs, as

well as all the important subcategories, such as DVD-R and CD-R discs.

The more money you have to spend, the better the performance and the more features you
get. For example, that $3,500 player is as solid as the rock of Gibraltar, and also plays DVD-
Audio and SACD discs. You can also splurge and go for a DVD megachanger, so you can store
your entire movie collection in a single machine, no disc-swapping necessary.

Record What You Want, When You Want

And then there's the issue of recording. There are many different ways to record television
programs. If you're in an old-school mood, you can search eBay for a deal on a old-tech video
cassette recorder. If you're more of a new-school guy, consider a DVD recorder, so you can
make your own DVD discs. And if you're *really* new-school, so new school you're ultra cool,
then you definitely want to go with a hard disk recorder—the ultimate in digital video
recording.

A hard disk recorder—sometimes called a digital video recorder (DVR) or personal video
recorder (PVR)—is simply a little computer with its own hard disk. The video signal comes
into the DVR and is recorded, digitally, onto the hard disk. When you play back the recording,
you're reading the stored file off the hard disk. It's actually nothing too fancy, if you're used to
computers; in the world of consumer electronics, however, this is really gee-whiz stuff.

What makes DVRs so appealing is the accompanying electronic program guide (EPG) and control over live TV. After all, a DVR doesn't do much more than what a VCR does (except with
much better picture quality, of course), so why is everyone all of a sudden raving about being
able to record their favorite television programs? Trust me on this one—it's all about the EPG,
which makes it *way* easier to schedule a recording than it was in the VCR era.

With a VCR you had to look up the start time of the show, program the VCR's timer, insert a
tape, and hope for the best. This was a bit of a stretch for the average non-techie consumer,
who couldn't even figure out how to make the VCR's digital clock stop flashing 12:00. It was
too much bother, so they didn't use the VCR to record at all. (And remember, the *R* in *VCR*
stood for *recorder*!) Instead, the VCR became a rather bulky and expensive movie playback
machine.

Well, now the DVD player has become the default movie playback machine, and the recording
function is finally being filled by the hard disk recorder—and the electronic program guide.
With an EPG all you have to do is scroll through the upcoming listings, highlight a selection,

and press a button on the remote control. Voila, the recording is scheduled, no tricky programming required. Even better, some EPGs let you search for programs by various criteria, or even schedule a whole season's worth of recordings at a single go.

The most notable EPG is TiVo, which costs you $12.95 a month to use, and is only available with specific TiVo-compatible units. Other DVRs offer other EPGs, such as the one offered by TV Guide, most of which are free. I still prefer the versatility and functionality of TiVo, but I also understand that zero dollars a month is a lot more attractive to most folks than $12.95 per month—especially when the basic hard disk recording functions are the same, regardless of which EPG is used.

Anyway, DVRs are all the rage, and can be found in a lot of different devices. You have the traditional freestanding DVR, as offered by TiVo and others; the combination DVR/DVD recorder, as offered by Panasonic and Sony; the combination DVR/cable box, offered by most cable companies today; the combination DVR/satellite receiver, offered by both DIRECTV and Dish Network; the DVR functionality of a Media Center PC; and the latest approach, the DVR built into a television set, as currently offered on a few Mitsubishi HDTV models.

Whichever route you take, make sure you like the EPG and that you have a big enough hard disk for all the programs you want to record. Don't settle for the basic 40GB models, which will only hold about 12 hours of programming in high-resolution mode (or about 40 hours in lower-resolution mode); I recommend at least an 80GB model, larger if you're a pack rat or record a lot of HDTV programming.

Put a PC in Your Living Room

Today's state-of-the-art home theater systems incorporate a lot of functions that seemingly require separate devices. If you want to record and play back television programming, you need a hard disk recorder; if you want to play prerecorded movies, you need a DVD player; if you want to house and listen to a large CD collection, you need one or more CD megachangers. Wouldn't it be great if you could replace all these different gadgets with one single device?

Well, you can, if you don't mind putting a PC in your living room. A properly equipped PC can do everything all these separate components can. It has a CD/DVD drive to play back and burn audio CDs and DVD movies; a TV tuner to play back television programming; and a hard disk to record and store audio and video files. One device, multiple functions. Kind of cool.

While you could place a normal desktop PC in your home theater system, this isn't an ideal solution, for a number of reasons. First, a desktop PC simply doesn't look like your other audio

and video components; the tall desktop design won't fit in a typical audio/video rack. And most desktop PCs are fairly noisy, thanks to those internal cooling fans, and you don't want all that annoying background noise when you're listening to your favorite music or movies.

What you need is a personal computer customized for living room use. This home theater PC—sometimes called a Media Center PC—should come in a case that mimics the form factor of traditional audio/video components, and it should be as quiet as possible, via the use of some sort of silent cooling system. Of course, the Media Center PC should also have the storage and computing capacity to do everything you need it to do—which means a built-in television tuner to receive TV broadcasts, a big hard disk to store all that programming, and a built-in CD/DVD drive to play back your CDs and DVDS. And it would be nice if all this were integrated with a remote control and onscreen interface that let you see and operate your system from across a large living room.

Fortunately, you don't have to look too far to find a device that fits these parameters. Today there are several manufacturers making affordable Media Center PCs for home use, at a variety of price levels. The best models are about 17" wide and a few inches tall, just like all your other audio/video components. Look for models with some sort of silent cooling system, one or more TV tuners (dual tuners let you record two programs at once, or watch one while you're recording another), and a really big hard disk. Personally, I think 200GB is the minimum if you're using the unit as a DVR; even more hard disk space is necessary if you plan on using the PC to store your entire CD collection in digital format.

Share Your Music with a Digital Media Server

A viable alternative to Media Center PC is a so-called digital media server. This is a device that lets you play digital audio files on your home audio system. You rip your favorite CDs to hard disk, and the media server accesses the hard disk to play individual songs and playlists. It's a great space-saver (you don't need to keep all your physical CDs in view anymore) as well as a way to get instant access to every song in your collection—including all the MP3 and WMA files you've downloaded from the Internet. (And if a digital media server sounds a lot like a Media Center PC without the video stuff, you're absolutely right.)

If you have most of your digital music stored on your desktop PC, consider a digital media hub instead. This is a device that doesn't have a built-in hard disk or CD drive; instead, it connects to your home network, accesses the digital audio files stored on your computer's hard disk, and then streams the music through your home audio system. This type of hub is typically a small and relatively low-cost device that connects directly to your home audio system; it plugs in to your home network via either wired or wireless connection.

When you're shopping for a digital media server or hub, take these points into consideration:

- If you get a self-contained digital media server, how big is its hard drive? (More hard disk space means you can store more CDs.)
- If you get a remote digital media hub, does it connect via Ethernet (wired) or WiFi (wireless)? And if it's WiFi, is it the slower 802.11b or the faster 802.11g, which you'll need to display videos and photos? (Or, heaven forbid, does it require a hard-wired Ethernet connection?)
- Can you connect multiple units to provide music to other rooms in your house?
- Does the unit have a built-in display or does it use your TV to display song information?
- Does it play audio only, or can it also stream videos or display digital photos and artwork?
- Can you control playback from the unit (or a remote control unit), or do you have to set everything up from your PC?

One final question. Do you really want a digital media server or hub, or would you be better off with a more full-feature (but also more complicated and more expensive) Media Center PC? Decisions, decisions...

Lots of Gadgets, One Remote

With all these different gadgets in your home theater systems, you're bound to end up with a coffee table full of remotes. There's the one for the TV, one for the A/V receiver, one for the DVD player, one for the digital video recorder, one for the Media Center PC, one for the cable box or satellite dish, and on and on and on. How do you deal with all those remotes?

Well, the easiest way to deal with remote control clutter is to do a little consolidation. The key is to combine all your operating functions into a single universal remote control unit. Most universal remotes have codes for the most popular audio/video components preprogrammed; other codes can be "learned" from the old remote. Once you have it programmed, the new remote can control four or more components, just by pressing the right buttons.

The best universal remotes feature some sort of LCD touch screen display. Typically, this display varies depending on which component you're trying to operate. Press the button for TV, and the touch screen changes to display the television controls. Press the button for DVD, and the screen displays the DVD's controls. And so on.

Even better are those remotes that let you program their functionality via your PC. It's really quite easy (and very cool) to design your own custom remote control layout on your PC, using the remote's supplied software, and then download that layout to your remote via a USB or serial connection. Some remotes, like Philips' Pronto line, even let you add your own custom graphics; go online to find all sorts of custom screens and logos to use.

Of course, ultra-programmability is useless if you can't figure out how to use the darned thing. So, don't be seduced by too many whiz-bang features; make sure that the remote is simple enough for everyone in your household to use, without consulting an instruction manual every time they want to change channels.

BIG-SCREEN TELEVISIONS

Samsung 50" DLP Rear Projection TV

Leo's pick

The most popular rear-projection technology today is digital light projection (DLP), and the most popular DLP sets are those from Samsung. I chose this particular Sammy model as my Leo's pick not because it has a better picture than competing models (it's just as good as the rest, but not noticeably superior), but because of the way it looks when it's turned off. And the way it looks is... well, really high-tech cool.

The HL-R5087 comes on a 1960s-hip chrome pedestal that makes it look much different from most rear projection sets today. In fact, the blogosphere has nick-named this set the Captain Kirk, for its *Star Trek*-like design. I won't argue with that; it's a cool TV to have in your high-tech living room. (And that's recognizing how terribly impractical the pedestal design is for arranging and connecting all your other audio/video equipment—in spite of Samsung's attempts to alleviate the problem with a component rack that rolls into place around the base of the unit.)

Design aside, this Sammy does DLP right—which is why they sell so many of them. This model uses Samsung's third-generation DLP technology, and the switching speed for the digital micromirror device (DMD) is twice as fast as previous models. Native resolution is 720p (1280 × 720); lower-resolution signals are upconverted to match, and 1080i signals are downconverted accordingly.

The DLP light engine uses a seven-segment 2.6" color wheel that spins at 10,800 RPM, faster than previous generations for a film-like picture without pixel breakup. Like all DLP models, you can expect a very bright, very colorful picture. Contrast is very good, and black levels are the best you'll find short of a traditional CRT.

You get all manner of inputs and outputs, as you might expect—2 composite video inputs, 2 S-Video inputs, 2 component video inputs, 1 DVI input, and 1 HDMI input, plus line audio and digital audio outputs. There's also a built-In NTSC/ATSC analog/digital tuner, and the set is digital cable ready with an active CableCARD slot.

To sum up, you get a state-of-the-art DLP rear projection set, complete with HDTV capability, in a cabinet that makes any living room look like the control room of the U.S.S. Enterprise. It's a set that will garner the admiration and (more important) the envy of all your friends and neighbors.

Model: HL-R5087 **Manufacturer:** Samsung (www.samsung.com) **Screen size:** 50" diagonal
Native resolution: 1280 × 720 **Display technology:** DLP **Dimensions:** 59.6" (w) × 21.8" (h) × 20.2" (d)
Weight: 82 lbs. **Price:** $3,499.99

Sony 60" LCD Rear Projection TV

If you're one of those who sees rainbows on DLP sets, consider this Sony rear projector that uses LCD technology. This is a big puppy, with a 60" screen; native resolution is a little better than 780p, at 1386 × 788 pixels. You also get an NTSC/ATSC tuner for over-the-air HDTV signals, a CableCARD slot for digital cable without the box, two component video inputs, and two HDMI inputs.

Model: KDF-60XS955 **Manufacturer:** Sony (www.sonystyle.com) **Screen size:** 60" diagonal **Native resolution:** 1386 × 788 **Display technology:** LCD **Dimensions:** 66 3/8" (w) × 39 5/8" (h) × 20 1/4" (d) **Weight:** 113.5 lbs. **Price:** $4,099.99

Pioneer 50" Plasma Flat Panel TV

While I'm not a fan of plasma sets (I don't like the burn-in), others are, and many of them really like this Pioneer PureVision plasma set. This set does a good job of minimizing reflected light, and uses 10-bit processing to deliver a palette of more than one billion colors. All the electronics are in a separate media receiver box, which includes NTSC and ATSC tuners, a CableCARD slot, three component video inputs, and two HDMI inputs.

Model: PRO-1120HD **Manufacturer:** Pioneer (www.pioneerelectronics.com) **Screen size:** 50" diagonal **Native resolution:** 1280 × 768 **Display technology:** Plasma **Dimensions:** 50" (w) × 29" (h) × 3 7/8" (d) **Weight:** 83.8 lbs. **Price:** $13,500

Sharp 45" Aquos Flat Panel LCD TV

If you want a flat panel display but don't want to worry about burn-in, turn to LCD technology—as found in this high-end Sharp Aquos model. This 45" LCD screen is as big as they come (so far) and is one of the few sets today to offer full 1080i (1920 × 1080) resolution. You also get 800:1 contrast ratio, 170° viewing angle, and a built-in NTSC/ATSC tuner and CableCARD capability. The speakers are detachable, so if you're running the sound through a separate audio/video system, you can leave them off to save a little space on the wall.

Model: LC-45GX6U **Manufacturer:** Sharp (www.sharpusa.com) **Screen size:** 45" diagonal **Native resolution:** 1920 × 1080 **Display technology:** LCD **Dimensions:** 42.67" × 25.39" × 3.72" **Weight:** 48.5 lbs. **Price:** $8,999

InFocus DLP Front Projector

True videophiles go for front projection systems, and this InFocus projector is a truly top-of-the-line machine. It uses three-chip DLP projection technology to deliver truly eye-boggling high-definition pictures at 1280 × 720 (720p) native resolution. Contrast ratio is an impressive 3000:1 and brightness is 2000 lumens, which means you get true blacks and an extremely bright picture. You can use the ScreenPlay 777 to project pictures up to 15 feet wide—something you just can't get with other technologies!

Model: ScreenPlay 777 **Manufacturer:** InFocus (www.infocushome.com) **Screen size:** Up to 15 feet **Native resolution:** 1280 × 720 **Display technology:** DLP **Dimensions:** 28.4" × 8.5" × 23.7" **Weight:** 44.4 lbs. **Price:** $24,000

AUDIO/VIDEO RECEIVERS

Denon AVR-5805

Leo's Pick

The heart and soul of any home theater system is its power and control center—the audio/video receiver. The ultimate home theater enthusiast needs a receiver that delivers the performance of separate components with the flexibility of multiple input/output configurations. This is what you get from Denon's AVR-5805, perhaps the finest A/V receiver ever made.

That's a bold claim, but until somebody builds a better mousetrap (and they will, of course), it's wholly accurate. There has been no other receiver in history that offers the combination of power, performance, and control provided by the AVR-5805. Let me elaborate.

First of all, this isn't a simple 5.1-channel receiver. The AVR-5805 delivers a total of 10 channels of amplification, at an impressive 170 watts per channel. But, you protest, you don't have a 10-channel home theater system? That's not the point. The 10 channels offered here can be split between two separate zones. This means you can run two fully functioning 5.1-channel home theaters in different rooms, or a 7.1-channel system in one room with a simple stereo system in another. You have full control over what's playing in zones A and B, and over the speaker configuration. So you can set up your main zone for five, six, or seven main channels (the sub is always separate, of course, since it's not amplified), and feed the leftover channels to one or more other zones. Or you can bi-amp five channels in your main room, for a stunning 340 watts per channel. Wowzers!

As you might suspect, all this configuration flexibility means you get a plethora of audio and video inputs and outputs. For inputs, you get 6 coaxial digital audio, 6 optical digital audio, 2 IEEE-1394 FireWire digital audio, 14 analog audio, 1 phono, 8 composite video, 7 S-Video, 6 component video, 1 DVI, and 3 HDMI. The selection of outputs is equally as impressive.

This puppy also happens to be THX Ultra2 certified, which means that George Lucas himself will come out and tweak your knobs for you. (Okay, not really on the George Lucas thing, but THS Ultra2 certification does reflect the quality sound reproduction you can expect.) Everything is controlled via a programmable universal remote control.

Model: AVR-5805 **Manufacturer:** Denon (www.usa.denon.com) **Power:** 170 watts × 10 channels
Dimensions: 17.1" (w) × 12" (h) × 20.5" (d) **Weight:** 92 lbs. **Price:** $6,000

Onkyo TX-NR1000

As good as the Denon AVR-5805 is, it's not alone in the rarified air of high-end A/V receivers. Case in point is Onkyo's TX-NR1000, which gives the AVR-5805 a pretty good run for its money. It's THX Ultra2 certified, with 150 watts per channel across seven channels. You get all the typical analog and digital audio/video inputs and outputs, including HDMI and IEEE-1394 connections. If you don't care about all the multi-room configurations offered by the Denon, save yourself a cool grand and check out this puppy.

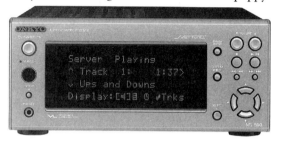

Model: TX-NR1000 **Manufacturer:** Onkyo (www.us.onkyo.com) **Power:** 150 watts × 7 **Dimensions:** 17 1/8" (w) × 8 11/16" (h) × 18 15/16" (d) **Weight:** 72.8 lbs. **Price:** $4,999.99

Yamaha RX-Z9

The RX-Z9 is Yamaha's entry into the super receiver market. It offers 170 watts per channel across seven channels, plus another two channels at 50 watts per (ideal for second-zone audio). The only thing the RX-Z9 lacks is HDMI video switching; it makes up for it with Yamaha's typically impressive array of digital signal processing modes. And, like the Denon and Onkyo models, this puppy is THX Ultra2 certified.

Model: RX-Z9 **Manufacturer:** Yamaha (www. yamaha.com/yec/) **Power:** 170 watts × 7 (plus 50 watts × 2) **Dimensions:** 17 1/8" (w) × 8 5/16" (h) × 18 7/16" (d) **Weight:** 66.1 lbs. **Price:** $4,499

Sunfire Ultimate Receiver II

I've long been impressed by Bob Carver's high-end audio offerings; Sunfire is Carver's latest company, and the Ultimate Receiver II shows what he can do in today's audio/video world. This is an A/V receiver made by die-hard audiophiles, so the sound's the thing—and the Ultimate Receiver does sound more musical than the similarly priced Denon/Onkyo/Yamaha models. Spec-wise, it's 200 watts per channel across seven channels, but the specs don't tell the real story. Try to arrange a demo for this puppy, and bring along your best CDs!

Model: Ultimate Receiver II **Manufacturer:** Sunfire (www.sunfire.com) **Power:** 200 watts × 7 **Dimensions:** 17" (w) × 5.75" (w) × 16.5" (d) **Weight:** 32 lbs. **Price:** $4,995

B&K AVR507 S2

Audiophiles know that B&K makes some of the best audio separates available; the AVR507 essentially combines B&K's most popular amplifier and pre-amp/processor into a single unit. As with the Sunfire, the sound's the thing, and I'll put the AVR507 up against any high-end receiver or similarly priced separate components out there. It's a beautiful-sounding receiver that just happens to do the audio/video thing. (Plus, the remote control is a custom version of the Home Theater Master 700, which is my favorite universal remote.)

Model: AVR507 S2 **Manufacturer:** B&K (www.bkcomp.com) **Power:** 150 watts × 7 **Dimensions:** 17" (w) × 7 1/2" (h) × 16 3/8" (d) **Weight:** 55 lbs. **Price:** $3,299.99

SPEAKERS

AV123 Rocket Onix System

When music is as important as movies, you need to move beyond the satellites-and-sub systems into full-range speakers. Yeah, they take up more space and your spouse might not like the way they look, but your ears will notice and appreciate the sonic difference. While you can spend some really big bucks on audiophile-quality speakers, the secret is to deal with a company that bypasses the traditional retail channel—and passes the distribution savings on to you. All of this is by way of introduction to AV123, a little company that designs high-end speakers, has them built to spec in China (although you wouldn't know that by their craftsmanship), and then sells them exclusively via their website.

These are, to put it mildly, *impressive* speakers, in terms of both sound and appearance. You might know of some speakers that sound impressive on the low end, or deliver good highs, but what you're actually hearing is the speaker coloring the music—which is something these speakers do not do. You get crystal clear sound, clearer than anything you're used to, but without any artificial coloration. When you listen to these speakers, you hear the music—not the speaker. It's something you have to hear to believe.

As for looks, photos don't do these puppies justice. The Rocket Onix line is constructed from South American Rosewood, and they're beautiful. Yeah, they're big (although bookshelf models are available), but these are speakers you want to show off. The wood grain is spectacular, and the tops and bottoms are piano black lacquer. Reinforcing the product's quality, AV123 ships out each speaker double-boxed and wrapped in a protective cloth bag; you even get a pair of cloth gloves to handle them with!

The system I've put together as my Leo's Choice is perfect for both music and movies. For front left and right we have the RS85s, four feet tall with six front-firing drivers and two rear-firing ports. The RSC200 center speaker (affectionately dubbed "Bigfoot"), is admittedly huge, but houses four front-firing drivers and one rear-firing port. The RSS300 surround speakers are a tad smaller, but still use four front-firing drivers in an adaptive-dipole design. Low bass comes from the UFW10 subwoofer, which has a 10" alloy cone woofer powered by a 500 watt (!) amplifier. Put them all together, and you have a $3,796 speaker system fit for the ultimate home theater—and for audiophiles everywhere. (Ask for a quote on which-ever speaker package you're interested in.)

Manufacturer: AV123 (www.av123.com) **Front left/right:** RS850 (2), 45.5" (h) × 15.6" (d) × 11.8" (w), 100 lbs., $1,999/pair **Center:** RSC200 (1), 12" (h) × 10.5" (d) × 25" (w), 46 lbs. $599 **Surround left/right:** RSS300 (2), 15.5" (h) × 6.5" (d) × 16.5" (w), 22 lbs., $599/pair **Subwoofer:** UFW10, 13" (h) × 13" (d) × 13" (w), 52 lbs., $599

Klipsch THX Ultra2 System

Klipsch is a company that makes speakers across the entire consumer and professional range. This THX Ultra2 system is at the top of their consumer line, even though it uses the same technology as the company's commercial theater systems. The KS-525-THX speakers employ a pair of 5.25" woofers and dual 5" square horn tweeter in what Klipsch calls a Wide Dispersion Surround Technology Array, for a fully immersed surround sound experience. Put it all together, and you have one fine-sounding $5,775 system.

Manufacturer: Klipsch (www.klipsch.com)
Front/center/surround: KS-525-THX (5), 20 lbs., $625 (each) **Subwoofer:** KW-120-THX, 80 lbs., $1,250
Subwoofer amplifier: KA-1000-THX, 500 watts, 27 lbs., $1,400

Polk Audio LSi25 System

What's interesting about the LSi25 floorstanding speaker is that it has its own built-in 10" powered subwoofer. This means you can save a few bucks by foregoing a separate sub—and avoid the hassle of placing that little speaker box somewhere out of the way. You'll supplement the LSi25s (front left and right) with a matching LSiC center speaker and two LSiFX surrounds. Package price is $4,849.85.

Manufacturer: Polk Audio (www.polkaudio.com)
Left/right: LSi25 (2), $2,999.95 (pair) **Center:** LSiC (1), $699.95 **Surround:** LSiFX (2), $1,149.95 (pair)

Definitive Technology Mythos System

For speakers as thin as your display, consider Definitive Technology's Mythos system. These are stylish speakers that you can either hang on the wall or sit on the floor or a tabletop. I recommend using the Mythos Two speakers for left and right front and surround, the Mythos Three as an under-the-screen center speaker, and the equally small (but not quite as flat) SuperCube 1 for the subwoofer. Total package price is $3,694.

Manufacturer: Definitive Technology (www. definitivetech.com) **Front/surround:** Mythos Two, $499 (each) **Center:** Mythos Three, $499 **Subwoofer:** SuperCube 1 (1), 1500 watts, $1,199

Mirage OMNISAT Micro System

If you want a *really* small speaker system that still delivers audiophile-quality sound, check out the Mirage OMNISAT Micro system. These tiny satellites fit in a 6" square space, weigh less than 3 lbs. each, and have 360° sound dispersion. Use the OMNISAT Micros for your front and surround channels and add an OMNI S8 subwoofer for the low bass. It's much better sound than you'll get from similar-looking systems aimed at the mass market, and at $1,250 for the package, it won't break the bank, either.

Manufacturer: Mirage (www.miragespeakers.com)
Front/center/surround: OMNISAT Micro (5), 2.35 lbs., $180 (each) **Subwoofer:** OMNI S8, 100 watts, $350

DVD PLAYERS

Denon DVD-5910

Leo's Pick

A $3,500 DVD player? *A $3,500 DVD player?* What on Earth could make a DVD player worth $3,500, when you can pick up fully acceptable models at your local Wal-Mart for less than $100?

Well, folks, here we enter into the world of the true videophile, where nothing but the absolute best will do. And this DVD player, pricey as it is, is the absolute best. It's all about performance, construction, and quality—albeit in quite subtle gradations.

Construction and quality first. Pick up the typical sub-$100 DVD player, and then try to heft this puppy. The DVD-5910 is not only physically bigger than a cheapie player, it's also noticeably heavier. (Forty-two pounds, if you're counting.) Put another way, the DVD-5910 feels like a higher-quality unit. And, believe it or not, weight is a reliable determinant of quality in the world of audio/video components; the better stuff almost always weighs more. It has to do with the quality of the parts used, and the quality of the construction. Trust me on this one.

Aside from sheer heft, the DVD-5910 packs a lot more of the latest technology inside the box than what you're probably used to. First of all, the player employs a Dual Discrete Video Circuit that uses separate and discrete video paths (for lower-noise signals). There's also a digital scaler with 10-bit processing, dual 14-bit, 216MHz video digital-to-analog converters (DACs), and 24-bit, 192kHz audio DACs. The drive mechanism uses vibration-resistant chassis construction to suppress outside vibrations and signal interference—which contributes to the unit's heft. Outputs include optical and coaxial digital audio, component video, DVI, and HDMI.

Even better, the DVD-5910 upconverts normal DVD video to high-definition video; you have your choice of 480p, 720p, and 1080i outputs. While DVD video isn't truly high-definition, upconverting to 720p or 1080i makes a noticeable difference in picture quality when played on an HDTV set.

Oh, one last thing. The DVD-5910 isn't just a DVD player. It also plays audio CDs, of course, as well as discs encoded in either the SACD or DVD-Audio formats. This makes the DVD-5910 a true universal player, and one with performance that's second-to-none.

Model: DVD-5910 **Manufacturer:** Denon (www.usa.denon.com) **Dimensions:** 17.1" (w) × 6.1" (h) × 17.1" (d) **Weight:** 42 lbs. **Price:** $3,500

Denon DVD-2910

If you want a better-than-average DVD player but think that spending $3,500 is just a little too extravagant, consider the DVD-5910's little brother, Denon's DVD-2910. This player offers many of the same features as its high-end sibling, but at less than a quarter of the price. So you get 720p/1080i upconversion, SACD and DVD-Audio playback, and a host of custom audio and video adjustments, as well as good solid (i.e., not plasticky) construction, at a price that won't break the bank too much. It's my recommended compromise between quality and price in this category.

Model: DVD-2910 **Manufacturer:** Denon (www.usa.denon.com) **Dimensions:** 17.1" × 4" × 12.5" **Weight:** 10.36 lbs. **Price:** $739

Sony DVP-CX985V Megachanger

If you have a fairly large movie collection, considering storing all your discs in a DVD jukebox, like Sony's DVD-CX985V. This megachanger will hold 400 DVD or CD discs; the onscreen display lets you quickly and relatively easily find and play the disc you want. And, of course, it offers progressive scan playback, as well as playback of SACD discs.

Model: DVP-CX985V **Manufacturer:** Sony (www.sonystyle.com.com) **Dimensions:** 17" (w) × 7.4" (h) × 21.1" (d) **Weight:** 19.2 lbs. **Price:** $399.95

Toshiba SD-3960

If you just want a basic no-frills DVD player, you can't go wrong with the Toshiba SD-3960. It offers a fair number of features, including progressive scan playback, component video output, playback of MP3 and WMA discs, and a built-in JPEG viewer. And, best of all, it doesn't weigh 42 pounds—or cost $3,500.

Model: SD-3960 **Manufacturer:** Toshiba (www.toshiba.com) **Dimensions:** 19 1/4" (w) × 2" (h) × 8" (d) **Weight:** 5 lbs. **Price:** $69.99

Panasonic PV-D4745

Now here's an interesting twist. Panasonic's PV-D4745 is a DVD player and a VHS tape player, all in one unit. The DVD player half offers progressive scan output; the tape player half is a 4-head VHS HI-Fi Stereo machine. Put together, this single unit is lower priced (and takes up less room on the shelf) than buying two separate units.

Model: PV-D4745 **Manufacturer:** Panasonic (www.panasonic.com) **Dimensions:** 16.9" (w) × 3.7" (h) × 10" (d) **Weight:** 8.2 lbs. **Price:** $119.95

VIDEO RECORDERS

Panasonic DMR-E500HS DVD Recorder/DVR

Leo's Pick

When you're looking at a hard disk recorder, it's all about disk size. The larger the hard disk, the more programming you can record and store. The last thing you want is a wimpy 40GB disk that can only store a handful of programs; that's been one of the drawbacks of TiVo's units, of late.

Well, take a look at the big hog of hard disk recorders. Panasonic's DMR-E500HS has a huge 400GB hard drive, big enough to hold more than 700 hours of programming (in EP-quality mode). It's hard to imagine filling up this puppy.

But the big hard disk isn't the only thing to like about this unit. The DMR-E500HS does double duty as both a hard disk recorder and a DVD recorder. This means you can record television programming to the hard disk, and then burn DVDs of those programs you want to archive. Or you can record directly to DVD, and use the hard disk as overflow if the program is longer than the DVD can hold. Recording from hard disk to DVD is made easier thanks to an onscreen editor, which lets you slice out commercials and insert chapter stops, titles, and menus. And it's all operable from the remote control unit.

Recording television programs is made easy thanks to the TV Guide electronic program guide. While the TV Guide EPG isn't quite as versatile as TiVo's EPG, it's free; there's no monthly subscription fees. Take that, TiVo!

And here's something else. The DMR-E500HS has an Ethernet network connection on the back. Why? So you can connect multiple units together over your home network, and serve up recorded video to different units around your home. Record a show on the main unit in your living room and then watch it later on a different unit in your bedroom. Neat!

There's even a memory card slot, so you can use the DMR-E500HS to view your digital photos. It accepts CompactFlash, MMC, SMC, and SD cards, which makes it a multiple media machine, in the best sense of the phrase.

Model: DMR-E500HS **Manufacturer:** Panasonic (www.panasonic.com) **Hard disk capacity:** 400GB
Dimensions: 16.9" (w) × 3.1" (h) × 11.9" (d) **Weight:** 11 lbs. **Price:** $999

Humax DRT800 DVD Recorder/TiVo DVR

If you want a combo DVD/hard disk recorder that uses proven TiVo technology (and the TiVo electronic program guide), take a look at the Humax DRT800. This unit has an 80GB hard drive, uses TiVo Series2 recording technology, and adds an easy-to-use DVD recorder. You can record programming to the hard disk, and then burn programs to DVD-R/-RW discs. You can even connect a digital camcorder (via FireWire) to save and burn your own home movies.

Model: DRT800 **Manufacturer:** Humax (www.humaxusa.com) **Hard disk capacity:** 80GB **Dimensions:** 16.5" (w) × 3" (h) × 12.8" (d) **Weight:** 9 lbs. **Price:** $499.99

LiteON LVW-5005 DVD Recorder

If all you want is a DVD recorder without all that hard disk stuff, check out the LiteON LVW-5005. LiteON maybe isn't as well known as Panasonic or Sony, but they make good stuff at affordable prices. The LVW-5005 can burn in a variety of formats, including DVD+R, DVD-R, DVD+RW, and DVD-RW— as well as CD-R, CD-RW, and VideoCD. It even has a built-in TV tuner, so you can record TV programming direct to DVD.

Model: LVW-5005 **Manufacturer:** LiteON (www.liteonamericas.com) **Dimensions:** 16.5" (w) × 2.7" (h) × 10.6" (d) **Weight:** 6.2 lbs. **Price:** $300

Sony DHG-HDD550 High Definition DVR

Okay, here's one to check out. The DHG-HDD550 is Sony's entry into the hard disk recorder market, and it's a good one. What's unique about the DHG-HDD550 is its ability to record HDTV programming, as well as its huge 500GB hard disk. (It can hold 60 hours of high-def video, or up to 400 hours of standard definition programs.) It uses the TV Guide electronic program guide, and has both component video and HDMI outputs for your high-definition television.

Model: DHG-HDD550 **Manufacturer:** Sony (www.sonystyle.com) **Hard disk capacity:** 500GB **Dimensions:** 16.94" (w) × 3.26" (h) × 14.05" (d) **Weight:** 12.57 lbs. **Price:** $999.99

TiVo Series 2 DVR

TiVo remains the name brand in hard disk recorders, primarily due to its powerful yet easy-to-use electronic program guide. (Which you pay for, in the form of a monthly fee.) TiVo offers three different Series2 recorders, in capacities ranging from 40 to 140GB. If you want to go the tried and true route (and I am a big TiVo fan), these are the DVRs to consider.

Model: TiVo Series 2 **Manufacturer:** TiVo (www.tivo.com) **Hard disk capacity:** 40GB, 80GB, 140GB **Dimensions:** 15" (w) × 3" (h) × 11.5" (d) **Price:** $199.99 (40GB), $299.99 (80GB), $249.99 (140GB)

MEDIA CENTER PCS

Niveus Media Center Denali Edition

Leo's Pick

Sooner or later, everyone will have a PC as part of their home theater system. What you want from a home theater PC is something that looks like a traditional audio/video component, something that sounds like a traditional audio/video component (i.e., no fan noise), and something that offers enough storage capacity and features to function as a combination DVD/CD player, digital video recorder, and digital audio jukebox. In other words, you want something like the Denali Edition Media Center PC from Niveus Media.

This is one honkin' big black box. The Denali Edition looks and feels like a high-end power amplifier, with its austere black metal faceplate; the unit stands an impressive 8.25" high, while its 17.5" width matches all your other system components. Operation is absolutely silent, due to the total absence of cooling fans. Instead, the entire case acts as a giant heat sink to disperse the normal heat build up. The only noise comes when the CD/DVD drive rotates, and that's not much at all.

In terms of performance, the Denali Edition delivers everything you'd expect from a high-end PC. It runs a 3.2GHz Pentium 4 processor with Hyper-Threading Technology, and comes with 1GB memory standard. The base unit comes with two 250GB hard drives; you can upgrade the configuration to include two 400GB drives, for a total of 800GB of hard disk storage. Video is courtesy an NVIDIA GF6600GT card; audio is Intel's High Definition 7.1-channel surround sound audio chip.

Speaking of video, the Denali Edition comes with three (!) separate television tuners. You get two NTSC (standard definition) tuners, and one ATSC (high-definition) tuner. Yes, that means you can record up to three programs simultaneously—or watch one and record two. Video output is via component video or DVI, while audio output is via analog, optical digital, or coaxial digital.

Naturally, the Denali Edition comes loaded with Windows XP Media Center Edition, and it works pretty good. You operate things via the included Media Center remote control, or with the Gyration wireless mouse and keyboard. I like the wireless keyboard; I've never gotten the hang of the "air mouse," but that's probably just me.

Bottom line, the Denali Edition is the biggest, most capable Media Center PC available today, and it's totally silent—if you have five grand to spare (yikes!). If your budget tends slightly less stratospheric, consider the Denali's Rainier Edition sibling, which offers similar silent operation in a smaller case, with fewer tuners, and with only a single hard disk. It'll only set you back three grand.

Model: Denali Edition HDTV **Manufacturer:** Niveus Media (www.niveusmedia.com) **Processor:** 3.2GHz Pentium 4 with Hyper-Threading Technology **Memory:** 1GB **Hard disk:** 500GB (250GB × 2) **TV tuners:** 2 NTSC, 1 ATSC (HDTV) **Dimensions:** 17.25" (w) × 8.25" (h) × 15" (w) **Weight:** 60 lbs. **Price:** $4,799

HP z552 Digital Entertainment Center

If spending five grand for the Niveus Media Center PC isn't quite your cup of tea, consider HP's z552 instead. At just fifteen hundred bucks, I think this could become the hit Media Center PC of the season; you get a lot of bang for what comes close to being mass market bucks. I'm talking a 200GB hard disk, dual NTSC TV tuners, Intel High Definition surround sound audio, DVD/CD burner, media card reader, and built-in WiFi and Ethernet networking. This puppy looks like a standard audio/video component, and it can replace your CD player, DVD player, and DVR device, no problem.

Model: z552 **Manufacturer:** HP (www.hp.com) **Processor:** Pentium 4 540J with Hyper-Threading Technology **Memory:** 512MB **Hard disk:** 200GB **TV tuners:** 2 NTSC **Dimensions:** 17" (w) × 4.4" (h) × 16.6" (d) **Price:** $1,499.99

Alienware DHS 5

Alienware is another strong contender in the Media Center PC market. The DHS 5 is unique in that it's based on the AMD Athlon64 chip instead of an Intel P4 processor, but that shouldn't affect performance one iota. The default 80GB hard drive is a little wimpy, but you can configure the DHS 5 with up to 800GB hard disk storage, 4GB memory, and a second NTSC TV tuner. (It comes with one tuner standard.) Unique to the Alienware machine is Discover Console technology, which enables you to automatically play CD/DVD-based PC games as you would on a video game console, no preloading necessary.

Model: DHS 5 **Manufacturer:** Alienware (www.alienware.com) **Processor:** AMD Athlon64 3000+ **Memory:** 512MB **Hard Disk:** 80GB **TV tuners:** 1 NTSC **Dimensions:** 17" (w) × 5.9" (h) × 18" (d) **Price:** $1,739

Shuttle Media Center XPC P8100m

Another approach to the living room PC is in a small form-factor box, like this one by Shuttle. While it doesn't have the traditional audio/video component form factor, it is small enough to tuck out of the way in a corner of your equipment rack, or on the bottom shelf of your TV stand. Otherwise, this small package delivers big-box performance, with a single NTSC TV tuner and 200GB hard drive. You can customize it with a dual NTSC TV tuner card, up to 960GB hard disk storage, and up to 2GB memory.

Model: P8100m **Manufacturer:** Shuttle (www.shuttle.com) **Processor:** 3.4GHz Pentium 4 550 with Hyper-Threading Technology **Memory:** 512MB **Hard Disk:** 200GB **TV tuner:** 1 NTSC **Dimensions:** 8" (w) × 7.4" (h) × 11.9" (d) **Weight:** 13.3 lbs. **Price:** $1,549

Sony VAIO RA834G

This Sony Media Center PC would be a perfect choice for a living room PC, if only it wasn't in the traditional desktop mini-tower configuration. What I like about it is its silent operation, thanks to water-cooling technology, and its upgradability to 2 terrabytes of hard disk space. (It comes with a 400GB standard.) In other words, its quiet and powerful—even if it looks a little out of place with your other equipment.

Model: RA834G **Manufacturer:** Sony (www.sonystyle.com) **Microprocessor:** 3.6GHz Pentium 4 560J with Hyper-Threading Technology **Memory:** 1GB **Hard disk:** 400GB **TV tuner:** 1 NTSC **Dimensions:** 7.4" (w) × 15.6" (h) × 15.3" (d) **Weight:** 34.2 lbs. **Price:** $2,099.99

DIGITAL MEDIA SERVERS

Sonos Digital Music System

Leo's Pick

A digital media server is like a Media Center PC that doesn't have all that PC stuff in it. The functionality is essentially the same; you use the server to store and access digital audio files, and then to play those files over your home audio/video system—or, in some cases, to multiple systems in multiple rooms.

My favorite digital media server is an odd little bird from Sonos. It's odd in that it's more like a digital media hub (which I'll talk about in a few pages); it doesn't store any media files but instead streams audio files from your desktop PC. But then it feeds music to multiple rooms, just like a good little whole-house audio system. As I said, a tad unusual, but unusually effective.

The main box in the system is the Sonos ZonePlayer, which connects to your main stereo speakers. It contains a 50 watt per channel amplifier, and connects to your home network via Ethernet. The ZonePlayer is controlled by handheld controller that looks more than a little like an Apple iPod. The controller has a big color LCD display, and you work the thing with an iPod-like scroll wheel. The nice thing about the controller is that it functions much like a traditional onscreen display; the color display lets you view song info, playlists, and even album cover art. To my mind, this is the coolest part of the system.

Surprisingly, even though the remote is wireless, it doesn't use standard WiFi technology. Instead, the remote (and all remote ZonePlayers) use a kind of wireless mesh networking technology. This actually makes connection and setup a real breeze; configuration is pretty much as easy as turning the thing on, no interference or device recognition issues.

To set up a whole-house system, just set up additional ZonePlayers in additional rooms. The individual ZonePlayers talk to each other via the wireless mesh network, and you can control all zones from each remote. It's so easy it's actually a little startling; all technology should be this user-friendly. (And remember, a zone doesn't have to be a room; think of your back deck as a zone with its own ZonePlayer.)

Sonos sells a variety of different packages. You can buy the ZonePlayers and remotes separately, or spend $1,199 for a package with two ZonePlayers and one controller. They also offer matching speakers, in case you don't have any of your own.

Manufacturer: Sonos (www.sonos.com) **Dimensions (ZonePlayer):** 10.2" (w) × 4.4" (h) × 8.2" (d) **Dimensions (Controller):** 6.5" (w) × 3.8" (h) × 0.95" (d) **Price:** $499 (ZonePlayer), $399 (Controller)

Escient Fireball DVDM-300 DVD and Music Manager

This is *the* system of choice for professional home theater installers, unusual in that it's based around both physical and digital media. FireBall manages, catalogs, and controls digital audio files, CDs, DVDs, Internet radio, you name it. It comes with its own 300GB hard drive for digital audio storage (in MP3 or FLAC lossless format), and you can connect up to three 400-disc CD/DVD changers. Connect optional MP-150 digital music players to set up a whole-house audio system.

Model: Fireball DVDM-300 **Manufacturer:** Escient (www.escient.com) **Dimensions:** 17 3/8" (w) × 4 5/8" (h) × 11 7/8" (d) **Weight:** 14 lbs. **Price:** $4,999

Yamaha MCX-1000 MusicCAST Digital Audio Server

Yamaha's MusicCAST is a media hub that functions as an audiophile-quality audio component. The MCX-1000 digital audio server serves as the base unit and has a built-in 80GB hard drive that can store up to 1,000 CDs (in MP3 format). Serve music to other rooms with one or more optional MCX-A10 client systems ($600 each), which connect wirelessly. There's a front panel display for song information; the obligatory wireless remote; and a full complement of analog, digital optical, and digital coaxial outputs.

Model: MCX-1000 **Manufacturer:** Yamaha (www.yamaha.com/ycc/) **Hard drive capacity:** 80GB **Dimensions:** 17 1/8" (w) × 4 3/4" (h) × 15 5/8" (d) **Weight:** 24.2 lbs. **Price:** $2,200

Denon NS-S100 Network Multimedia Server

Denon's NS-S100 is another digital media server designed for the professional installation market. It's a Linux-based device that functions as a high-end audio/video receiver, PVR, and digital audio manager; it can store and serve television programming, digital music, digital photos, and so on. It comes with two 120GB hard drives, one fixed and one a removable "mirror" for backup and archiving. Whole-house operation is possible via an Ethernet connection to your home network, using individual NS-C200 client units.

Model: NS-S100 **Manufacturer:** Denon (www.usa.denon.com) **Hard drive capacity:** 240GB (120GB × 2) **Price:** ~$4,000

DVICO TViX M3000 Digital Movie Jukebox

This is a promising device for those of you who want to store and stream digital movies. The TViX unit lets you rip CDs and DVD to the unit's hard drive, then play back movies and music through your home theater system. You can order the unit with anywhere from 120GB to 300GB of hard disk storage; go with the largest capacity, as DVDs are disk hogs. Video output is via your choice of composite video, S-Video, or component video; audio out is optical digital or coaxial digital.

Model: M3000U **Manufacturer:** DVICO (www.tvixusa.com) **Dimensions:** 4.8" × 6.8" × 2.7" **Weight:** 42.3 oz. **Price:** $274.99 (120GB), $289.99 (160GB), $329.99 (200GB), $369.99 (250GB), $409.99 (300GB)

DIGITAL MEDIA HUBS AND EXTENDERS

Roku SoundBridge M2000 Network Music Player

Leo's Pick

You don't have to have a separate PC or digital media server in your living room to experience digital audio on your home theater system. Another approach is to use a digital media hub, which lets you stream audio files from your desktop PC through your audio/video receiver. All you have to do is hook the hub up to your home network and you're ready to go.

Case in point is Roku's SoundBridge, a cool-looking network music hub contained in a slim cylindrical aluminum tube. The M2000 is a full 17" wide, to fit with your other audio components, and has a large built-in display.

For such a small device, the SoundBridge unit does quite a lot. It supports MP3, WMA, AAC, WAV, AIFF, FLAC, and Ogg Vorbis audio files; it streams Internet radio; and it even has built-in support for Apple's iTunes. The M2000 connects to your PC via wired Ethernet or wireless WiFi connection, and features the standard complement of audio outputs—analog RCA, optical digital, and coaxial digital.

You control everything with the included wireless remote control; you can browse by song, album, artist, genre, or composer. Song and artist information is displayed on the big 512 × 32 pixel vacuum-fluorescent readout; it's a full 12" wide, so you won't have to squint. That's big enough to display up to four lines of text.

If you're into the whole-house audio thing, just put a SoundBridge unit in all your rooms. You can connect up to ten SoundBridge units to a single computer (just five if you're running iTunes,

sorry). Once connected, each individual unit can select different music to play. Pretty cool, and really easy to install and use.

Model: SoundBridge M2000 **Manufacturer:** Roku (www.rokulabs.com) **Dimensions:** 17" (w) × 2.75" (h) × 2.75" (d) **Weight:** 2.75 lbs. **Price:** $499.99

Apple AirPort Express

Here's something a lot of people don't know: You can use Apple's AirPort Express as a budget digital media hub. You don't get a display, which means you need to queue things up on your computer, but it's a quick and easy digital media solution—especially if you're an iTunes user. The AirPort Express works with both PCs and Macs, and connects to your PC via 802.11g WiFi wireless connection.

Model: AirPort Express **Manufacturer:** Apple (www.apple.com) **Dimensions:** 3.7" × 2.95" × 1.12" **Weight:** 6.7 oz. **Price:** $129

Onkyo NC-500 Network Audio Receiver

As the name implies, Onkyo's NC-500 is actually an audio receiver with networking capabilities. Connect the NC-500 to your home network (via Ethernet), and you can serve music from your PC to your living room—or to multiple rooms in your house. And, unlike traditional digital media hubs, this puppy's a full-fledged receiver, which means it has its own built-in amplifier (25 watts × 2 channels); hook up a pair of speakers, and you're ready to rock and roll.

Model: NC-500 **Manufacturer:** Onkyo (www.us.onkyo.com) **Dimensions:** 8 1/16" (w) × 3 9/16" (h) × 11" (d) **Weight:** 8.6 lbs. **Price:** $399

Slim Devices Squeezebox2 Wireless

Slim Devices' Squeezebox2 is unique in that it's a Linux-based network music hub. It's also capable of playing the widest variety of digital file formats: MP3, WMA, AAC, Ogg Vorbis, Apple Lossless, WMA Lossless, FLAC, WAV, and AIFF, as well as raw pass-through of uncompressed PCM audio. The Squeezebox2 is a low-profile unit with built-in display; it connects to your PC via wireless WiFi (802.11g) or wired Ethernet. You can synchronize multiple players for whole-house audio!

Model: Squeezebox2 Wireless **Manufacturer:** Slim Devices (www.slimdevices.com) **Dimensions:** 8.5" (w) × 1.9" (h) × 4.5" (d) **Price:** $299

Linksys WMCE54AG Media Center Extender

If you have a Media Center PC somewhere in your house (doesn't have to be in your living room; we could be talking about a desktop model here), you can serve audio and video to any room in your house with a Media Center Extender. This Linksys device is one such unit; it works via wired Ethernet or wireless 802.11a/g WiFi, and transmits music, videos, and photographs from your main Media Center PC. It comes with its own remote control, of course; operation is facilitated by the easy-to-use onscreen display.

Model: WMCE54AG **Manufacturer:** Linksys (www.linksys.com) **Dimensions:** 17" (w) × 2" (h) × 12.25" (d) **Weight:** 5.7 lbs. **Price:** $299.99

UNIVERSAL REMOTE CONTROLS

Philips iPronto

Leo's Pick

The more components you have in your home theater system, the more remote controls you accumulate. And it's not just remote clutter that's a problem; for many operations you have to turn on the TV, switch to a specific input, turn on your A/V receiver, switch to a specific input *there*, then turn on the playback device and press play. This type of multi-stage operation typically involves three (or more) individual remotes, which is a real pain in the palm.

A better solution is to use a universal remote that can operate multiple devices and be programmed for multiple-step operations. That's what we'll look at in this section, starting with this remote that looks (and acts) more like a tablet PC—the Philips iPronto.

No question about it, the iPronto is the hands-down winner for the most sophisticated consumer-grade remote control today (not counting big whole-house models sold by home theater installers, of course). This funky unit combines a color touch screen remote control, a wireless Internet browser, and an electronic program guide into a single device. A big device, mind you, but a single device nonetheless.

The biggest piece of real estate is occupied by the 6.4" color VGA (640 × 480) touch screen display, which has a fully customizable user interface. Arranged around the perimeter of the display are eight direct-access buttons you can use to navigate screen layouts, as well as five programmable control buttons for volume up/down, channel up/down, and mute.

Because the display is fully customizable, you can design your own interfaces. You do this via the iProntoEdit PC editing software, which lets you create your own pages of controls for each of the devices in your system. You can also add channel logos and other multimedia content you download from the Internet, which is uber-cool.

But the iPronto is more than a simple remote—it's also your own guide to what's playing. It uses WiFi wireless technology (connected to any always-on broadband Internet connection) to acquire TV programming information for its built-in electronic program guide. That same WiFi connection also lets you use the iPronto as a tablet web browser to surf the Internet and send and receive email. Also cool is the fact that the iPronto includes built-in stereo speakers, a microphone, and a headphone jack. It's almost like a mini-media player.

Naturally, the iPronto replaces all the other remotes in your house. It learns infrared codes from other remotes and has an MMC slot and a USB port for future upgrades. It's a power hog, as you might expect; good thing it uses a rechargeable lithium-ion battery and comes with its own external charger unit. But man oh man, will the neighbors be impressed when they see this puppy sitting on your living room coffee table!

Model: TSi6400 **Manufacturer:** Philips (www.pronto.philips.com) **Dimensions:** 9.4" × 7" × 0.9" **Weight:** 31.4 oz. **Price:** $1,699

Philips ProntoPro NG

Okay, the iPronto is probably overkill for most folks, but you gotta like the idea of a customizable color touch screen remote—which is what you get, for half the iPronto's price, from Philips's ProntoPro NG. This is a sleek unit with a high-resolution 3.8" color LCD touch screen display. Like the iPronto, you use Philips' proprietary software to create your own screen layouts on your PC and then download them to the ProntoPro NG. And, so you don't have to worry about replacing batteries all the time, it comes with its own docking cradle/charger. Cool!

Model: TSU7000 **Manufacturer:** Philips (www. pronto.philips.com) **Dimensions:** 6.1" × 3.6" × 1.1" **Price:** $999.99

Philips RC9800i WiFi Touch Screen Controller

This Philips remote isn't part of the Pronto line; in fact, it takes a different approach to the issue of control. First, its activity based rather than component based, so it uses a lot of multiple-device macros. Second, it doesn't just control your audio/video equipment, it can also control a variety of Universal Plug and Play devices on your PC system. Third, it works via WiFi in addition to traditional infrared. And fourth, because of the WiFi connection, it displays its own electronic program guide. In other words, it's like a blend of the iPronto and the ProntoPro, but in a traditional remote form factor, sort of.

Model: RC9800i **Manufacturer:** Philips (www. homecontrol.philips.com) **Dimensions:** 5.86" × 3.97" × 0.94" **Price:** $499

Home Theater Master MX-700

As popular as the Pronto line is, some people (like me!) prefer hard buttons to touch screen controls. That's why I'm such a big fan of the Home Theater Master MX-700. It has a big LCD screen, but it's just for display, not for touch-screen control; instead, operation is via traditional push buttons. The MX-700 can control up to 20 components, and each component can have up to four pages of controls. Programming is easy enough with the Windows-based software; the MX-700 can learn commands from other remotes, and be programmed for multiple-step, multiple-device macros. Best of all, the unit's backlit GemStone buttons are tougher and more responsive than traditional rubber buttons—and much, much better IMHO than an unresponsive touch screen.

Model: MX-700 **Manufacturer:** Home Theater Master (www.hometheatermaster.com) **Dimensions:** 9" × 3" × 1.3" **Weight:** 8 oz. **Price:** $499

Logitech Harmony 880

The Harmony 880 is unique in two ways. First, you program it via a series of forms on Harmony's website; just fill in the blanks with the equipment you have, and all the appropriate codes are downloaded via USB. Second, it's activity-based rather than equipment-based; press the Watch DVD button and the remote turns on your TV, switches to the proper video input, turns on your DVD player, and starts playback. You also get a nice color screen and rechargeable battery and docking station—and it costs about half the price of other high-end programmable remotes.

Model: Harmony 880 **Manufacturer:** Logitech (www.logitech.com) **Dimensions:** 8.1" × 2.3" × 1.3" **Price:** $249.99

MORE COOL HOME THEATER GADGETS

JVC JX-S777 Audio/Video Switcher

You can buy cheaper audio/video switchers, but they won't switch everything this baby does. This is the first A/V switcher with full digital video, component video, and digital audio connections. Here's what you get. Inputs: eight composite/S-Video/audio, two component video, and two digital optical audio. Outputs: five composite/S-Video/audio, two component video, one digital optical audio. Plus, you get three FireWire DV input/output connections. You control them all via front-panel buttons or with the wireless remote control.

Model: JX-S777 Manufacturer: JVC (www.jvc.com) Dimensions: 17 3/16" (w) × 4 1/8" (h) Weight: 8.4 lbs. Price: $799.95

Polk Audio XRt12 XM Component Tuner

If you're an XM satellite radio junkie, you don't want your listening to stop when you get out of your car. There's tons of good programming on XM, and now you can listen to it on your home audio system, thanks to Polk's XRt12 XM tuner. It sits in your equipment rack like any other audio component and connects to your audio receiver. You do have to run a wire to a remote satellite antenna (either outside or near a window), but from then on it's like using any other audio component. It's XM radio in your living room, at the highest possible quality.

Model: XRt12 Manufacturer: Polk Audio (www.polkaudio.com) Dimensions: 17" (w) × 2.3" (h) × 10.5" (d) Weight: 5 lbs. Price: $299.95

Monster Reference PowerCenter HTS3500 MKII

If you've spent a few grand or more on a quality audio/video system, you don't want to plug your stuff straight into a standard wall outlet. Monster's PowerCenter is a line conditioner that serves to filter out line noise as well as isolate noise between components. The HTS3500 (other models are available) filters 10 AC outlets, 3 coaxial connections, and 1 phone line connection. It's sized to look like a standard audio component, and fit comfortably in your equipment rack.

Model: HTS3500 MKII Manufacturer: Monster Cable (www.monstercable.com) Dimensions: 17 1/8" (w) × 3 7/8" (h) × 12" (d) Weight: 4.9 lbs. Price: $399.95

Couch Potato Tormentor

Here's a gadget for the spouse of the ultimate home theater enthusiast. The Couch Potato Tormentor is the anti-remote, a small device that interferes with your television viewing. It randomly changes the channel your spouse is watching, which leads to all manner of hilarity (and possible spousal conflict). Use at your own risk!

Model: Couch Potato Tormentor Manufacturer: For Play Electronics (www.couchpotatotormentor.com) Price: $14.95

Surround Sound Tube Headphones

Surround sound is great, but what do you do if your spouse or neighbors want you to turn down the sound? Well, with the Surround Sound Tube Headphones you can turn off the speakers and get full surround sound from headphone listening. Five headphone drivers surround your head in a halo-like tube of sound, replicating the five separate channels in a Dolby Digital or DTS soundtrack. The Tube headphones are currently shipping in Europe only; check with the manufacturer for U.S. availability.

Model: THS 2004-5 **Manufacturer:** TubeSurround Corporation (www.tubesurround.com) **Price:** ~$190

Sony MDR-DS8000 Surround Sound Headphones

Sony's MDR-DS8000 replicates a six-channel surround sound experience in a single set of wireless headphones. Not only do you get surround sound without the speakers, you eliminate the cord from the phones to your receiver. Sony uses infrared technology so you can sit up to 33 feet away from the receiver. There's also a Gyro head-tracking system that rotates the soundwave when you rotate your head—a really neat and practical effect.

Model: MDR-DS8000 **Manufacturer:** Sony (www.sonystyle.com) **Price:** $799.99

Premiere MovieLounger Bijou Theater Seating

Let's face it, here's what you really want—movie theater seating for your home theater system. Premiere makes a full line of MovieLounger seating; the Bijou series is a Euro-deco style chair, ideal for a contemporary home theater system. The chair's a wall-hugger recliner, natch, with cup holders in each arm. It's available in loveseat or couch configuration; contact the manufacturer for more details.

Model: Bijou **Manufacturer:** Premiere (www.premierehts.com) **Price:** $2,000+

D-Box Quest Motion Simulator Chair

Here's another approach to home theater seating—one that moves. D-Box's Quest is a motion simulator chair, which means that it moves back and forth to simulate the onscreen action. Imagine watching a car chase, and having your chair throw you right and left as the cars corner down the streets. For best effect, the Quest chair works with special motion-coded movies; there are currently 400 major titles available. Contact the manufacturer for specific seating configurations.

Model: Quest **Manufacturer:** D-Box (www.d-box.com) **Price:** $5,000+

10

The Ultimate Gadget Geek

HOW TO BECOME THE ULTIMATE GADGET GEEK

I've done a lot of talking (actually, a lot of writing) throughout this book on how to become the ultimate game player or the ultimate road warrior or the ultimate home theater enthusiast, and so on. But when it comes right down to it, all these things are just different types of gadgets, and what all this is really about is becoming the ultimate gadget geek, period. The category doesn't matter; if you want to become the ultimate gadget geek, all gadgets are good and all gadgets are desirable.

So we come to the final category in this book, which is about those various gadgets that we haven't covered yet—those gadgets that don't fall into any particular category. That doesn't make these gadgets any less useful (or any more useful, for that matter), it just means we haven't covered them yet, that's all.

What kinds of gadgets are we talking about? It's a wide and varied bunch, let me tell you. Here's just a sampling:

- **High-tech clothing**, which doesn't necessarily mean battery-powered beanies. (Although those are fun, too!) Most high-tech clothing today is actually clothing designed to carry other high-tech gadgets, with lots of pockets and pouches and wiring channels. Some high-tech clothing comes pre-wired—or, more accurately, pre-wireless, with built-in (or sewn-in) Bluetooth access. Other high-tech clothing melds state-of-the-art technology with traditional functionality, such as those ubiquitous high-tech watches. In any case, technology is nosing its way into the clothing industry, and there's more interesting stuff on the way.

- **Desktop radios**, which don't necessarily sound all that high-tech, though you'd be surprised. Here we're looking at some very high-performance table radios, including several models with built-in satellite radio tuners. We're also seeing the tip of the HD Radio iceberg. (HD Radio, for those of you not yet keeping track, is the new digital format that promises much higher quality sound for traditional AM and FM stations.)

- **Home gadgets**, which is a fairly broad category, I grant you. Some of these gadgets are kitchen gadgets, a subcategory I've always had a fondness for. I'm actually a pushover for those stylish-if-somewhat-impractical Scandinavian can openers and German blenders, you know, the ones that look like something other than what they really are and that you can never quite figure out how to use. (I once had a can opener that was so stylish that I never figured out which end was up!) So there's a little of that here, as well as a few gadgets that wouldn't look out of place in your living room, such as high-tech weather stations and digital picture frames. Bottom line, there's no room in the house safe from the high-tech gadget invasion!

- **Other cool gadgets**, which is my catch-all category for stuff that just didn't fit anyplace else. This is a real dog's dinner, as my English friends like to say, with everything from videophones and GPS dog finders to robotic floor cleaners and synthesized saxophones. (The term *dog's dinner*, by the way, refers to the mash-up of leftovers that you used to feed to your dog before you got suckered into those expensive designer dog foods created specially for different stages of your dog's development; I don't know about your dog, but mine likes leftovers just as well.)

What is it about these gizmos that make them so attractive to us gadget geeks? It's a combination of things, really. First off is the technology involved. The best gadgets do something beyond the ordinary, push the envelope beyond the traditional, and are just plain new in what they do. That's why, back in the early 1960s, the coolest gadget was the AM transistor radio. It seems old hat now, but that little portable gizmo was the height of high-tech at the time. How something that small—and without a power cord!—could actually receive radio signals was mind-boggling. That little Japanese radio was the Apple iPod of its day. The latest technology is always cool.

It also helps that the gizmo is attractively designed. Depending on the current trends, that might mean rounded corners, bright colors, and lots of shiny surfaces. (Of course, design tastes change; in the 1950s, cool design meant big faceplates and useless fins, go figure.) Apple seems to be driving consumer electronics design today; there are a lot of products that look suspiciously related to our old pal the iPod. But still, cool design makes for a cool gadget.

Finally, small is cool. The coolest cell phones and portable music players are the smallest ones. You don't want to be weighted down with a big clunky thing, no matter what kind of technology is inside. So when you're looking for the coolest gadget on the shelf, look for the smallest one.

Most of the gadgets in this section are readily available to the average consumer. Some gadgets are still in the prototype stage, however, which means they may or may not ever make it to market. Still other gadgets are available in Europe but haven't yet made it to the U.S.; there are also a few gadgets marketed to professionals that might not be available to us regular consumers. Remember to check the manufacturers' websites before you go harassing the pimply-faced kid at Best Buy. (Or just go ahead and harass the pimply-faced kid anyway; he probably deserves it.)

So now its onward and upward to some of the oddest and most fun gadgets in the entire book. Count yourself as the ultimate gadget geek if you already own three or more of these gizmos!

WEARABLE GADGETS

SCOTTeVEST Sport TEC Technology Enabled Clothing

Leo's Pick

If you're a true gadget geek, you carry around a bunch of different gadgets on your person—a cell phone, PDA, iPod, GPS unit, digital camera, and who knows what else. The problem is, where you tuck away all these gadgets—without bulging out your pockets or dragging down your belt?

The answer comes in the SCOTTeVEST line of technology enabled clothing. Company founder Scott Jordan has created a line of clothing specially designed to hold all manner of electronic devices, while still remaining sleek and stylish. It's quite an accomplishment.

Let's take a look at a few popular pieces of SCOTTeVEST clothing, starting with the Three.0 Cotton Jacket. On the outside, it looks like a typical waterproof jacket, nothing special. However, the jacket consists of an outer shell and a fleece inner coat that zips into it. Hidden within the outer jacket are a whopping 30 pockets, while the inner lining has 12 more pockets. While the shear number of pockets is impressive, it's how they work that really counts. Most of these pockets are special hanging pockets that attach to the body of the garment only at the opening; this enables the pocket's contents to hang freely within the interior space of the clothing, thus eliminating unsightly tucks and bulges. You can load yourself up with dozens of different devices, and it won't look like you're carrying.

In addition, many of these pockets are actually pockets in pockets, which let you change the size to accommodate different-sized devices. Nearly every pocket can be zippered closed, for added security. (You don't want your PDA falling out as you bounce jollily down the street now, do you?)

Similar design is the TEC Sport Jacket. To the casual observer, it looks like a classic blue blazer. Inside, however, you have dozens of hidden pockets and pockets in pockets. The TEC Sport Jacket also features what SCOTTeVEST calls a Personal Area Network, which is a series of holes and passages that link all the pockets to one another through the jacket's lining. This lets you string together power cords, earphones, antennas, and the like, without anyone seeing the wires.

All of these features can also be found in the SeV Hidden Cargo Pants. What looks like a standard pair of khakis hosts eleven layered pockets, which you fasten closed with small magnets. (No annoying Velcro here!) Like the other items, you can pack your pants full of all sorts of fun stuff, and no one will notice. It's like being a stealth nerd.

Model: Sport TEC **Manufacturer:** SCOTTeVEST (www.scottevest.com) **Price:** $299.99 (TEC Sport Jacket), $189.99 (Three.0 Cotton Jacket), $99.99 (SeV Hidden Cargo Pants)

Suunto N3i Smart Watch

Suunto's N3i looks like a normal wrist watch with a big LCD display. The display is for all the information you'll receive from Microsoft's MSN Direct service, which delivers news, weather, sports, and stock information, as well as instant messages from your online buddies. You also get an online calendar and appointment scheduler and Internet-accurate time—all of which requires you to subscribe to the MSN Direct service, which costs $9.99 per month. But then you'll be connected continuously—the ultimate wireless wired guy.

Model: N3i **Manufacturer:** Suunto
(www.suuntowatches.com) **Price:** $299.99

Venexx Perfume Watch

I can't help it; this gizmo reminds me of something the Joker would wear, although he'd probably fill it with laughing gas or acid or some other concoction that the Batman would find similarly sinister. For you and me, we get to fill this watch with perfume—yes, perfume. Turn the bezel downward and the sprayer appears; press the button to spray a burst of your favorite fragrance. Yeah, I have no idea why anyone would want to spray perfume from a wrist watch, but what do I know? It's a neat little gadget, in any case.

Model: Various **Manufacturer:** Venexx
(www.venexxusa.com) **Price:** $89.95

The HUB Snowboarding Jacket/MP3 Player

I like high-tech clothing, which is why I'm looking forward to production versions of this prototype snowboarding jacket. The HUB contains its own MP3 player, a microphone sewn into the collar (for voice recognition control), and a Bluetooth module. The jacket connects wirelessly to a fabric keyboard embedded into the sleeve of the jacket, and to speakers built into the matching helmet. It's everything the high-tech snowboarder needs! (Check with the manufacturer for U.S. availability.)

Model: The HUB **Manufacturer:** O'Neill
(www.oneilleurope.com) **Price:** ~$650

GloThong Illuminated Thong Underwear

Not all high-tech clothing has to be nerdly practical; high-tech can also be fun, as evidenced by this illuminated thong underwear. The GloThong is an electroluminescent thong with lightweight waterproof rechargeable battery. The glowing underwear holds a charge for about an hour and a half, and there's a detachable plug for recharging. It comes in lime green, turquoise, royal blue, and lipstick red—and in both female and male versions.

Manufacturer: GloThong (www.glothong.com)
Price: $69.96

DESKTOP RADIOS

Tivoli Model One

Leo's Pick

You don't always have room for a full-blown audio system, complete with mongo speakers; sometimes a desktop radio will have to do. Well, you can forget those twenty-buck cheapie models you find at Wal-Mart, and move instead to the Rolls Royce of desktop radios, the Tivoli Model One. This is one cool and classy gizmo, with great sound and great looks, great for both bedroom and office use.

The Tivoli Model One is the table radio that the radio pros use; it was designed by audio legend Henry Kloss. As you would expect from any Kloss-designed product, the Model One is constructed from the highest-quality components and built to exact quality requirements. It's also the height of simplicity, with just three knobs to its name. The big tuning knob is the most important one, of course. It's an analog tuning knob (none of this digital nonsense for the Tivoli folks) with geared-down 5:1 tuning. This means that tuning is incredibly sure and accurate. It even lights up (amber) when you've achieved proper tuning for a given station.

The Model One is an AM/FM radio, of course, with built-in AM and FM antennas. There's also an auxiliary input you can use to connect a CD player or similar device, a record output you can use to record your favorite programs, and a headphone jack for private listening.

Once you have a station tuned in, you can sit back and enjoy surprisingly rich sound. The Model One uses a 3" speaker, mated with a multi-stage frequency contouring circuit that adjusts the speaker's output over half-octave increments. The resulting sound is full and warm; the Model One's sound is much larger and deeper you'd expect from such a small device. (In fact, it's the sound more than anything that makes this the choice of the pros.)

That great sound comes out of an equally great-looking cabinet. The Model One is housed in a furniture-grade, handmade wood cabinet. (No cheap plastic here.) It's available in cherry, walnut, maple, black, and silver finishes.

Of course, the Model One's single speaker delivers only mono sound. If you want stereo sound, choose the Tivoli Model Two, which adds a separate matching speaker to the main unit, for $159.99. Or if you want to wake up to music, go with the Model Three, which takes a Model One and tacks on a cool-looking analog alarm clock, for $199.99.

Model: Model One **Manufacturer:** Tivoli Audio (www.tivoliaudio.com) **Dimensions:** 8 3/8" (w) × 4 1/2" (h) × 5 1/4" (d) **Weight:** 5.5 lbs. **Price:** $99.99

Tivoli Model Satellite

If you like the Tivoli Model One and you like satellite radio, check out the Tivoli Model Satellite. This is essentially a Model One AM/FM radio with added SIRIUS satellite tuner, which lets you listen to all that great SIRIUS programming in your bedroom or den. What more can I say? It's a perfect match!

Model: Model Satellite **Manufacturer:** Tivoli Audio (www.tivoliaudio.com) **Dimensions:** 8 3/8" (w) × 4 1/2" (h) × 5 1/4" (d) **Weight:** 6.5 lbs. **Price:** $299.99

Grundig Porsche Design P7131

If XM radio is more your style, check out this new desktop radio from Grundig and Porsche Design. It combines an AM/FM tuner, shortwave radio, and XM satellite radio tuner, all in a very stylish device. There's also two full-range speakers, a powered sub-woofer, and a digital clock radio with his-and-her dual alarms.

Model: P7131 **Manufacturer:** Grundig (www.grundigradio.com) **Dimensions:** 8.5" × 5" × 5.6" **Weight:** 6 lbs. **Price:** TBA

Polk Audio I-Sonic

Here's another XM radio for home use. Polk's I-Sonic receives XM satellite radio, standard analog AM/FM radio, and the new digital AM and FM HD Radio. It also has a built-in CD/DVD player, and an auxiliary port you can use to connect your iPod or similar device. Connect it to your TV to watch DVDS, or just settle back to listen to practically about any type of audio entertainment available.

Model: I-Sonic **Manufacturer:** Polk Audio (www.polkaudio.com) **Dimensions:** 14.5" × 9.75" × 4.75" **Price:** $599

Cambridge Soundworks CD 740

If you don't much care about satellite radio or high-definition AM/FM, then check out this great-sounding tabletop radio/CD player from Cambridge Soundworks. The room-filling sound comes from a large subwoofer hidden inside a small vented enclosure. The music comes from your choice of AM, FM, or CDs. You can control it all from the front panel, or from the included wireless remote control.

Model: CD 740 **Manufacturer:** Cambridge Soundworks (www.cambridgesoundworks.com) **Dimensions:** 4 15/16" (h) × 14" (w) × 9 7/8" (d) **Weight:** 12 lbs. **Price:** $349.99

HOME GADGETS

Eva Solo Magnetimer Kitchen Timer

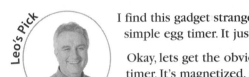

I find this gadget strangely appealing, even though it's nothing more than a simple egg timer. It just looks so cool—plus, it's magnetic!

Okay, lets get the obvious out of the way. The Magnetimer is a simple round timer. It's magnetized, so you can stick it to any metal surface. When it's time to time, just slap it to the stainless steel fronts of your fancy-schmancy high-end appliances, and you're ready to start the countdown.

The timer itself is made of stainless steel and silicone rubber, which provides a nice visual contrast. The rubber base also ensures that the Magnetimer won't scratch your fancy-scmancy stainless steel appliances, which is important.

All that said, there's really nothing fancy about this gizmo other than its looks and its stick-to-itiveness. Just twist the dial to set the timing interval, and it starts its countdown. It's charmingly old-school analog, so there aren't any buttons to push or switches to set. It's really just a big timer knob, not much bigger than the all the eggs you'll be boiling with it.

But it looks neat—and it's magnetic!

Model: Magnetimer **Manufacturer:** Eva Solo (www.evasolo.com/products-minutur.html) **Price:** $35

Oregon Scientific AWS888 Weather Forecaster

I'm a fool for these weather station gizmos. The AWS888 from Oregon Scientific is especially neat in that it sports a 3.8" full-color display which can show current conditions and forecasts with photo-image animations. Set up remote sensors outdoors to measure temperature, humidity, and barometric pressure; the time and forecasts come from a wireless connection to the U.S. atomic clock.

Model: AWS888 **Manufacturer:** Oregon Scientific (www.oregonscientific.com) **Price:** $249.95

VIOlight Toothbrush Sanitizer

Cleanliness is next to godliness, so who wants a heathen toothbrush? The VIOlight is a toothbrush sanitizing system that uses a germicidal UV light bulb to kill 99.9% of the nasty bacteria found between your bristles; the entire process takes less than ten minutes. It doubles as an ordinary mild-mannered toothbrush holder, so no extra counter space is necessary.

Model: VIOlight **Manufacturer:** VIOlight (www.violight.com) **Price:** $49.95

VoiSec Refrigerator Voice Recorder

Need to leave a message for your spouse or your kids—or to yourself? Then check out the VoiSec digital voice recorder. It's a small button-shaped device that you can stick on the front of your refrigerator; press the button to record a message, or lift the lid for playback. This may be the most useful gadget in the entire book!

Model: VoiSec **Manufacturer:** VoiSec (www.voisec.se/pages/voisec.html) **Dimensions:** 1.6" (diameter) × 0.71" (h) **Price:** ~$40

Wallflower 2 Multimedia Picture Frame

Show off your digital photos with this digital picture frame. The Wallflower 2 connects to your PC via WiFi, downloads the pictures you've selected, then displays them in a rotating slideshow. The color screen is a big 14.1", which makes the Wallflower 2 look like a traditional picture frame. You can store 30GB of photos, movies, or music files on the device's built-in hard disk.

Model: Wallflower 2 Standard Edition **Manufacturer:** Wallflower Systems (www.wallflower-systems.com) **Dimensions:** 18.5" × 15.5" × 3.5" **Price:** $899

MORE COOL GADGETS

Motorola Ojo Personal Videophone

Leo's Pick

When I was a kid, the two things they promised us for the future were picture phones and flying cars. Well, the future's here and I'm still waiting on my flying car, but the age of the picture phone is finally upon us.

Our friends at Motorola bill the Ojo as a personal videophone, which describes exactly what it is. The Ojo has a built-in video camera to take pictures of you as you talk, and an LCD display to show pictures of whomever it is you're talking to. (Assuming that the person you're calling has their own Ojo, of course.) It's just the type of device they were talking about forty-odd years ago.

Now here's the complicating factor, sort of. You see, you can't use the Ojo on regular phone lines. Nope, if you want to videophone your friends, you have to use a VoIP Internet phone service—which is all the rage today, anyway. (The Ojo will just make it more so.) Connect the Ojo to your broadband Internet connection and you can dial anyone else with a similar VoIP connection, with full-motion MPEG4 video at 30 frames per second.

Let's face it, the Ojo is really just several existing technologies glued together into a single convenient device. You could build your own videophone with a webcam, microphone, and speaker system, all connected to a PC and a broadband modem. Of course, that would be a lot more bulky and a lot less convenient than using the Ojo, but still—you get the point. It's all about converging technologies.

Enough ranting, let's get back to the Ojo. It's actually a fairly stylish device, centered around a 7" vertical 16:9 LCD display. (Actually, this would more accurately be described as a 9:16 aspect ratio, wouldn't it?) The vertical display enhances the face-to-face experience—you're viewing in portrait mode, instead of the normal TV-like landscape mode. You can monitor what your caller sees with the picture-in-picture mirroring, and close the lens when you need a little privacy. You don't even have to disturb the framing by holding a handset up to the side of your head; the Ojo includes a built-in two-way speakerphone, as well as a hands-free wireless handset, if you choose to go that route.

So now that the picture phone has finally become reality, you should rush right out and buy one—or two or three, since you'll need to equip all your friends and relatives with compatible devices. But I still want to know—where the heck's my flying car?

Model: Ojo **Manufacturer:** Motorola (www.motorola.com/ojo/) **Dimensions:** 14" × 8.5" × 7.5" **Weight:** 2.5 lbs. **Price:** $799.99

Sleeptracker Watch

Wake up at the wrong time and you're grumpy all day. Better to ease yourself awake at the optimal time during your sleep cycle, which is what the Sleeptracker does. It looks like a normal wrist watch, but it actually monitors your sleep cycles for those almost-awake moments—and then gently wakes you when you're most alert. It's a neat idea, and helps to keep you on your game in the morning.

Model: Sleeptracker **Manufacturer:** Innovative Sleep Solutions (www.sleeptracker.com) **Price:** $149

ClockBall Rolling Timepiece

Look, all I can say about the ClockBall is that it looks pretty neat. It's a clock, sort of (more accurately a "rolling timepiece"), designed by a French firm, which may or may not explain things. You tell the time by how it rolls around the floor, which really isn't very practical at all, but still. It moves at about a centimeter an hour, within a black square frame. It's probably the most unique desk clock you'll come across—if you can keep it from rolling off your desk.

Model: ClockBall **Manufacturer:** NEOS (www.clockball.net) **Dimensions:** 3.5" (diameter) **Price:** ~$50

Laserpod Light

Throw out your lava lamp, something cooler has finally arrived. The Laserpod uses three lasers and three blue and purple LEDs, projected through a crystal diffuser, to create one heck of a light show. Just make sure you're playing a Jimi Hendrix album when you turn it on!

Model: Laserpod **Manufacturer:** Nebula Gifts (www.laserpod.com) **Price:** $100

Citizen TASER X26c Pistol

Neighbors bugging you? Then take them out hard with this portable TASER pistol. As you no doubt know, the TASER is a non-lethal weapon that uses electric bolts to temporarily override the target's central nervous system, reducing him or her to a heap of quivering Jell-O. The X26c is a handheld TASER gun with a range of 15 feet and a laser sight for more accurate targeting. It can even penetrate up to 2" of clothing, and you don't need a permit to use it. (Why does that frighten me?)

Model: TASER X26c **Manufacturer:** TASER International (www.taser.com/self_defense/) **Dimensions:** 6.0" × 3.2" × 1.3" **Weight:** 7 oz. **Price:** $999

MORE COOL GADGETS

Siemens Com-Badge Home Communicator

Leo's Pick

Here's a piece of future tech that I want on the waiting list for. It's *Star Trek: The Next Generation* meets the smart home, and it couldn't be cooler.

What the Siemens folks have come up with is the Com-Badge, a small communicator device you wear on the front of your shirt. You control the Com-Badge via voice recognition; it interfaces with other devices in your home via Bluetooth wireless technology. Plus—and this is the big deal—you get to look like Captain Picard on the Enterprise, thumping yourself in the chest and saying "Make it so" to your new high-tech toaster.

When programmed properly, the Com-Badge should make it possible to control all sorts of different functions in your house, from opening the garage door to turning on the living room lights. Just press the badge and say "Open the garage door" or "Turn on the living room lights." The Com-Badge contains both a microphone and a miniature speaker, and Siemens claims that it will be able to recognize 30,000 individual words, which is no mean feat.

It's certainly no stretch of the imagination to see the thing used for wireless telephone conversations, or as part of an in-house intercom system. (That's right, you can press the Com-Badge and carry on a conversation with other Com-Badge-equipped users in your house—or to anyone anywhere, via phone.) Siemens also envisions a connection with your email inbox; the Com-Badge's voice recognition system would read your incoming emails and recite the text to you, no matter where you are in the house. This really is becoming quite *Star Trek*-like, isn't it?

Oh, and in case it matters, Siemens says that for "fashion conscious consumers, an additional version of the badge will be available which can be worn like a piece of jewelry, to make sure users are always in style." If they really want to boost sales, they'll make a version shaped like a Star Fleet communicator badge. That's really what we want, isn't it?

Model: Com-Badge **Manufacturer:** Siemens (communications.siemens.com) **Price:** TBA

Dermabond Topical Skin Adhesive

Throw out all your Band-Aids; they're *so* twentieth-century! Instead, you can bond your wounds with Dermabond adhesive, the same stuff that doctors are now starting to use after surgery. Dermabond eliminates the need for stitches, seals out infection-causing bacteria, and disappears naturally as the wound heals. And, unlike traditional bandages, you don't have to worry about keeping a Dermabonded wound dry. It's what cosmetic surgeons prefer!

Model: Dermabond **Manufacturer:** Johnson & Johnson (www.dermabond.com) **Price:** $22.95/vial

Global Pet Finder

When Fido runs away, find him fast with the Global Pet Finder. This is a small GPS tracking device that attaches to your pet's collar; you can track your lost pet by accessing the Global Pet Finder website or by calling F-O-U-N-D from your cell phone. Two caveats—it's for dogs only (not cats), and you need to subscribe to the Global Pet Finder Service ($17.99/month). Other than that, it's a neat use of existing technology to keep your pets from getting lost.

Model: Globalpetfinder **Manufacturer:** GPS Tracks (www.globalpetfinder.com) **Weight:** 5 oz. **Price:** $349.99

GoDogGo Automatic Fetch Machine

Here's another gizmo for your doggie—an automatic fetching machine. Actually, the GoDogGo looks like one of those automatic tennis ball shooting machines, with a big green bucket of balls on the top. All you have to do is train Fido to fetch the tennis balls—and, if you're really good, to put the balls back in the bucket!

Model: GoDogGo **Manufacturer:** GoDogGo (www.buygodoggo.com) **Price:** $149.95

OpenX Plastic Package Opener

I *despise* the hard plastic packaging that most gadgets come packed in today. This packaging defies the laws of physics; I've tried scissors, knifes, even hedge clippers, and nothing seems to get it open. That's what attracted me to the OpenX, a little plastic device that combines a small blade (to puncture the plastic) and a larger blade (to rip open the package from the puncture point) that actually opens up most of these impossible packages. My only beef? The OpenX itself comes in an impossible-to-open plastic package!

Model: OpenX **Manufacturer:** OpenX (www.myopenx.com) **Price:** $4.95

MORE COOL GADGETS

iRobot Scooba Robotic Floor Washer

Leo's Pick

In last year's *Gadget Guide* I sang the praises of the Roomba robotic vacuum cleaner, a great gadget for keeping your carpets clean. But what if you have tile or wood floors, instead of carpet?

Help is now at hand. The folks behind the Roomba have just come out with a similar product for hard floors, called the Scooba. The Scooba is a self-propelled cleaning robot that vacuums, washes, and dries wood and tile floors in a single pass. Like the Roomba, the Scooba wriggles around your floor like one of those pool-cleaning thingies, in a seemingly random pattern that ultimately covers your entire floor space. Unlike the Roomba, the Scooba is designed for all types of sealed hard floors, and can clean wet spills in addition to normal dirt and grime.

The Scooba uses a specially formatted cleaning solution, developed by Clorox, to get your floors sparkling clean. It uses only fresh water and cleaning solution from a clean tank, so it never spreads dirty water on your floor. It circles around and picks up the dirty solution, leaving your floors both clean and dry.

If the Scooba is anything like the Roomba, I think it will be the smash hit of the holiday season. (iRobot has sold more than 1.2 million Roombas to date, by the way.) It's great for anyone who doesn't like cleaning, doesn't have time for cleaning, or isn't very good at cleaning (like me!). It's also a dream come true for older consumers and those with physical disabilities; no more mopping and scrubbing required!

Model: Scooba **Manufacturer:** iRobot (www.irobot.com) **Price:** TBA

Robosapien V2 Toy Robot

The Robosapien is a surprisingly advanced toy robot, capable of shuffling around aimlessly and making farting noises—just like a lot of programmers I know. The new Robosapien V2 is bigger than the original (almost 32" tall), with more advanced movements. He can bend over, lie down, twist back and forth, and track movement via infrared optical sensors. There's even a new stereo sound detection system that allows him to respond and react to noises. Plus, the Robosapien V2 has a new, edgier look—kind of like a Power Ranger with big claws for hands.

Model: Robosapien V2 **Manufacturer:** WowWee (www.robosapienonline.com) **Price:** $200

Hokey Spokes LED Bicycle Spoke Lights

Apparently kids today no longer think putting playing cards in their bicycle spokes is cool. Instead, they need a set of LED bicycle spoke lights, like those sold by Hokey Spokes. (Love that name!) These are transparent blades that attach to your bicycle spokes; as the blades spin, a small microprocessor modulate the internal LCD lights so that custom images and text appear in thin air, thanks to the old persistence-of-vision effect. I gotta admit, these things are cooler than flipping playing cards!

Model: Hokey Spokes **Manufacturer:** Illumination Design Works (www.hokeyspokes.com) **Weight:** 6 oz. **Price:** $29.95

Yamaha WX5 MIDI Wind Controller

Yamaha's WX5 is a MIDI controller for woodwind players. It looks sort of like a flute but fingers like a saxophone, and connects to your computer via MIDI. You can run the WX5 through any MIDI tone generator or synthesizer, to make it sound like a trombone or guitar or piano—or even a saxophone. It has a 16-key layout, high-resolution wind sensor for volume control, and thumb-controlled pitch bend wheel. It's great for current woodwind players, or even for newbies who want to play around a bit.

Model: WX5 **Manufacturer:** Yamaha (www.yamaha.com) **Dimensions:** 24" × 2.4" × 2.8" **Weight:** 18.3 oz. **Price:** $749.95

Maytag Skybox Vendor

Haven't you always wanted your own custom vending machine? Well, that's what Maytag's Skybox Vendor is, short of a functioning coin box. Just load it up with your favorite beverages, insert the appropriate selection cards, and get ready for liquid refreshment fun. You can customize the SkyBox with different selection cards, as well as interchangeable front and side display panels—just like a commercial vending machine. It can hold up to 64 12-ounce cans or 32 12-ounce glass or plastic bottles, your choice of beverages.

Model: Skybox Vendor **Manufacturer:** Maytag (www.skyboxbymaytag.com) **Dimensions:** 33.5" (h) × 24" (w) × 22.1" (d) **Weight:** 117 lbs. **Price:** $499

Index

E

F

G

H

I

J

K

N - O

P

Q - R

S

T

W

X - Y - Z